C000099613

THE COOKTIONARY®

A French Dictionary for Cooks

GEE GREVILLE

THE COOKTIONARY

* A-Z *

Illustrations by Michael Logan

frang📖livres

FRANGLIVRES
90 rue de Flandres
60490 Conchy-les-Pots
FRANCE

Copyright © Gee Greville 2003

Illustrations copyright © Michael Logan 2003

Cover design by Christian Duclairoir

All rights reserved. No part of this book may be reproduced
by any means, electronic or mechanical, including photocopy
or any information storage and retrieval system without
permission in writing from the copyright owner.

ISBN 2-9520074-0-3

Dépôt Légal en France Octobre 2003
Imprimé en Grande Bretagne

COOKTIONARY is a Registered Trade Mark

Typeset from the publisher's disk
by Scriptmate editions

Manufactured in the UK by
BOOK IN HAND LTD, 20 Shepherds Hill, London N6 5AH

CONTENTS

CODES & ABBREVIATIONS

(.. à)	à comes after the word
(à la ..)	à la comes before the word
/..	Original word is repeated
/	Separates similar words
;	Separates alternative translation
[ ]	(in English text) French word
[ ]	(in French text) Literal translation
[ ]	Word that may be omitted from the description
=	Equals; Equivalent to
...	Undefined word
abbr.	Abbreviation
AOC	*Appellation d'origine contrôlée* = Licenced to use place name of origin
btls	Bottles
cl	Centilitres
esp.	Especially
(fam.)	Familiar, colloquial word
Lit.	Literally
ltrs	Litres
Med.	Med.
ml	Millilitres
opp.	Opposite
orig.	Originally
pron.	Pronounced
sp.	Speciality
(term)	Culinary term
trad.	Traditional; Traditionally
yrs.	Years old

To TOM

Most grateful thanks to Jacqueline Gabaut.
Special thanks also to
Mike Logan,
Christian Duclairoir,
Phil Gooda,
James Pugh,
Probyn Miers,
Ann Kritzinger
and the many friends who
have made helpful suggestions.

… with my father in mind …

PREFACE

Once I began cooking seriously in my new French kitchen, I was impatient to use real French recipes and browse through French cookery magazines.

Of course, in the beginning, there were words I didn't know and translations I couldn't find. Often in a hurry, I would guess—but I knew that to guess the meaning of a culinary word could be disastrous, even dangerous, so I had to search beyond my everyday French dictionary. New-found words were jotted down in a small notebook on the kitchen table.

Thus THE COOKTIONARY was born.

Settling into an adopted country is a mixture of hard work and good luck. It is the same with entertaining, and both are most rewarding. For us, however, entertaining presented another challenge—the need to make polite conversation, often about food, but always in French! The small notebook expanded to include more than just culinary words.

THE COOKTIONARY is not a 'cookery book'. It is a series of dictionaries for cooks who live or holiday in France. It is designed to be the definitive reference in an Anglo-French kitchen—for family cooks, professional chefs, restaurateurs, B.& B. hosts, wine buffs, students, holidaymakers, even kids of cooks!

A-Z is the first book in THE COOKTIONARY series and contains over 6000 French gastronomic, culinary and household words translated into English—words used in recipes, cookery magazines and food advertising, on packaging, kitchen equipment and restaurant menus.

Whatever the reason for being in France, THE COOKTIONARY is an essential ingredient for every bookcase, briefcase and suitcase. Details of other books in THE COOKTIONARY series can be found on page 181.

Gee Greville

AB: agriculture biologique Organic farming (See also *Bio*)

Abaisse Sheet of rolled-out pastry; Layer of sandwich cake, etc.

Abaisser to Reduce (heat, price, etc.); (term) to Roll out pastry

Abats Offal: edible items from animal carcass (head, feet, heart, liver, etc.)

Abats blancs White offal: head, stomach, brains, sweetbreads, udders & feet

Abats rouges Red offal: liver, heart, lungs, spleen, tongue & kidneys

Abatte Thick knife used to flatten meat

Abattis Giblets: heart, liver, gizzard, head, neck, etc. of poultry

Abattoir Slaughterhouse

Abeilles / Essaim d' .. Bees / Swarm of bees

Abîmer / S'.. to Damage, to Spoil / to Go bad, to Go off

Ablette Bleak: freshwater fish used in *friture*

Abondamment Copiously; Heavily; Thoroughly (wash, etc.)

Abondance Abundance, Plenty; *AOC* cow's-milk cheese of Haute-Savoie

Abondant, -e Abundant, Plentiful, Thick, Lush

Abordable Accessible, Available; Reasonable (price)

Aboukir Sponge cake with chestnut cream & coffee icing

Abricot Apricot

Abricotage Glazing (esp. with apricot jelly)

Abricoter (term) to Glaze (with jam/jelly)

Abricotine Apricot & brandy liqueur

Abricot-pays Fruit of the West Indies used for jam & juice

Abricots (oreillons d'..) Apricot halves (resembling ears)

Absinthe Wormwood: bitter herb orig. used for *pastis*, etc.

AC (See *AOC*)

Acajou Mahogany

Acanthe Acanthus plant

Acariens Mites, Dust mites

Acarne Sea bream *[pagre]*

Accéder to Comply with; to Have access to

Accolade (en ..) Dish of contrasting foods

Accommoder (term) to Prepare a dish; to Adapt

Acéré, -e Sharp

Acétomel Vinegar & honey syrup for preserving fruit

Achard Achar: spicy fruit & vegetable pickle

Achatine Snail of the Far East

Achats Purchases, the Shopping

Ache de marais Smallage, Wild celery

Acheter en gros to Buy in bulk

Acide Acid, Sour, Tart; Acidic

Acide acétique Acetic acid (found in vinegar)

Acide aminé Amino acid (found in protein)

Acide citrique Citric acid (found in citrus fruit)

Acide lactique Lactic acid (found in milk)

Acide malique Malic acid (found in fruit)

Acide tartrique Tartaric acid (found in wine)

Acides gras Fatty acids (lipids)

Acidifier to Turn sour

Acidité Acidity, Tartness

Acidulé, -e Tangy, Slightly acid

Aciduler to Acidulate with vinegar or lemon juice

Acier / .. inoxydable Steel / Stainless steel

Acra, Akra Small spicy vegetable /fish fritter, sp. of Caribbean cuisine

Acre Acrid, Pungent, Sharp

Acreté Acridity, Pungency, Sharpness

Addition Bill (esp. of a restaurant) [note]

Adhérer to Adhere, to Stick, to Cling

Adoucir to Sweeten; to Soften (water, etc.); to Soothe

Advocaat Dutch liqueur made with egg yolks

Aérer / Aéré, -e to Air (ventilate) / Aired

Afart Trad. feast before midnight mass in Ariège

Affaire (bonne/mauvaise) Good/bad deal

Affamer / Les affamés to Starve / The starving

Affiche Price tag, Sticker, Poster

Afficher to Display, to Show

Affiler to Sharpen (blade, etc.)

Affiner to Ripen, to Mature; to Refine

Affriander (term) to Make a dish look attractive & enticing

Affrioler to Tempt, to Entice (with titbits)

Affriter to Prove a pan with salt/oil before use

Affûter to Sharpen, to Grind (knife, etc.)

Affûteuse Sharpener [aiguiseur]

AFNOR: association française de normalisation French trading standards authority

Africaine (à l'..) N. African-style: with sautéed/steamed vegetables

AFSSA: agence française de sécurité sanitaire des aliments French food safety agency

Agapes Feast; Copious meal

Agar-agar Extract of seaweed

Agenaise (à l'..) Agen-style: often with its famous prunes

Agiter to Stir; to Shake

Agneau Lamb

Agneau blanc Pale-fleshed lamb (3-4 months-old)

Agneau de lait Spring lamb (6 weeks-old & not yet weaned)

Agneau gris Lamb (4-5 months-old & fat no longer white)

Agnelet Baby milk-fed lamb (30-40 days-old)

Agnelle Ewe lamb

Agnès Sorel Mistress of Charles Vll; Soup & garnish of mushrooms, pickled tongue & chicken

Agréable Pleasant, Nice

Agrémenter to Embellish, to Adorn

Agricole Agricultural (land, produce, etc.)

Agriculteur Farmer, Market gardener

Agriculture Farming, Agriculture

Agriculture biologique Organic farming

Agroalimentaire Food production

Agrume Variety of plum, esp. used for Agen prunes

Agrumes Citrus fruit

Aigle de mer [*sea eagle*] Skate (in Brittany)

Aiglefin Haddock [*églefin*]

Aïgo boulido [*boiled water*] Garlic soup of Provence

Aïgo sau d'iou *Bouillabaisse* made with potatoes

Aigre Sour, Bitter, Tart

Aigre-doux Bittersweet; Sweet & sour

Aigrelet, aigrelette Rather sharp, Sourish

Aigrelette Sharp sauce

Aigreur / Aigreurs d'estomac Sourness / Heartburn

Aigrir to Turn sour

Aiguebelle Liqueur from this monastery near Montélimar

Aiguière Ewer

Aiguille Needle; Garfish

Aiguille à brider Trussing needle

Aiguille à larder/piquer Larding needle

Aiguillette Thin trip of meat (esp. duck) taken from the fillet

Aiguillette baronne Cut of beef: top end of rump

Aiguiser to Sharpen, to Grind (knife); to Whet the appetite

Aiguiseur, Aiguisoir Knife sharpener [*affûteuse*]

Ail / Tête/gousse d'.. Garlic / Bulb/clove of garlic

Aile Wing

Aile de raie Skate wing

Aileron Fin of fish; Pinion (wing tip) of fowl

Ailes de lapin Front legs of a rabbit (which resemble chicken wings)

Aïllade Another word for *aïoli*; Oiled bread rubbed with garlic

Aillée Green centre of garlic clove; Rubbed with garlic; Garlic & ground almond paste

Ailler to Prick/rub with garlic

Aillet Young garlic shoot

Aimant / Pourvue d'.. Magnet /Magnetic force

Aïoli Garlic mayonnaise of Provence

Aïoli garni / Grand aïoli Provençal dish of salt cod, shellfish & vegetables served with *aïoli* / Copious/meat version of *aïoli garni*

Airelle Cranberry [*canneberge*]

Aisément Easily

Aïvar East European condiment of dried peppers

Aixoise of Aix-en-Provence or Aix-les-Bains

Ajouter to Add; to Adjust

Alambic Alembic: complex still, used for distilling brandy

Albacore Yellow fin tuna

Alberge Variety of peach used for jam making

Albert (sauce ..) Butter sauce with horseradish, mustard, cream & egg yolks (for braised beef)

Albigeoise (à l'..) Albi-style: garnish of stuffed tomatoes & potato croquettes served with meat joints

Albufera (à l'..) Various rich dishes (often with *foie gras*)

Albufera (sauce ..) Sauce with sweet pepper butter

Alcazar Gâteau with almond meringue & apricot *marmelade*

Alcool / Alcoolique Alcohol, Spirit / Alcoholic

Alcool blanc Eau-de-vie, Schnapps

Alénois Variety of cress

Alevin Fry: young fish

Alfalfa Lucerne: clover-like fodder-plant *[luzerne]*

Algérie (vins d'..) Algerian wines

Algérienne (à l'..) Algerian-style: with sweet potatoes & tomatoes

Algue Algae, Seaweed, Dulse

Alicot, Alicuit Trad. rich poultry stew of the SW

Aligot Sticky purée of *Tomme fraîche* cheese, potato, garlic & cream, sp. of Rouergue; Another name for *Tomme fraîche*

Aligoté Dry white wine of Burgundy (used with *crème de cassis* for *kir*)

Aliment, Alimentaire Food, Feed

Aliment pour animaux Pet food

Alimentation Diet, Food stuff/supply/industry

Alimentation saine Healthy diet

Alise Rowanberry: fruit of mountain ash used for jam, etc.

Alkékenge Cape gooseberry, Strawberry tomato

Allache Large sardine

Allant au four *[goes in oven]* Ovenproof

Alléchant Tempting, Enticing, Alluring

Allégé, -e Light; Low fat, Low sugar; Diet (product)

Alléger to Lighten, to Make less heavy; to Simplify

Alléluia Trad. Easter cake of the SW

Allemande (à l'..) German-style: often with game; Dish with *sauce allemande*

Allemande (sauce ..) Classic white sauce base made with stock (esp. for fish, offal, chicken & egg dishes)

Allergie / Allergique Allergy / Allergic

Alliage Alloy; Combination

Allier to Combine; to Go well together

Allonger *[to stretch]* to Extend; to Thin (sauce, etc.) with liquid; to Water down (coffee, etc.)

Allume-feu Fire-lighter; Spill; Cigarette lighter *[briquet]*

Allume-gaz Gas-cooker lighter

Allumer to Switch on, to Light up

Allumettes *[matches]* Cheese straws; Potato matchsticks

Alose Shad: bony fish similar to herring

Alouette / .. de mer Lark, Skylark / Snipe, Sandpiper

Alouette sans tête *[lark with no head]* Rolled veal/beef stuffed with sausage meat & cooked in sauce

Aloyau Sirloin of beef

Alpage Mountain pasture; Movement of herds to high ground for summer grazing

Alphonse Lavallée Variety of large black dessert grape

ALSACE Region in the NE with the Rhine as its border with Germany; known for its (mostly white) wines & a rich cuisine of goose, sausages, fish, *foie gras* & sauerkraut/*choucroute*

Alsacienne (à l'..) Alsace-style: with *choucroute*, ham & dumplings, cooked in Riesling wine

Altérer to Spoil, to Impair, to Adulterate (food, etc.)

Alu, Aluminium Tin foil

Alvéole / Plat à alvéoles Small cavity/ hole / Special dish for cooking & serving snails

Amande / .. mondée Almond; Kernel / Blanched almond

Amande (lait d'..) Blancmange mix; Iced & glazed cake made with almond paste

Amande aboukir Glazed petit four made with almond paste

Amande de mer Clam *[palourde]*

Amandes (pâte d'..) Almond paste: ground almonds mixed with icing sugar & glucose syrup

Amandine Classic almond sponge-cake tart

Amasser to Pile up, to Heap up, to Gather up

Amateur de ... Lover of ..., Connoisseur

Ambiante / Température .. Ambient, Surrounding / Room temperature

Ambrosie Ambrosia: food of the gods

Améliorer to Improve, to Make (something) better

Amender to Amend, to Correct

Amener to Bring

Amer, amère / Amertume Bitter, Sour / Bitterness

Américaine, Armoricaine (à l'..) Elaborate (lobster) dish with shellfish sauce (not from the USA or Brittany!)

Ame Soul

Amiante Asbestos

Amidon Starch

Ammoniaque Ammonia solution

Amollir / S'.. to Soften, to Make soft / to Go/become soft

Amorphe Passive, Lifeless

Amourettes Spinal marrow of beef/veal (prepared like brains)

Amovible Detachable, Removable, Interchangeable

Amuse-gueule Cocktail snack

Anacarde Cashew fruit *[pomme de cajou]*

Ananas Pineapple

Anchois / .. de Norvège Anchovy / Sprat

Anchoyade Anchovy & garlic paste of Provence

Ancienne (à l'..) Traditional-style: often with onions & mushrooms

Andalouse (à l'..) Andalusia-style: with Spanish sausage, rice & tomatoes

Andouille Cold sliced chitterling sausage with regional variations, esp. of Guéméné & Vire

Andouillette Hot chitterling sausage with regional variations, esp. of Cambrai, Lyon & Troyes

Andouillette à la ficelle String of small *andouillettes*

Aneth Dill

Ange de mer Angel shark (resembles skate)

Angélique Angelica

Anges à cheval Angels-on-horseback: oysters wrapped in bacon

Angevine (à l'..) Anjou-style: often veal/lamb/pears/plums

Anglaise (à l'..) English-style: often plain boiled or poached (See also *Assiette anglaise*)

Angourie [des Antilles] Prickly cucumber of the Caribbean

Anguille / Anguillette Eel / Elver *[civelle]*

Anguille de mer Conger eel *[congre]*

Anguille des sables Sand eel *[équille]*

Angurie Watermelon jam, sp. of Bugey

Animelles Animal testicles *[rognons blancs]*

Anis / Anisé, -e Anise, Aniseed / Flavoured with anise

Anisette Aniseed-flavoured liqueur (*pastis*, etc.)

ANJOU Region in the Loire Valley renowned for its soft fruit, still & sparkling wine

Anna (pommes ..) Potatoes sliced & sautéed in a covered pan

Annuler to Cancel

Anone Custard apple (tropical fruit)

Anorexie Anorexia: distaste for food (opp. of *appétit*)

Anse Handle (of pot, basket, etc.)

Anthropomorphiques (gâteaux ..) Trad. [Easter] cakes of various regions & depicting popular local figures

Antiadhésif, antiadhésive Non-stick

Antiboise (à l'..) Antibes-style: Provençal dishes using eggs, tomatoes & fish

Anti-éclaboussures Splash-/spatter-proof

Antigel *[antifreeze]* (fam.) Brandy

Antigrippe *[anti-'flu]* (fam.) Chaser: spirit drunk after beer

Antillaise (à l'..) Caribbean-style: often with rum

Anversoise (à l'..) Antwerp-style: often with hop shoots

AOC: appellation d'origine contrôlée Strictly controlled licence to use name of the place (village, region, etc.) from which produce (wine, cheese, poultry, fruit, etc.) originates

AOP: appellation d'origine protégée As *AOC* but with wider European coverage

Aoûtat Harvest mite *[trombidion]*

Aoûtiens People who holiday in August

Apéro, Apéritif Drink before a meal (*apéritif* = that stimulates the appetite)

Apiculteur, apicultrice / Apiculture Bee-keeper / Bee-keeping

Aplatir to Flatten, to Beat flat (escalope, etc.)

Apogée Peak, Climax

Appareil Equipment; (term) Preparation/mix of ingredients (esp. in cake making)

Appareil ménager Household appliance

Appenzelle Semi-hard Swiss cow's-milk cheese

Appertisation Method of preserving food by heat sterilization (invented by Nicolas Appert in 1783)

Appesantir to Make heavier

Appétissant, -e / Peu .. Tempting, Appetizing / Unappetizing

Appétit / Appétits Appetite / (term) Spring onions & chives (because they stimulate the appetite)

Apprêt Preparation (of & for a dish)

Appuyer to Press on/down/against

Apre Acrid, Pungent, Tart

Apron Small river fish of perch family

Apyrène Fruits without stone/pips

Aqueux, aqueuse Watery

AQUITAINE Region in the SW (called Guyenne when it belonged to the English)

Arabe Arab, Arabic, Arabian

Arabica Species of coffee (milder than *robusta*)

Arachide (huile d'..) Groundnut/peanut oil (Peanuts = *cacahuètes*)

Araignée *[spider]* Prize piece of meat from ox hock

Araignée à friture Skimmerspoon (to remove food from deep-fryer)

Araignée de mer Spider crab

Arapède Limpet

Arbois Wine of the Jura

Arboriculteur Nurseryman

Arbouse Arbutus, Strawberry tree

Ardennaise (à l'..) Ardennesstyle: often game with juniper

ARDENNES (les ..) Hilly & wooded region, bordering Belgium, with a cuisine of game, berries & mushrooms

Ardoise Slate, Blackboard

Arêtes Fish bones

Argent, Argenterie Silver, Silverware

Argenteuil (crème ..) Cream of asparagus soup

Argentin Scabbard fish

Argot de cuisine Kitchen slang: colourful jargon used in bars & restaurants (*gros bonnet, picrate, frometon*, etc.)

ARIEGE *Département* in the Pyrenees

Ariégeoise (à l'..) Ariège-style: chicken/mutton & stuffed cabbage

Arlequins *[harlequins]* (term) Food arranged decoratively

Arlésienne (à l'..) Arles-style: with aubergines, tomatoes & courgettes

Armagnac *AOC* brandy of Gascony (*XXX* = 3 yrs.; *VO* = 5-10 yrs.; *VSOP* = up to 15 yrs.; *Hors d'âge* = at least 25 yrs.)

Armer to Reinforce; to Wind on (timer, etc.)

Armillaire couleur de miel Honey/Bootlace fungus

Aromates Herbs & spices

Aromatique Aromatic

Aromatiser / Aromatisé, -e to Flavour / Flavoured

Arôme Flavour, Aroma; (wine term) Specific grape smell

Arracher to Tear/pull out/up/away, to Extract

Arrêter *[to stop]* (term) to Quickly stop something cooking by adding cold water, draining or removing from pan

Arrière-cuisine Scullery

Arrière-goût After-taste

Arroche Orache: spinach-like plant often used with sorrel

Arrondir to Make round, to Round off

Arroser *[to water]* to Baste, to Sprinkle with liquid; to Drink a toast

Art Art, Skill, Knack

Art de la table Table decoration/arrangement

Art floral Flower arranging

Artichaut (fonds/cœurs d'..) Artichoke hearts

Artichaut [poivrade] *[globe]* Artichoke

Artichaut de Jérusalem/hiver Jerusalem/winter artichoke *[topinambour]*

Artichaut japonais Chinese artichoke *[crosne]*: tiny curled tuber (sweeter than Jerusalem artichoke)

Artisan / Artisanale Craftsman / Cottage industry, Handicraft

ARTOIS Region in the North (part in Belgium) with a cuisine similar to that of Flanders

Arts ménagers Home economics

As de pique *[ace of spades]* (fam.) Parson's nose *[croupion]*

Aspartame (brand name) Artificial sweetener

Asperge / Pointes d'.. Asparagus / Asparagus tips

Asperger to Sprinkle, to Spray

Asperges picnic Mini asparagus (usually tinned/jarred)

Aspergille Variety of snail

Aspérité Roughness, Not smooth

Aspic de ... Dish of cold food set in aspic jelly

Aspirateur Vacuum cleaner

Assaisonner / Assaisonnement to Season / Seasoning

Assation (term) to Cook food in its own juice

Assembler to Assemble, to Arrange

Assiette / Assiettée Plate, Small dish / Plateful

Assiette anglaise *[English plate]* Dish of assorted cold meats

Assiette assortie Dish of various hors d'œuvre

Assiette calotte [*skull-cap*] Salad/dessert plate/dish

Assiette creuse [*shallow*] Soup/dessert bowl/dish

Associer to Join, to Connect

Assoiffé, -e Thirsty

Assorti, -e Assorted, Mixed

Assouplir (s'..) to Become soft/supple

Asticots Maggots

Astringent (wine term) Excessive tannin

Astuce / Astucieux, astucieuse Trick, Ruse / Crafty, Clever, Astute

Athérine Sand-smelt: small sea fish

Atre Hearth, Fireplace

Attabler / S'.. to Seat (guests) at table / to Be seated at table

Attaque First impression

Attaquer [*to attack*] (term) to Launch (into), to Tackle

Atteler to Harness, to Yoke (oxen)

Attendre / S'.. to Wait / to Expect (something to happen)

Attendrir / Attendrisseur to Tenderise, to Soften / Meat mallet

Attendu (term) Food that has to 'rest' or be hung before preparation

Atténuer to Reduce (heat, etc.), to Lessen, Diminish

Attignole Cold meatball, sp. of Normandy

Attriau Rustic flat sausage made with pork liver & veal

Aubaine Boon, Windfall, Godsend

Aubépine Hawthorn, May-bush

Auberge Country restaurant, Inn

Aubergine Aubergine, Eggplant

Aubrac (bœuf d'..) Beef cattle of the Massif Central

AUGE (Pays d'..) Region of Normandy known for *calvados* & cider

Auge Trough

Augouts Bouquet garni in Saône-et-Loire

Aulx [*plural of* ail] Garlic bulbs

Aumônière [*almoner's purse*] Food wrapped in another; Dessert of apple/pear in pastry

AUNIS Old province around La Rochelle on the west coast

Aurore Various dishes containing tomato purée

Aurore (sauce ..) *Sauce velouté* flavoured with tomato purée

Aussitôt Immediately, Straight away

Aussitôt que possible As soon as possible

Autant de/que As much/many as

Auto-cuiseur Pressure cooker

Automne / Automnal, -e, automnaux Autumn / Autumnal

Autre / Entre autres Other, Another / Amongst others

Autrefois In the past, In the old days [*jadis*]

Autrichienne (à l'..) Austrian-style: often with paprika

Autruche Ostrich

Auvergnate (à l'..) Auvergne-style: often with cheese, pickled pork, bacon, cabbage, & potatoes

AUVERGNE Mountainous region in the heart of rural France noted for its beef cattle, cheese & charcuterie

Avaler to Swallow

Avant Before, Beforehand, First

Avant-veille / Avant-hier Two days before / The day before yesterday

Avarié, -e Spoiled, Rotten, Damaged

Aveline Filbert: cultivated hazelnut

Avenir Future

Averti, -e Experienced, Well-informed

Avertir to Warn, to Notify, to Advise

Avocat Avocado pear

Avoine / Flocons d'.. Oats / Oat flakes, Rolled oats

Avoine (farine d'..) Oatmeal

Azyme Unleavened bread, Matzo

WHITE AUBERGINES

Baba Light sponge soaked in alcohol (rum or Kirsch)

Babeurre Buttermilk [*lait baratte, lait de beurre*]

Babines Chaps, Chops, Lips

Bac / .. à glaçons Tub, Container, Sink / Ice-tray

Bacon Cured loin of pork (English-style bacon = *lard*)

Bactéries Bacteria

Badiane Star anise: tropical fruit with aniseed-flavoured seeds

Badigeonner to Paint, to Coat lightly, to Cover

Badoise (à la ..) Baden-style: game dishes of German cuisine

Baeckoffe, Backenoff Alsatian stew (trad. cooked, in a pot sealed with dough, in the baker's oven)

Bâfrer to Guzzle

Baguette THE classic French bread loaf/stick

Baguettes Chopsticks

Baies Berries

Baigner to Bathe, to Soak

Bailler [*to yawn*] (term) Shellfish (oysters, etc) that open before cooking (& must be discarded)

Bain d'huile Marinade of oil used for preserving (esp. fish)

Bain de friture Oil of/for a deep-fryer

Bain-marie Double-saucepan or oven pan of hot water; Sterilizing unit

Baiser [*kiss*] Petit four meringues sandwiched with cream

Baisser to Lower, to Reduce [heat]

Baisure Kissing crust: soft join between batch-baked loaves

Bajoues Cheeks, Jowls

Balai / Balayette Broom / Small brush

Balance Weighing scales; Shrimp net

Baleine Whale

Baliste Triggerfish: Med. fish resembling tuna

Balle Ball, Ball-shaped

Ballon [*balloon*] Small ball; Balloon wine glass; Hot-water tank

Ballot Bundle, Pack

Ballotter to Toss, to Shake

Ballottine Boned, rolled & stuffed meat/poultry

Balthazar Champagne bottle size (16 btls)

Baluchon Bundle, Parcel

Bamboche, Bamboula Big party, (fam.) Bash

Bamboche (en ..) [*spree*] Cod pieces cooked in very hot fat

Bambolles Apple fritters (esp. of the Loire Valley)

Bambou (pousses de ..) Bamboo shoots

Bamia, Bamya Okra, Ladies' fingers: tropical plant used in Caribbean cuisine

Ban des Vendanges Proclamation (in wine regions) of date on which grape harvest can begin

Banane / .. plantain Banana / Plantain banana

Banc Bench

Bannette Dolicho bean: small haricot bean

Banon Soft Provençal cow's-/goat's-/ewe's-milk cheese wrapped in chestnut leaves

Banquet Banquet, Feast

Banquette Banquette seat, Covered bench

Banquette (faire ..) to Be a wallflower

Banyuls Sweet dessert wine of Roussillon

Baptême Baptism, Christening

Baquet Tub, Bucket

Bar Bass, Sea perch

Baraquets Thick flat *haricots verts* of the Languedoc

Baratte Churn

Barbadine Variety of passion fruit (used as a vegetable)

Barbaque (fam.) Poor quality meat (possibly origin of barbecue)

Barbe à papa [*daddy's beard*] Candyfloss

Barbe de capucin Variety of curly endive

Barbeau, Barbillon Barbel: fresh-water fish

Barberon Salsify (in the South)

Barbette River turbot

Barboteur [*paddler*] Common name for domestic duck

Barbotine Tansy

Barbouille (en ..) [*smear*] Chicken/rabbit cooked in red wine with its blood added at the last moment

Barbue Brill

Bardane Burdock

Barde / Barder Bard / to Bard: cover with strips of fat/bacon

Barigoule Stuffed artichokes of Provence

Baril, Barrique Barrel, Cask, Drum

Baron Joint of lamb comprising both legs & saddle

Barquette Boat-shaped tartlet; Light puff-biscuit

Barquette (en ..) In a pack/packet

Barre Bar (of chocolate, etc.)

Barreau Bass of Brittany

Bas, basse Low; Bottom (of oven)

Bas morceaux Bottom cuts: meat used for stews, etc.

Baselle Basella, Vine spinach

Basilic Sweet basil

Basquaise (à la ..) Basque-style: with tomatoes & smoked ham

BASQUE (Pays ..) Basque country: in the SW corner with its own language, Atlantic resorts & Pyrenean border with Spain

Basse-cour Farm-yard, Poultry-yard

Basses-côtes Cut of beef (chuck/blade) used for grills/stews

Basset Decorative butter mould

Bassin / Bassinet Basin, Bowl / Small [metal] basin

Bassine / .. à confitures Pan / Preserving pan

Bassine à friture Deep-frying container

Bâtard [*bastard*] Short fat French bread loaf

Bâtarde (sauce ..) Hot butter sauce for vegetables & boiled fish

Batavia Batavian endive (salad green)

Bâton *[stick]* Short bread stick; Small cake

Bâton de Jacob Jacob's stick: small éclair

Bâtonnet Stick, Rod; Stick-shaped petit four

Bâtonnet de poisson Fish finger

Battant Hinged section (of door/window); Leaf of table

Batte à côtelette Steak batt: used to flatten escalopes, etc.

Batterie de cuisine Cooking equipment/utensils; Kitchen staff

Batteur Blender, Whisk *[fouet]*

Battre / Battu, -e to Beat, to Whip / Beaten, Whipped

Battre en omelette to Beat eggs (as for an omelette)

Baudroie, Beaudroie Monkfish *[lotte]*

Baume / .. des champs Balm, Balsam / Wild mint

Bavarois Bavarian cream: egg custard with gelatine & cream

Bavaroise Frothy drink of tea, coffee or chocolate with alcohol

Bavette Cut of beef: undercut of sirloin for grilling & stewing; Large bib (esp. for eating lobster)

Baveux, baveuse Runny (omelette, etc.), Moist, Sloppy

Bavoir Child's bib

Bazine Semolina dumpling

BEARN Region of the Pyrenees adjoining the Pays Basque, with a similar cuisine, heavy cheeses & *Jurançon* wines

Béarnaise (à la ..) Béarn-style: often game & poultry dishes with mushrooms & spicy vegetables

Béarnaise (sauce ..) Hot butter & egg yolk sauce for grills

Béatilles Giblet stew, sp. of the *Lyonnais*

Beaufort Mountain cow's-milk cheese of Savoie (French equivalent of Swiss Gruyère/*Fribourg*)

BEAUJOLAIS (le ..) Wine-growing region of southern Burgundy, between Mâcon & Lyon; Easy-drinking wine from this region that produces much more than *nouveau*

Beaumes-de-Venise *AOC* fortified sweet wine of the Vaucluse

Beaumont Pasteurized cow's-milk cheese of Haute-Savoie

Bec *[beak]* Spout of jug or teapot, etc.

Bécasse Woodcock

Bécasseau Young woodcock; Sandpiper

Bécassine Snipe

Béchamel (sauce ..) Basic white sauce

Bécharel (pâté de ..) Garlic pie, sp. of Brittany

Bêche-de-mer Sea slug, Sea cucumber

Bectance, Becquetance (fam.) Food, Grub, Nosh

Becter, Becqueter *[to peck]* to Eat very little ('like a bird')

Bécune Barracuda, Sea pike

Bedon / Un gros .. (fam.) Tummy / Large fat man

Bégot, Béglon, Béglin Sweetie, Bonbon

Beignet / .. au sucre Fritter / Doughnut

Beignets de crevettes Prawn crackers

Belge Belgian

Belle Hélène (poire ..) Poached pear with hot chocolate sauce

Bellevue (en ..) Dish of lobster & cold chicken in aspic

Belon Flat oyster of Brittany

Bélouga, Béluga White whale producing caviar

Bénédicité Grace (said before a meal)

Bénédictine Herb liqueur of Fécamp in Normandy

Bénédictine (à la ..) Dish using salt cod & potato purée

Benincase Gourd-melon: variety of squash

Bercy (à la ..) Various dishes with wine or shallot butter

Bergamote Bergamot: small yellow oily-skinned orange; Variety of round pear; Barley sugar sweet

Bergamote (thé à la ..) Earl Grey tea

Berger / Bergère (à la ..) Shepherd / Shepherdess-style: various regional dishes with lamb/poultry

BERGERACOIS Wine growing region around Bergerac in the Dordogne

Berle Water parsnip

Berlingot Boiled 'humbug'

sweet; Pyramid-shaped milk container

Berny Croquette potatoes rolled in chopped almonds; Garnish of tartlet filled with lentil purée

Berrichonne (à la ..) Berry-style: meat joints with cabbage & chestnuts, or potatoes with onion & bacon

BERRY Old province, around Bourges in the centre of France, with a rustic cuisine of soups & stews

Berthous Dish of melted cheese served (trad. on a special *assiette à berthous*) with boiled potatoes, sp. of Savoie

Besan Chickpea flour (used in Indian cuisine)

Besoin Need, Want, Necessity, Requirement

Bestiaux Cattle, Beasts

Bestiole Bug, Insect, Small animal

Besugo Basque name for red mullet [*rouget*]

Bétail Cattle, Livestock

Bêtise [*blunder*] Mint-flavoured boiled sweet with (orig. errant) air bubbles

Bette Swiss chard, Spinach beet [*blette*]

Bettelman Alsatian version of bread & butter pudding

Betterave / .. à sucre Beetroot; (fam.) Red wine / Sugar-beet

Betterave crapaudine Variety of beet with 'warty' skin (like a toad/*crapaud*)

Beuchelle Type of giblet/offal stew of Touraine

Beugnon Fritter of Berry

Beurré Variety of pear

Beurre / Beurré, -e Butter / Buttered; (fam) Drunk, Plastered

Beurre allégé Low-fat butter

Beurre Bercy Butter sauce with shallots & bone marrow

Beurre blanc Butter sauce with white wine & shallots

Beurre citronné Lemon butter sauce

Beurre clarifié Clarified butter

Beurre Colbert Tarragon & meat glaze added to *beurre maître d'hôtel*

Beurre composé Compound butter: softened butter to which various ingredients have been added

Beurre d'amande Paste of butter & ground almonds

Beurre d'escargot Paste of butter, garlic & parsley (for snails)

Beurre d'Isigny *AOC* butter from Normandy

Beurre de cacahuète Peanut butter

Beurre de Gascogne Purée of veal kidney fat & blanched garlic

Beurre de homard Lobster butter: pounded cooked lobster meat & eggs added to softened butter

Beurre de karité Shea butter: made from tropical fruit seed

Beurre de Marseille Name sometimes used for olive oil

Beurre de Montpellier Butter sauce with herbs, garlic, gherkins & hard-boiled egg

Beurre de moutarde Butter blended with strong mustard

Beurre de noisettes Paste of butter & ground hazelnuts

Beurre de Provence Another name for *aïoli*

Beurre demi-sel Lightly salted butter

Beurre doux *[sweet]* Unsalted butter

Beurre Echiré *AOC* butter from the Deux-Sèvres

Beurre en pommade *[ointment]* Butter beaten smooth & used as base for butter creams & sauces

Beurre fondu Clarified butter, lemon juice, salt & white pepper

Beurre fouetté Whisked (low-fat) butter

Beurre hôtelier Softened butter, parsley, lemon juice & duxelles

Beurre landais Balls of butter rolled in breadcrumbs & grilled

Beurre maître d'hôtel Softened butter, parsley & lemon juice

Beurre manié Kneaded butter & flour (used to thicken)

Beurre marchand de vin Butter whisked into reduced red wine, shallots, chopped parsley & lemon juice

Beurre meunière *Beurre noisette* with lemon juice

Beurre monté Butter whisked into reduced liquid & seasoned

Beurre mousseux Butter creamed with lemon juice & water

Beurre noir Clarified butter, capers, parsley & vinegar

Beurre noisette Butter heated until nut brown in colour

Beurre vert Butter flavoured with spinach juice

Beurrée Buttered bread in various regions

Beurrer to Butter, to Add butter; to Cover with butter

Beurrier / .. cloché Butter-dish / Covered butter-dish

Beursaudes Cracklings: residue from melted pork fat

Beuverie Drinking session

Biarrote (à la ..) Biarritz-style: garnish of potatoes & Ceps

Biche Doe: female deer

Bicolore Two-coloured/-toned

Bicot Kid (goat) *[chevreau]*

Bidoche (fam.) Bad/inferior meat

Bidon Can, Drum (container); (fam.) Belly

Bien-être Well-being, Welfare

Bienfait / .. du ciel Gift, Blessing, Boon / a Godsend

Biens de consommation Consumer goods

Bière / .. blonde / ..brun / .. rousse / .. blanche Beer / Lager / Brown ale / Stout / White/wheat beer

Bière de gingembre Ginger beer

Bière pression/en fût Draught beer

Bifteck Steak (not necessarily beef)

Bigarade Little bitter/Seville orange

Bigarade (sauce ..) Orange sauce for duck & game

Bigarreau White-heart cherry

Bigarrure / Bigarré, -e Medley (of colours) / Multicoloured

Bigne Fritter of the Auvergne

Bigorneaux Winkles, Periwinkles

Bigouden Almond-flavoured biscuit of Brittany *[galette]*

Bille a Marble, Small ball

Billes en céramique Blind-baking beans

Billot Butcher's block, Thick chopping board

Bio, Biologique Organic: without artificial additives

Bique / Biquet Nanny goat / Kid (goat) *[bicot]*

Bis, -e Greyish-brown (colour); Unbleached (flour, etc.)

Biscotte Rusk, Crispbread

Biscotte Parisienne Light almond biscuit

Biscuit Biscuit; Sponge cake; Biscuit-ware: unglazed porcelain

Biscuit à la cuiller *[spoon biscuit]* Sponge finger

Biscuit glacé Ice cream cake

Biscuit roulé Sponge roll

Biseau (couper en ..) to Cut on the slant/bevel

Bison Bison, Buffalo *[buffle]*

Bisque Shellfish paste used as base for fish soup

Bisque de ... Shellfish soup (crayfish, lobster, etc.)

Bistre Yellowish-brown

Bistrot Bistro: unsophisticated 'local' bar/restaurant

Bistrouille, Bistouille Mix of

coffee & brandy; Cheap bandy

Biterroise (à la ..) of Béziers in the Languedoc

Bitoke Type of thin hamburger

Bitter Bitters: aromatic bitter alcohol (*Suze*, etc.)

Blaff Creole dish of fish/shellfish served with rice & beans

Blanc, blanche White

Blanc (à ..) Food (onions, etc.) cooked without browning; Blind-baked pastry case (for raw/cream fillings)

Blanc (au ..) Dish (esp. poultry & veal) in a white sauce

Blanc d'œuf Egg white

Blanc d'œuf en neige Whisked egg white

Blanc de ... Dish/piece of white meat/fish/vegetables

Blanc de blancs White wine made from only white grapes

Blanc de cuisson White stock: flour, water, seasoning, lemon juice or white vinegar (used for offal/vegetables)

Blanc de noirs White wine made from black grapes

Blanchaille Whitebait

Blanchiment (term) 'White' stage of blending butter, sugar & flour, etc.; Bleaching

Blanchir to Blanch, to Scald; (term) to Cream egg yolks with sugar

Blanc-limé White wine with lemonade

Blanc-manger Blancmange

Blanquette de ... Various dishes made with only white meat

Blanquette de Limoux Sparkling white wine of the South

Blanquette de veau Classic veal dish with cream & white wine

Blatte Cockroach [*cafard*]

Blé / Blé noir Wheat / Buckwheat [*sarrasin*]

Blé en herbe Wheat in the blade (not yet 'in ear')

Blé tamisé Sifted flour

Blennie Blenny: small river fish of the South

Blet, blette Over-ripe, Soft (fruit, etc.)

Blette Swiss chard, Spinach beet [*bette*]

Blettir (se ..) to Become over-ripe (fruit, etc.)

Bleu Blue; Very rare (meat); General term for blue cheese

Bleu (au ..) Fish (esp. trout) cooked in boiling water & vinegar (turning the skin blue)

Bleu de ... Blue cheese from various regions, notably *Auvergne, Bresse, Causses, Corse*, etc.

Bleue du Nord (race ..) Thick-set breed of cattle of the North that are cream-coloured with 'blue stains'

Bleuet, Bluet Cornflower; (sometimes) Blueberry [*myrtille*]; Bluebottle (fly)

Blini Russian pancake (served with caviar, etc.)

Blond, -e Pale, Fair, Blond, Light

Blonde d'Aquitaine (race ..) Large cream-coloured beef cattle of the SW

Blondir (faire ..) to Lightly brown in butter/oil

Bocage Hedged pasture (esp. in Normandy)

Bocal, bocaux Jar, Preserving bottle

Bock Beer glass; Glass of beer

Bœuf Beef; Ox; Stargazer: Med. fish

Bœuf à la mode Boiled beef (often with a mushroom sauce)

Bœuf gros sel Boiled/braised beef

Bœufs Oxen, Bullocks

Bogue Boops: Med. fish; Chestnut husk

Bohémienne (à la ..) Various dishes named after comic opera

Boisson / .. sucrée Drink, Beverage / Soft drink

Boissons non comprises Drinks not included (in price)

Boîte / En .. Tin, Can, Box / Tinned, Canned

Boîte à sel Salt box: lidded box/jar for cooking salt

Boîte à thé Tea caddy

Boîtes empilables Stacking-boxes

Bol Bowl, Basin

Bôle Rape in Périgourdine

Bolet Boletus mushroom

Bolet jaune Slippery Jack mushroom

Bolet orangé Orange birch boletus mushroom

Bombe Ice cream dessert & its stainless steel mould

Bombe insecticide Fly spray

Bombé, -e Distorted, Lumpy

Bombine Salt pork & black pudding stew of the Ardèche

Bombonne, Bonbonne Demi-john *[dame-jeanne]*

Bon Good; Voucher

Bon accord Good match, Goes well with ...

Bon enfant (term) Jovial, Fun, Easy-going, Casual

Bon marché Good value, Not too expensive

Bon vivant One who enjoys the good life

Bonbonnière Candy/sweetie box

Bonbons, Bonbecs Sweets, Candies

Bon-chrétien Variety of pear

Bondard, Bonde, Bondon Creamy cow's-milk cheese from Normandy

Bondelle Houting (fish)

Bonifier to Improve

Bonimenteur *[smooth talker]* Showman, Street crier

Bonite, Boniton Bonito, Skipjack tuna

Bonne affaire Good deal

Bonne bouffe (fam.) Good food, Good eating place

Bonne femme (à la ..) (term) Simple/homely dish

Bonnet d'électeur/prêtre Variety of squash

Bonnet d'évêque (fam.) Parson's nose *[croupion]*

Bon-prime Coupon; Gift token

Bontemps (sauce ..) Sauce made with cider & mustard

Borassus Palmyra: palm tree of Asia & Africa

Borborygmes Rumblings, Gurgling (of stomach)

Borchtch, Bortsch Borsch: vegetable & beetroot soup, orig. of Russia/Poland

Bord Border, Edge, Brim

Bordeaux (vins de ..) Wines of Bordeaux in the SW that include many world-famous names: Fronsac, Graves, Médoc, Pomerol, Sauternes, St-Emilion, etc.

Bordeaux clairet Pale red (not *rosé*) wine of Bordeaux

Bordeaux rouge Red wine of Bordeaux, Claret (orig. a mispronunciation of *clairet* = pale red wine)

BORDELAIS Region around Bordeaux in the SW

Bordelaise (à la ..) Bordelais-style: with red wine, bone marrow & shallots

Bordure Border of potato, rice etc. round a dish

Borie Shepherd's hut in the Luberon (now holiday homes!)

Bosser (fam.) to Work

Botte Bunch, Bundle

Bottereau Fritter of Nantes

Bouc Billy goat (*Bouc émissaire* = scapegoat)

Boucage / Boucaner Smoke-drying / to Smoke-dry (fish, meat, etc.)

Boucaud, Boucot Common/brown shrimp

Bouche Mouth; Opening; Vent; Manhole

Bouche à oreille (de ..) (term) By word of mouth

Bouche bée (être ..) to Gape; to Show astonishment

Bouché, -e Capped, Stoppered; Bottled (esp. cider); Blocked

Bouchée Mouthful; Small *vol-au-vent*; Savoury petit four

Bouchée à la reine Small *vol-au-vent* filled with chicken & mushroom in a cream sauce

Bouchées au chocolat Chocolates

Boucher Butcher; to Plug, to Block up; to Fill (gaps)

Bouchère (à la ..) Butcher's wife-style: with garnish of bone marrow; Marinated veal chops

Boucherie Butcher's shop; Butchery

Boucherie chevaline Horse-meat butcher

Bouchon [*traffic jam*] Cork, Stopper, Cap; Plug; Trad. tavern of Lyon

Bouchon de paille Bundle of straw (orig. on tavern signs, hence *bouchons* of Lyon)

Bouchonné Corked (wine)

Bouchots Mussels cultivated on racks suspended between poles (*bouchots* in Poitou)

Bouclé, -e Curled, Ringed

Boucler to Fasten; to Finish off

Boudin antillais Spicy Caribbean sausage

Boudin blanc White-meat sausage with regional variations

Boudin noir Black pudding, Blood sausage

Bouffe (fam.) Nosh, Grub; Informal meal amongst friends

Bouffer / Bouffi, -e (fam.) to Eat, to Stuff oneself / Puffy

Bouffis Bloaters: lightly smoked young herrings

Bouge *[hovel]* (fam.) Dive (bar, etc.)

Bougie Candle

Bougras Vegetable soup of Périgord

Boui-boui (fam.) Low-class/bad restaurant, etc.

Bouillabaisse Classic fish stew of Provence (orig. of Marseille)

Bouillant, -e Boiling; Boiling hot

Bouillante (fam.) Soup (which should be boiling hot!)

Bouilleture, Bouilliture Thick eel stew of Anjou & Poitou

Bouilleur de cru Licensed home-brewer of *eau-de-vie*

Bouilli Boiled beef (dish)

Bouillie Baby cereal (mix), Porridge, Gruel

Bouillie claire Skilly: thin soup/broth (of prison, etc.)

Bouillinade Fish stew *[bouillabaisse]* of Roussillon

Bouillir / Bouilli, -e to Be boiling / Boiled

Bouillir (faire ..) to Boil something

Bouilliture d'anguilles Eels cooked in garlic & white wine, sp. of Poitou-Charentes

Bouilloire Kettle

Bouillon Stock; Stock cube; Broth; (fam.) Restaurant

Bouillon gras/américain Beef tea; Meat stock

Bouillonner to Boil up, to Bubble up, to Froth up

Bouillons / A gros .. / A petits .. Bubbles / to Boil rapidly / to Simmer

Bouillotte Hot-water bottle

Bouillotter to Simmer

Boujaron Tot, Dram: 6 cl (rum measure for a sailor)

Boulanger / Boulangerie Baker / Bakery, Baking

Boulangère (à la ..) Baker's wife-style: dish with sliced potato & onion topping

Boulangerie-pâtisserie Shop that sells bread & cakes

Boule / Boule de cuisson Ball, Sphere / Cooking ball

Boule de Berlin German-style doughnut

Boule de naphtaline Mothball

Boule-de-neige *[snowball]* Small round cake coated in cream; Ice cream dessert; Field mushroom

Boulette *[pellet]* Croquette, Rissole, Meatball; Various ball-shaped cheeses

Boulette d'Avesnes Soft cheese of Picardy made with buttermilk & herbs, rolled in paprika

Boulette de Cambrai Cone-shaped herby cow's-milk cheese of the North

Boulghour, Bulghur Bulgur/cracked wheat

BOULONNAIS Region around Boulogne-sur-Mer in the North with a cuisine rich in fish & shellfish

Boulot Whole apple wrapped in pastry

Boulot, boulotte Fat, Plump, Dumpy

Boulotter (fam.) to Eat; to Gain one's daily bread (*boulot* = job)

Boum *[bang!]* [teenage] Party

Bouquet Bunch, Posy, Bouquet;

(wine term) Nose; Prawn (with whiskers like a goat/*bouc*) [*crevette rose*]

Bouquet garni Bunch/bag of mixed herbs

Bouquetière [*flower-girl*] (term) to Arrange vegetables round a joint, etc.

Bouquin [*old book*] Old hare; Old he-goat

BOURBONNAIS Province in the centre of France, jutting into the Auvergne & with a similar cuisine

Bourbonnaise (à la ..) Bourbonnais-style: rustic dishes with vegetables, chestnuts & fruit

Bourdaloue (poires ..) Poached pears in almond cream or rice

Bourdane Apple dumpling

Bourdelone Dessert of hot poached fruit

Bourdelot Stuffed apple/pear wrapped in pastry, sp. of Normandy

Bourdon Bumblebee

Bourg Small market-town (= borough)

Bourgeois Snapper (fish)

Bourgeoise (à la ..) Simple family-style dish served with garnish of small vegetables

Bourgeon Bud, Tip, Spear (of plant, etc.)

BOURGOGNE (la ..) Burgundy: wine-growing region, running N-S, roughly from Dijon to Lyon

Bourgogne (vins de ..) Huge variety of top-quality wines known simply as Burgundies

Bourguignonne (à la ..)

Burgundy-style: with onions, bacon, mushrooms &, of course, red wine

Bouribout Chicken/duck stew with grapes

Bourrache Borage

Bourratif, bourrative Filling, Stodgy

Bourrellerie Leather goods, Saddlery, etc.

Bourrer / Se .. to Cram / to Guzzle, to Stuff oneself

Bourriche Hamper, Large basket/box (esp. for oysters)

Bourricot, Bourrique (fam.) Donkey

Bourride Fish soup with vegetables of Provence (authentically with monkfish & egg yolks)

Bourriol Thick potato pancake of the Auvergne

Boursault Pasteurized cream cheese

Boursin Cream cheese of Normandy

Boursouflé, -e Swollen, Bloated

Boursoufler to Puff up, to Blister

Bouse Dung, Cowpat

Bout End, Tip; [tiny] Piece, a [little] Bit

Bout (au .. de) After (a time/period), At the end of (a period)

Bout des doigts Fingertips

Boutargue 'White caviar' of Provence: grey mullet/tuna roe

Bouteille / .. à gaz Bottle / Gas cylinder

Bouteille isolante Vacuum (Thermos) flask

Bouteillerie Buttery: domain of the butler & where wine, ale, bread & butter, etc. are kept

Boutique Small speciality shop

Bouton de guêtre *[gaiter button]* Smallest Field mushroom

Bouts (fermé aux deux ..) Closed/tied at both ends

Bouts (par petits ..) A bit at a time, Little by little

Bouvier Drover, Herdsman

Bouzy (mostly) Red wine of Champagne

Bovine (viande ..) Beef, Ox

Bovins Cattle

Boyaux Intestines, Guts, Bowels; Casing (for sausages, etc.)

Braconner / Braconnier to Poach (game, etc.) / Poacher

Braderie Street market; Clearance sale

Bragance *[Braganza]* Garnish of croquette potatoes & tomatoes; Dessert of orange-flavoured Genoese cake with custard cream

Braisage Braised dish; Braising

Braiser to Braise: cook slowly in a sealed pan (orig. placed in the embers/*braises*)

Braisière Braising pan, Stew-pot (trad. cast iron)

Branche (en ..) On the stalk (leaf vegetables, tomatoes, etc.)

Brancher to Perch, to Roost; to Plug in, to Connect (up)

Branchies Gills (of fish) *[ouïes]*

Brandade Classic dish of puréed salt cod *[morue]*, milk & olive oil, sp. of Provence &

Languedoc (garlic & puréed potatoes are often added)

Brassage Brewing

Brasser to Toss (salad); to Stir/mix up; to Brew (beer, etc.)

Brasserie Brewery; Restaurant that serves food continuously

Brayaude Dish with ingredients of the Auvergne; Nickname for an *Auvergnat*, who trad. wears breeches/*braies*

Brebis Ewe; Abbr. for ewe's-milk cheese

Bréchet Wishbone

Bredèle Spiced biscuit of Alsace, trad. hung on the Christmas tree

Bréjau Piece of salt pork used in *soupe Bréjaude*

Bréjaude Cabbage & ham soup of Limousin

Brème / .. de mer Bream / Sea bream

Bresaola Dried & salted beef (orig. of Italy)

Bressane (à la ..) Bresse-style: dishes using the renowned AOC corn-fed *poulet de Bresse*

BRESSE Region in the east, bordering Lyon, best known for its free-range & corn-fed poultry

Brestois Apricot & almond sponge cake of Brest

BRETAGNE Brittany: the rugged coastal region jutting out into the Atlantic & English Channel

Breton of Brittany; Large rich glazed cake

Bretonne (à la ..) Brittany-style: often with haricot beans

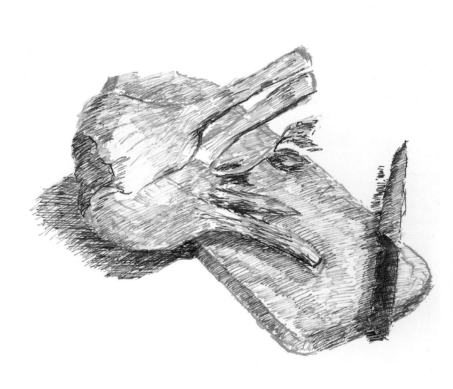

Bretzel Pretzel

Brick (See *Brik*)

Brider to Truss (poultry, etc.)

Brie Large disc of soft cow's-milk cheese from various regions around Paris (Meaux, Melun, Coulommiers, Montereau, Nangis & Provins)

Brigade de cuisine Kitchen staff

Brignolet, Bricheton (fam.) Bread

Brik Small item rolled/folded in *pâte à brik*, sp. of Tunisia

Brik (pâte à ..) Wafer thin pastry used for *briks*

Brillat-Savarin Cream cheese of Normandy; Chef & gastronome (1755-1826)

Brin, Brindille Twig, Sprig

Brinde Glass of wine drunk as a toast

Brioche *[paunch]* Soft bun/loaf made with butter & eggs (*Faire une brioche* = to drop a brick!)

Brioche (pâte à ..) Dough of flour, yeast, water/milk, eggs, butter [& sugar] used for the trad. soft bun *[brioche]* & numerous regional cakes & casings

Brioche à tête Trad. double-ball *brioche* bun (considered the most authentic, so also called *brioche parisienne*)

Brioche aux raisins Teacake

Brique *[brick]* Carton (for/of milk/juice, etc.); (fam.) Piece of bread

Briquet / Gaz à .. Lighter / Lighter fuel

Briser to Break, to Shatter, to Crush

Bristol Bristol board, Cardboard

Broc Pitcher, Large jug

Broccio, Brocciu Goat's-milk cheese of Corsica

Broche *[brooch]* Spit; Small meat skewer

Broche à tremper Dipping pin (for coating small items)

Brochet / .. de mer Fresh water pike / Barracuda fish

Brocheton Small pike

Brochette / En .. Skewer / Spit-roasted; On a skewer

Brochettes Food on skewers, Kebabs

Brocoli Broccoli

Brosse Brush; Broom *[balai]*

Brou / .. de noix Husk / Liqueur made from walnut shucks (husk covering shell); Walnut stain

Broue Froth; Head of beer

Brouet Broth; (fam.) Coarse/weak soup/stew

Brouette Wheelbarrow; Barrowful

Broufade Provençal beef stew with anchovies

Brouillade Mix of ingredients; Scrambled eggs

Brouillé, -e Mixed, Scrambled (eggs, etc.)

Broussaille Scrub, Undergrowth; Tousled

Brousse Ewe's-milk cheese of Provence; Bush; The Bush

Broutard, Broutart Calf grazed in pasture

Brouter to Graze, to Nibble

Broyé Large crumbly cake of Poitou; Maize flour gruel of Béarn

Broyer / Broyeur to Grind, to Crush, to Pound / Grinder

Broyeur d'ordures Waste disposal unit

Bruche Weevil

Brugnon Variety of nectarine

Brûlant, -e Burning; Scorching

Brûlé, -e Burnt, Flamed

Brûler to Burn, to Scald; to Roast (coffee)

Brûler (se ..) to Burn oneself

Brûlerie de café Coffee shop/merchant

Brûleur Burner, Gas-ring

Brûlot Flamed alcohol added to beverage or food

Brûlure / .. d'estomac Burn, Scald / Heartburn

Brun, -e Brown, Dark

Brunir to Brown

Brunissage, Brunisseur Browning

Brunoise Diced vegetables braised in butter

Brunoise (en ..) Mixed vegetables cut into small cubes/dice

Brut, -e Rough, Raw, Unrefined, Unsweetened, Dry

Bruxelloise (à la ..) Dish garnished with Brussels sprouts

Buanderie Laundry; Launderette

Bucarde Cockle

Buccin Whelk *[bulot]*

Bûche / .. de Noël Log; Log-shaped; Swiss roll / Yule log

Buffet Sideboard, Dresser; Food set out on a long table

Buffet de gare Station buffet/restaurant

Buffet froid Cold buffet: meal set out on a sideboard/*buffet*

Buffle Buffalo

BUGEY Small region in the East & one of the centres of French gastonomy with a rich cuisine of poultry, game, river fish, dairy produce & pâtés

Buglosse Bugloss: herb similar to borage

Bugne Large fritter of Lyon

Buisson *[bush]* Food presented in pyramid/dome shape

Bulle / Bulleux, bulleuse Bubble / Bubbly

Bulot Sea snail

Bunyettes Deep-fried *galettes* of Roussillon

Burette Cruet set *[huilier]*

Burlat Variety of cherry

Buron Rustic bistro in the Auvergne (orig. a shepherd's hut); Trad. name for dairy in the Cantal region

Buronnier Local name for a cheese maker in the Auvergne

Buvable Drinkable; to Take orally (medicine)

Buvette Station/theatre bar; Mobile bar at stadiums, etc.

Byrrh Bitter wine-based aperitif

C

Cabardès Red & rosé wine from the Aude

Cabaret Night-club show; Modest bar; Tea trolley

Cabas Two-handled shopping bag/basket

Cabécou *[little goat]* Tiny fresh (mainly) goat's-milk cheeses made in various regions of the SW *[Rocamadour]*

Cabernet Sauvignon Black grape variety (often blended with Merlot & Cabernet Franc), used esp. for the red wines of Bordeaux

Cabillaud, Cabillard Cod

Cabosse Bruise, Dent, Bump; Fruit of cocoa tree

Caboulot (fam.) Café, Bar, 'Pub'

Cabri Kid, Young goat in Corsica *[chevreau]*

Cacahuètes, Cacahuettes Peanuts

Cacao Cocoa (bean/powder: origin of chocolate)

Caddie Supermarket trolley

Cadence Cadence, Rhythm

Cadole Stone shelter for vineyard workers in Champagne

Caen (à la mode de ..) Tripe cooked in cider, sp. of Caen in Normandy

Cafard Cockroach *[blatte]*

Café Coffee; Cup of black coffee; a Café; Coffee-coloured

Café (faux ..) Decaffeinated coffee

Café (pause ..) Coffee break

Café à la chaussette *[sock]* Coffee made by slow filtering

Café allongé Black coffee with added hot water

Café au lait White coffee

Café brûlot Coffee flamed with brandy; Brandy-soaked sugar lump put into coffee

Café calva Black coffee with a measure of Calvados

Café complet Coffee served with a croissant

Café crème Small black coffee served with cream

Café décaféiné Decaffeinated coffee

Café express Espresso (strong Italian-style) coffee *[express]*

Café filtre Filter coffee

Café frappé Strong black coffee blended with crushed ice & ice cream

Café gallois *[Welsh coffee!]* Irish coffee

Café glacé Iced coffee

Café liégeois Coffee dessert with cream or ice cream

Café lyophilisé Freeze-dried instant coffee

Café moulu Ground coffee

Café noisette Black coffee with cream & Kirsch

Café serré Extra strong black coffee

Café soluble/en poudre Instant coffee

Caféine Caffeine: substance found in coffee, tea & cola

Cafeteria, Cafétéria Type of café/restaurant (often self-service) selling snacks & non-alcoholic drinks

Cafetière Coffee-making machine

Cageot Crate, Display tray (for fruit, etc.)

Cagette Small crate/case

Caghuse Cold knuckle of pork, sp. of Picardy

Cagibi Store cupboard

Cagouilles Snails in Charente [petits gris]

Cahors Strong deep red wine of the Dordogne

Caille Quail

Caillé Curd; Junket; Small ewe's-milk cheese

Caillebotte Cream cheese; Dish with cream cheese

Cailler (se ..) to Curdle; to Congeal

Caillette Small pork & green vegetable sausage of the SE

Caisse Cashier; Box, Case, Crate

Caissette Small box; Small paper case

Caissette (en ..) In a case (hors d'œuvres, petits fours, etc.)

Caisson Crate (for bottles)

Cajasse Cold dessert of rum-flavoured batter with fruit, sp. of Sarlat in Périgord

Cajou (pomme/noix de ..) Cashew fruit/nut

Cake English-style (usually fruit) cake

Calamar, Calmar Squid [encornet]

Calcaire Limescale

Calculette Pocket calculator

Calebasse Calabash: fruit of gourd family

Calendo (fam.) Camembert cheese

Caler/ Se .. to Wedge, to Steady; to Stall / to Be full

Calibre Size, Calibre

Calissons Diamond-shaped iced sweetmeats of Provence

Calvados, Calva Cider brandy of Calvados in Normandy

Camarguaise (à la ..) Camargue-style: with rice & ingredients of Provence

CAMARGUE (la..) Marshland in the Rhône delta renowned for its wild horses, black bulls, salt & rice

Camelot / Camelote Street vendor / Cheap shoddy goods

Camembert Soft cow's-milk cheese of Normandy

Camomille Camomile: used for herbal teas

Campagnard, -e of the Country [side], Rustic

Campagne Country, Country-side; Campaign; Season

Camphre Camphor

Canapé Bite-sized bread/toast with savoury topping

Canard Duck; Drake; (fam.) Sugar lump 'dunked' in coffee/alcohol; (fam) One's daily newspaper

Canard de Barbarie Barbary duck: large duck, which can weigh more than 4 kg

Canard de Nantes/Challans Duck (orig. from the Vendée): crossbreed of wild & farmed varieties

Canard de Pékin Small fatty duck used in Chinese cuisine

Canard de Rouen Duck from

Normandy (killed by smothering to avoid bleeding & giving special flavour)

Canard laqué Peking duck: Chinese dish of roasted duck glazed with sweet-&-sour sauce

Canard sauvage / .. siffleur Wild duck / Widgeon

Canardière Duck pond

Cancalaise (à la ..) Cancale-style: with its renowned oysters, prawns or *sauce normande*

Cancoillotte Strong-tasting cheese paste (made with low fat *metton* cheese), sp. of Franche-Comté

Candissoire Wire grid & tray used when glazing small items

Cane / Caneton Female duck / Male duckling

Canette Female duckling; Trad. thick bottle for beer or lemonade; Tin can

Canne Reed; Cane; Stick

Canne à sucre Sugar cane

Canneberge Cranberry *[airelle]*

Cannelé, -e Fluted

Canneler to Make decorative grooves in fruit, etc. before slicing

Cannelés Little fluted cakes, sp. of Bordeaux

Cannelle Cinnamon

Cannelure Groove, Channel

Canon Round cut of beef (esp. *onglet*); (fam.) Small glass of red wine

Cantal *AOC* cow's-milk cheese of the Auvergne

Cantaloup Cantaloupe melon

Cantine Canteen, Cafeteria

Caoua (fam.) Coffee *[kawa]*

Capelin Caplin: fish mostly used in soups

Capillaire Maidenhair fern

Capilotade Type of hash made with cooked meat/chicken

Capitaine Threadfin: sea fish related to mullet

Capitaine rouge/blanc Emperor bream *[empereur]*

Capiteux (wine term) Sensuous, Heady

Câpres Capers

Caprin Caprine: pertaining to goats

Capsule / .. à vis Bottle top; Cap; Seal / Screw-top cap

Capucin Savoury tartlet filled with cheese-flavoured choux pastry; Hare *[lièvre]* over 1 year

Capucine Nasturtium

Caquelon Earthenware cooking pot with glazed interior (*toupin* in the SW)

Caquette Southern dish of fried blenny

Carafe / .. de vin Decanter, Jug of water / Jug of wine

Carafon Small *carafe*

CARAIBES (les ..) The Caribbean (Islands) (See *Créole*)

Carambole Carambola: star-shaped tropical fruit

Caramel / .. dur / .. mou Caramel / Toffee / Fudge

Caramélisé, -e Caramelized

Caraméliser to Caramelize: turn sugar into caramel, coat with caramel or glaze vegetables, etc.

Caramote Large Med. prawn [*crevette rose*]

Carapace Shell (of lobster, etc.)

Caraque 'Scroll' made of chocolate, to decorate cakes, etc.; Rich chocolate cake decorated with cream

Carbonade Beef stew with regional variations (cooked with beer in Flanders, with wine in Provence)

Carcasse Carcass (of animal)

Cardamome Cardamom

Carde Chard: variety of beet; Inner leaves of cardoon/*cardon*

Cardinal Fish dish with lobster garnish/sauce; Dessert with red fruit; Variety of black dessert grape

Cardinaliser to Cook shellfish (which turns red) in stock

Cardine Megrim (fish)

Cardon Cardoon: prickly plant related to the artichoke

Carême Lent

CAREME (Antonin) Celebrated Parisian chef (1783-1833); many dishes bear his name

Carence Deficiency

Cari Curry (in French cuisine, often a stew with curry flavours or meat with a curry sauce) [*curi*]

Carmin Carmine, Cochineal: food colouring (E120)

Caroline Savoury éclair filled with cheese/ham/fish mousse

Carotte Carrot

Caroube Carob: sweet bean used in food industry

Carpaccio Paper-thin slices of raw meat/fish/fruit (orig. Italian dish of raw beef in olive oil)

Carpe Carp

Carré Square; Piece (of chocolate); Loin, Rack (of lamb); Best end of neck

Carré de l'est Square cheese, with sticky rind, of Lorraine

Carré de Lille Gingerbread of the North

Carreau Tile; Windowpane; Trivet; Small square; Check(ed)

Carrelet Plaice [*plie*]

Cartagène Liqueur wine of Languedoc-Roussillon

Carte (à la ..) Free choice from menu (i.e. not set meal/*menu*)

Carte (la ..) The menu card (*Menu* = set meal)

Carte brasserie *Brasserie* menu (trad. available all day)

Carte des vins Wine list

Carthame Safflower, Bastard saffron

Cartilage Gristle

Carton [cardboard] Box

Cartouche Cartridge

Carvi (grains de ..) Caraway (seeds)

Cascher Kosher [*kascher*]

Caséine Casein: milk protein

Caser to Find a place for, to Put away

Casier / .. à bouteilles Bin, Rack / Bottle rack

Casier à langoustes Lobster pot

Cassant, -e Crisp, Brittle

Cassate Cassata: Italian ice cream cake

Casse-croûte [*crust breaker*] Snack; Snack bar

Casse-museau [*jaw breaker*] Hard cheese & almond biscuit

Casse-noix/noisettes Nutcrackers

Casser / Cassé, -e to Break, to Snap, to Crack (nuts) / Broken

Casser la croûte [*to break the crust*] to Have a snack, to Snack

Casserole Saucepan, Pan (*Poêle* = frying pan; *Cocotte* = stew pan)

Casserole russe Trad. copper saucepan (used in catering)

Casserons Small squid of Charentes [*encornets*]

Cassis Blackcurrant; Wine of Provence

Cassis (crème/liqueur de ..) Blackcurrant liqueur (base for *kir*)

Cassole Earthenware cooking pot (esp. for *cassoulet*)

Cassolette Small heatproof container; Dish cooked in it

Cassonade Soft brown sugar

Cassoulet Classic Languedoc stew with haricot beans

Castor Beaver

Catalane of Catalogne (region shared with Spain in eastern Pyrenees) with a trad. cuisine of hearty soups & stews, spicy flavours & strong sweet wines

Catalyse (four à ..) Catalysis oven: with self-cleaning lining

Catigot Fish stew with regional variations

Cauchoise (à la ..) Caux-style: often with hare/rabbit

Caudière, Caudrée Fish soup/stew of the North

Cavaillon Melon from this town in Provence

Cave / Caveau [*vault*] Cellar, Wine cellar (Caves = *grottes*) / Small cellar

Cave d'appartement Portable cellar: small temperature-controlled cabinet on shock absorbers

Caveau de dégustation Wine cellar reception room/area

Caviar Sturgeon roe; Hors d'œuvre of vegetable purée (esp. aubergine)

Caviar blanc (fam.) Mullet roe [*boutargue*]

Caviste Cellarman: in charge of wine cellar in a restaurant, etc.

Cawcher Kosher [*cascher*]

Cébette Young spring onion (before bulb has formed)

Cédrat Citron: large variety of lemon

Céleri (branche/à côtes) Celery

Céleri (pied de ..) Head of celery

Céleri-rave Celeriac

Céleri-rémoulade Shredded celeriac in mayonnaise

Célestine (poulet ..) Fricassee of chicken, sp. of Lyon

Cellier Larder, Store-cupboard; Store

Cendrés [*in cinders*] Various small cheeses rolled in ashes

Cène (la ..) The Last Supper

Centrifugeuse Electric juice extractor

Cépage (vin de ..) Varietal wine: named after the variety of grape from which it is made

Cèpe [de Bordeaux] Cep: prized wild mushroom

Cèpe bai Bay Bolete mushroom

Céphalopodes Cephalopods: molluscs with a distinct head (cuttlefish, squid, etc.)

Cercle à tarte Ring mould for tarts & flans

Céréale Cereal; Corn crops

Céréalier, céréalière Cereal farm/farmer

Cerf / .. commun Stag / Red deer

Cerfeuil Chervil

Cerises / .. jubilé Cherries / Cherries flambéed with Kirsch

Cerisette Cherry-flavoured drink/sweet

Cerisier / Cerisaie Cherry-tree / Cherry-orchard

Cerneaux Shelled walnuts; Green walnuts

Cerner to Shell, to Husk (walnuts, etc.); to Score with fork or sharp knife

Cernier Grouper, Stone Bass (large tuna-like fish)

Cervelas Saveloy sausage (orig. made with *cervelles*/brains) with regional variations

Cervelle de canut [*silk-weaver's brain*] Whipped cream cheese with herbs, garlic, shallots &, for special occasions, white wine & olive oil, sp. snack of Lyon (famed for its silk)

Cervelles Brains (The brain = *le cerveau*)

Cervoise Barley beer

Céteau Small sole

CEVENNES (les ..) Rocky unpopulated region in the Massif Central (R.L. Stevenson country!)

Cévenole (à la ..) Cévennes-style: with chestnuts/mushrooms

Chabichou Small goat's-milk cheese of Poitou-Charentes

Chablis Renowned white wine of Burgundy

Chabot Bullhead, Sea devil: fish with large head

Chabrot, Chabrol (faire ..) To add a dash of red wine to the last of one's soup

Chacun, -e Each one, Every one

Chai Wine store/cellar (esp. of Bordeaux where there are no underground cellars)

Chai (maître de ..) Cellar master (in charge of a *chai*)

Chair / .. à saucisse Flesh / Sausage meat

Chair de crabe Crabmeat

Chaise d'enfant High chair

Chaland Customer

Chaleur Heat, Warmth

Chaleureux, chaleureuse Warm, Hearty

Challans Variety of duck from the Vendée

Chalosse (bœuf de ..) Beef cattle from this region of Gascony

Châlot Apple cake made with sweet bread & eggs

Chalumeau [*blowlamp*] Flexible/bendy straw [*paille*]

Chalumeau à cocktail Swizzle stick

Chalut / Chalutier Trawl (of fish) / Trawler

Chambord Classic dish of large stuffed fish (carp, salmon, etc.)

Chambord (sauce ..) Sauce made with fish stock & red wine

Chambrer (term) to Allow wine to reach room temperature

Chameau / Chamelle Camel / She-camel

Chamois Small mountain goat [*isard*]

Chamoure Trad. pumpkin pie of Lyon

Champ / En plein .. Field / In open country

Champagne Bubbly, Champers: known as a celebration wine the world over, made by a complex & strictly-controlled method in a defined area of Champagne

CHAMPAGNE (la ..) Region, NE of Paris, where the poor chalky soil produces vines used to make the world-famous sparkling wine, *le champagne*, as well as some still wine

Champenois of Champagne; With champagne or wine of Champagne

Champêtre [*of the fields*] Rural, Rustic, Country-style

Champignon Mushroom, Fungus

Champignon de Paris/couche Cultivated/button/cup mushroom

Champignon vénéneux Toadstool

Champignonnière Mushroom bed

Champignons (aller aux ..) to Go mushroom picking

Champigny Puff-pastry tart with apricot jam or *compote*

Champoreau Black coffee laced with spirit

Chancir to Go Mouldy

Chandeleur Candlemas (2 Feb.): celebrated with pancakes

Chanteau Hunk (of bread, etc.)

Chanter to Sing; to Crow; (term) to Sizzle (esp. butter, etc.)

Chanterelle Another name for *girolle* mushroom

Chantilly (crème ..) Sweet-ened/flavoured whipped cream

Chantilly [à la ..] With whipped cream

Chanvre Hemp

Chaource Creamy cow's-milk cheese of Champagne

Chapeau [*hat*] Cap (of mush-room), Top, Layer of pastry on a pie/*tourte*, etc. (N.B: *chapeau melon* = bowler hat!)

Chapelet [*rosary*] String of onions

Chapelure Dried breadcrumbs (Fresh breadcrumbs = *panure*)

Chapon Capon: castrated cock bird; Scorpion fish; Knob of dry bread rubbed with garlic (used to flavour salads)

Charançon Weevil

Charbon / .. de bois Coal / Charcoal

Charbonnée Charcoal grilled; Stew thickened with blood

Charbonnier Coley, Coalfish

Charcuter to Mangle meat (by bad carving)

Charcuterie Delicatessen (orig. only pork meat products & shop selling them)

Charcutier, charcutière Pork butcher

Charcutière (à la ..) Dish with pork, ham & sausages, etc.

Chardon Thistle (related to cardoon/*cardon*)

Chardonnay White grape variety used esp. in Burgundy wines & champagne

Charentais Variety of melon

Charentaise (à la ..) Charente-style: often with Cognac

CHARENTE *Département,* inland from Charente-Maritime, with a simple cuisine of high-quality ingredients

Chargouère Turnover, Pasty

Chariot *[carriage]* Trolley (esp. for cheese & desserts); Supermarket trolley *[caddy]*; Cart, Truck

Charlotte Hot dessert of fruit purée in mould lined with bread; Puréed fish/vegetables set in a mould; Variety of potato

Charlotte russe Cold dessert of Bavarian cream/mousse set in a mould lined with sponge fingers

Charmille Arbour

Charnière Hinge, Join

Charnu, -e Fleshy, Plump, Thick, Meaty

Charolaise (à la ..) Charolais-style: often a beef dish or with cauliflower/turnips

Charolaise (race ..) Breed of beef cattle from Burgundy

Charron Cartwright, Wheelwright

Charrue Plough

Chartres (à la ..) Various dishes cooked with tarragon

Chartreuse Green/yellow herb-flavoured liqueur of Grenoble; Spectacular dish of game birds & layered vegetables

Chasse Hunt; Hunting; Shooting

Chasse au lièvre Hare coursing

Chasse-café (fam.) Spirit taken after coffee

Chasselas Variety of white dessert & wine grape (called *Fendant* in Switzerland, where it represents 30% of the vines)

Chasseur Hunter; Various dishes & a sauce, with mushrooms, tomatoes & shallots

Châtaigne Sweet chestnut with twin fruits in the husk (*marron* has a single fruit)

Châtaigne d'eau Water chestnut *[macre]*

Châtaigne de mer Sea urchin *[oursin]*

Château *[castle]* Wine estate (esp. of Bordeaux)

Châteaubriand Thick fillet steak

Châteauneuf-du-Pape Strong (mostly) red Côtes-du-Rhône wine from around Avignon (once a Papal city)

Châtelain Castellan, Lord of the manor

Châtelaine (à la ..) Dish garnished with chestnuts/artichokes

Châtrer *[to castrate]* (term) to Remove bitter-tasting gut of shrimp by twisting tail from head

Chaude Plum tart

Chaudeau Orange tart

Chaud-froid Elaborate dish of white meat, poultry or fish that is prepared hot & served cold in sauce/aspic

Chaud-froid (sauce ..) Brown/white sauce used to coat *chaud-froid* ingredients

Chaudière Boiler

Chaudin Pig's intestine (used as sausage skin)

Chaudrée Fish soup/stew of the Vendée

Chaudron Cauldron: large cooking pot

Chaudronnerie (petite ..) Pots & pans

Chauffage Heating; Heater

Chauffe-assiettes Plates warmer

Chauffe-eau Water-heater

Chauffe-plats Hot plate

Chauffer to Heat, to Warm

Chaufroiter (term) to Prepare sauce for a *chaud-froid*

Chaume / Chaumière Thatch; Stubble / Thatched roof

Chausson *[slipper]* Turnover, Pasty

Chayote Custard marrow

Cheddar Cheddar (& often French name for Cheshire) cheese

Chef Head, Boss, Chief, Leader; Chef

Chef cuisinier/de cuisine Chef, Head/master cook

Cheminée *[chimney]* Pie funnel (for steam to escape)

Chemise (en ..) *[in a shirt]* Food (potato, garlic, etc.) cooked in its skin/wrapping (ham, napkin, etc.)

Chemiser (term) to Line mould with fat, paper, etc.

Chêne Oak

Chenet Firedog

Chenin blanc White grape variety used in Loire wines

Cheptel / .. ovin/porcin Livestock / Sheep/pig population

Cheptel bovin Beef/dairy herd, Head of cattle

Cher, chère / Pas .. Dear, Costly / Cheap, Inexpensive

Chère Cheer, Fare, Good living

Chester French name for Cheshire cheese

Chevaine, Chevesne Chub: fish used for stews

Cheval Horse; Horsemeat

Cheval (à ..) *[on horseback]* Egg/oyster, etc. placed on top of steak/hamburger, etc.

Chevaler to Arrange food by overlapping slices, etc.

Chevalière (à la ..) Elaborate dish with garnish of crayfish & oysters

Chevaline (boucherie ..) Horse butcher

Chevaucher (se ..) to Overlap

Cheville *[ankle]* Butcher's hook

Chèvre Goat; Abbr. for goat's-milk cheese; Small crab *[étrille]* in Brittany

Chevrette Kid: young goat; Local name for shrimp *[crevette]*; Trivet; Chemist's jar

Chevreuil Venison; Roedeer, Roebuck

Chevreuil (en ..) Meat prepared & served as venison

Chevrier Goatherd

Chevriers Flageolets beans

Chicon (fam.) Chicory *[endive]*

Chicorée [frisée] Curly endive (salad green)

Chicorée à café Chicory root

Chicorée de Bruxelles Belgian endive *[witloof]*

Chicorée rouge Radicchio: variety of Italian chicory

Chicot *[stump]* (fam.) Hunk (of bread)

Chien de mer Dogfish *[saumonette]*

Chiffon Duster, Cloth, Rag (Fabric = *tissu*)

Chiffonnade Ingredients shredded/sliced paper-thin

Chiffonné, -e *[crumpled]* Tired (lettuce, etc.)

Chimique Chemical, Synthetic, Man-made

Chinchard Horse mackerel, Scab

Chinois Conical-shaped sieve *[passoire]*

Chinois confit Small bitter orange crystallized or preserved in brandy

Chinois, -e Chinese

Chinon Red, white & rosé wine of Touraine in the Loire Valley

Chipiron Squid in the Pays Basque *[calamar]*

Chipolata (à la ..) Garnish of chipolatas, chestnuts & vegetables

Chipoter to Nibble (food)

Chips Potato crisps

Chique Type of cheese fondue made with *crème fraîche*, chives & garlic, sp. of the Vosges; Mint-/lemon-flavoured almond bonbon

Chiqueter (term) to Press/score edge of pastry, etc.

Choc des verres Clink of glasses

Chocart, Choquart Large apple turnover

Chocolat / Chocolats Chocolate: basic mix of cocoa & sugar (quality depends on % of cocoa/*cacao)* / Chocolates

Chocolat (bouchées au ..) Chocolates

Chocolat (truffes en ..) Chocolate truffles

Chocolat à croquer Eating chocolate

Chocolat à pâtisser Confectioner's chocolate

Chocolat au lait Milk chocolate

Chocolat blanc White chocolate

Chocolat chaud Hot chocolate drink

Chocolat de couverture Coating (quick melting) chocolate

Chocolat de ménage/à cuire Cooking chocolate

Chocolat en poudre Chocolate powder

Chocolat fin/extrafin/surfin/ supérieur Superfine chocolate

Chocolat menier Quality dessert chocolate

Chocolat noir dessert Plain dessert chocolate

Chocolat noir/bitter/noir amer Dark/bitter chocolate

Chocolat praliné Chocolate with praline chips

Chocolatier Chocolate shop

Chocolatière Chocolate pot (for serving hot chocolate)

Choisy Dish/soup with lettuce

Choix / Au .. Choice, Selection / Of your choice

Chope Tankard, Mug

Chopine Small bottle (orig. 0.46 ltr.)

Choquart Apple & raisin turn-over, sp. of Brittany

Chorizo Dry spicy Spanish sausage with pimento

Chou, choux Cabbage; Small bun/puff made with choux pastry

Chou (salade de ..) Coleslaw

Chou cabus White cabbage

Chou chinois/de Chine Chinese cabbage/leaves

Chou de mai Spring cabbage/greens

Chou de Milan Savoy cabbage

Chou farci Stuffed cabbage (classic dish of the South using Savoy cabbage)

Chou frisé Curly kale

Chou pommé Firm round (white) cabbage

Chou rouge Red cabbage

Choucroute Sauerkraut: pickled cabbage; Classic Alsatian dish of sauerkraut with meat/fish

Chouée Dish of cabbage & vegetables cooked in pork fat

Choufleur Cauliflower

Choufleur romano Green coned cauliflower

Chou-marin Sea kale

Chou-navet [cabbage-turnip] Swede [rutabaga]

Chouquette Small choux bun sprinkled with sugar

Chou-rave Kohlrabi: (German for) cabbage-turnip

Choux (pâte à ..) Choux pastry: batter mixture, boiled & baked

Choux à la crème Cream puffs

Choux au fromage Cheese puffs

Choux brocolis Broccoli

Choux de Bruxelles Brussels sprouts

Choux palmistes Palm hearts

Christe-marine Samphire [salicorne]

Christophine Another name for *chayote* (squash)

Chroniqueur gastronomique Cookery correspondent; Restaurant-guide writer

Chuchotement [whispering] Hiss of pressure cooker valve

Chuinter to Hiss, to Sizzle

Churrasco Spicy stew

Chutes [falls] Trimmings (of pastry, etc.)

Cible / Ciblé, -e Target / Targeted

Ciboule Spring/Welsh onion

Ciboules de Chine Chinese chives

Ciboulettes Chives [civettes]

Cicatrice / Cicatriser Scar / to Heal

Cidre Cider (trad. served in a stoneware cup/*moque*)

Cidre bouché *[corked]* Bottled cider

Ciel et terre *[sky & earth]* Potatoes *[pommes de terre]* with apples *[pommes en l'air]*; Black pudding *[boudin noir]* with pears

Cigale de mer Squill-fish (similar to lobster)

Cime Top, Summit

Cimier Haunch of venison *[gigue]*

Cinghalaise (à la ..) Sri Lankan-style: cold fish or white meat with curry-flavoured vinaigrette

Cinq-épices Five spices of Chinese cooking (cinnamon, clove, fennel, pepper, star anise)

Ciron Cheese-mite

Ciseaux / Cisailles Scissors / Shears

Ciseler to Snip (herbs); to Make incisions (in fish)

Citerne Cistern, Tank

Citrique Citric (acid)

Citron / .. vert Lemon / Lime

Citron pressé Drink of fresh lemon juice with sugar & water

Citronelle Lemon balm

Citronnade Lemonade

Citronner / Citronné, -e to Sprinkle with lemon juice; to Rub with cut lemon / Lemon-flavoured

Citronnier Lemon-tree

Citrouillat Sweet/savoury pumpkin pie of Berry

Citrouille Pumpkin *[potiron]*

Civelles Elvers

Cives Garlic chives

Civet / .. de lièvre Rich game/seafood stew / Jugged hare

Civettes Chives *[ciboulettes]*

Clafoutis Batter cake with fruit (trad. cherries)

Claie Rack for cooling cakes, storing fruit, etc.; Shelf in oven/fridge

Clair, -e Clear; Thin (soup); Light (colour)

Claires Salt marsh oyster beds; Oysters raised in *claires*

Clairet Pale red wine of Bordeaux & Médoc (the word 'claret' came from *clairet*)

Clairette White grape variety of the Midi; Sparkling white wine (made from *Clairette* & *Muscat* grapes) of the South

Clairette-de-Bellegarde Dry white wine of the Gard made from *Clairette* grapes

Clairette-de-Die Sparkling white wine of theDrôme

Clam Clam: smooth-shelled mollusc *[palourde]*

Clamart Various dishes containing green peas

Claper (fam.) to Eat

Clapier Rabbit hutch

Clapotons Sheep's trotters in Lyon

Claquebitou Savoury goat's-milk cheese dip/spread, sp. of Burgundy

Claqueret Whipped cream cheese of Lyon

Claquin Whipped cream cheese of Mâcon

Clarifier to Clarify (butter, stock, etc.)

Clarté Clarity, Clearness, Limpidity

Clavaire Clavaria: woodland mushroom

Clavelin Dumpy 62 cl bottle used for *Vin Jaune* of the Jura

Clayette Small *claie* (rack/tray for storing fruit, etc.)

Clayon Basket/tray for draining cheese, drying fruit, etc.

Clémentine Clementine (citrus fruit)

Clémenvilla Large cousin of clementine

Climat *[climate]* (wine term) 'Growth' in Burgundy (See also *Cru*)

Clin d'œil Wink of an eye, In a flash

Cloche *[bell]* Bell-shaped cover for dish/plate

Cloche maraîchère Salad bell, Glass cloche

Cloison Partition

Cloporte Woodlouse

Cloquer to Blister

Clore / Clos, -e to Seal, to End with / Finished, Ended

Clos Enclosure; [walled] Vineyard, esp. in Burgundy

Clous de girofle Cloves (*clous* = nails)

Clouter to Stud (onion with cloves, etc.)

Clovisse Mediterranean clam

Coagulant Coagulant, Clotting agent

Coaguler to Congeal, to Clot; to Curdle

Cobaye (servir de ..) to Be a guinea pig

Cocagne (pays de ..) Cockaigne: land of milk & honey

Coccinelle Ladybird

Cochenille Cochineal: carmine red dye

Cochon / .. de lait Pig / Suckling pig

Cochonnailles (fam.) Pork products *[charcuterie]*

Cochonnet Piglet

Cocktail Cocktail (drink); Cocktail party; Small/bite-size item; Fruit/prawn cocktail

Coco Liquorice water: refreshing drink made from liquorice-flavoured water & lemon juice; Child's word for egg

Coco (noix de ..) Coconut

Coco-fesse Giant chickpea of the Seychelles

Cocos White beans in purple pod (used whole when young)

Cocotier Coconut palm

Cocotte Ovenproof dish with lid & two handles; Casserole, Stew; Child's word for hen

Cocotte (en ..) Cooked/baked (esp. eggs) in a small *cocotte* dish

Cocotte-minute Pressure cooker

Cocotter (fam.) to Stink, to Pong

Code barres Bar code

Codonat Quince in Provence *[coing]*

Cœur Heart; Heart-shaped cheese

Cœur (à ..) (term) Soft cheese in perfect condition (Lit. ripe through to its 'heart')

Cœurs de palmier Palm hearts

Coffre Chest, Bin, Safe; (term) Body of lobster

Coffret Small box, Casket

Cognac World-famous brandy of Charente (See also *Armagnac*)

Coin cuisine Cooking area

Coing / .. du Japon Quince / False quince, Japonica

Cointreau Orange-flavoured liqueur of Angers

Col Neck (of bottle, etc.); Mountain pass

Colbert Egg & bread-crumbed fried fish

Colbert (sauce ..) Spicy sauce of meat glaze & butter with Madeira (for vegetables, grills & fish)

Colère (en ..) *[in a rage]* Fish (esp. whiting) served with its tail in its mouth

Colimaçon *[spiral staircase]* Snail *[escargot]*

Colin / Colinot Hake *[merlu]* / Small hake

Collation Snack, Light meal

Colle *[glue]* State of softened gelatine ready to dissolve

Coller *[to stick]* to Add gelatine; to Use gelatine as sealant

Collet, Collier Neck, Scrag, Collar

Colombe Dove *[tourterelle]*

Colombine Small cheese croquette

Colonel (le ..) (fam.) Livarot cheese (wrapped in five strips of grass)

Colonne *[column]* Apple-corer

Coloquintes Decorative (nonedible) squashes

Colorants Colouring agents

Colorer to Colour, to Add colour

Colvert *[green collar]* Mallard (wild duck)

Colza Rape (seed used to make oil)

Comble Heaped measure, Highest point

Combler to Fill [up], to Fill to the top

Comestible / Comestibles Edible / Food, Provisions, Victuals

Comice Variety of pear

Comice agricole Regional agricultural show

Commander / Sur commande to Order / Made to order

Commis [de cuisine] Kitchen/chef's assistant

Commis voyageur Travelling salesman

Commun, -e Common, Ordinary, Usual

Communard Cook in charge of food for the kitchen staff

Commune Community, District

Complet, complète Complete, Whole, Wholemeal, Full (N.B: I'm full = *Je n'en peux plus*)

Composé, -e Shaped, Formed, Moulded; Consisting of

Composer to Concoct, to Invent

Compote Food stewed until it disintegrates (esp. fresh/dried fruit, game, sweet peppers & onions)

Compoter (term) to Cook ingredients very slowly

Compotier Large fruit dish on raised base; Fruit bowl

Comprendre to Understand; to Include

Compris (service/tout..) Service/everything included (in price)

Comptoir Counter, Bar (of café)

Comté Cow's-milk cheese with small holes of Franche-Comté; County (of Nice, etc.)

COMTE de NICE Region around Nice (once a 'county')

Comtoise (à la ..) Franche-Comté-style: often freshwater fish or meat cooked in wine

Concasser to Crush, to Pound, to Cut bones, etc.; (term) to Chop (herbs, etc.)

Concentré, -e Concentrated (liquids, etc.)

Conchage Process in manufacture of chocolate

Concher to Pipe (with forcing bag)

Concocter to Concoct

Concombre Cucumber

Concorde Garnish of vegetables for joints of meat

Conçue Imagined, Conceived

Condé Various dishes, soups & desserts dedicated to the great general of Chantilly (1621-86)

Condiments Seasonings, Herbs, Relish, etc.

Confectionner to Make up, to Prepare (ingredients, etc.)

Confiote Child's word for jam *[confiture-compote]*

Confire to Preserve (in fat, syrup, etc.); to Pickle; to Candy

Confiserie Confectionery; Sweet factory/shop

Confiseur, confiseuse Confectioner

Confit, -e Preserved, Pickled, Candied; Potted (meat, etc.)

Confit de canard/oie Pieces of duck/goose preserved in duck/goose fat, sp. of the SW

Confiture / .. d'orange Jam, Preserve / Marmalade

Congélateur / Congelé, -e Freezer / Frozen

Congolais Coconut rock: coconut meringue biscuit

Congre Conger/sea eel

Connaisseur, connaisseuse Expert, Connoisseur

Conque Conch (shell)

Conseil / Conseiller Advice / to Advise; to Recommend

Conservation en boîte Bottling; Canning

Conserver to Preserve, to Seal in

Conserves Preserves, Pickles; Tinned/bottled foods

Consistance Consistence, Consistency

Consommation Consumption; Drinks, etc. (in bar/café)

Consommé Clear soup made from meat/poultry/fish stock; Beef tea

Consommer to Consume; to Accomplish

Constat Official report; Assessment

Contenance Capacity, Volume

Contenant Packaging

Conteneur Container

Contenir to Contain, to Hold, to Accommodate

Contenu Contents

Contiser (term) to Encrust chicken/fish fillets with sliced truffle

Contrée Land (country), Clime, Region

Contre-filet Part of beef sirloin [*faux-filet*]

Conversation Little almond tartlet

Convier to Invite

Convives Guests, Table companions; Restaurant covers

Convivial, -e Sociable, Friendly, Festive

Copa, Coppa Dried spicy pork sausage of Corsica & Italy

Copeaux [*wood shavings*] Scrolls (of pastry/chocolate)

Copieux, copieuse Copious, Hearty Substantial, Plentiful

Coprah Copra: coconut kernel (used for its oil)

Coprin chevelu Shaggy Inkcap mushroom

Coq Cockerel, Cock bird; Ship's cook

Coq d'Inde Turkey cock

Coq de bruyère Capercaille, Wood/black grouse

Coque Shell (of egg, nut, etc.); Cockle; Easter cake of the South

Coque (à la ..) In its shell

Coquelet, Jeune coq Young cockerel

Coquelicot Poppy [*pavot*]

Coqueret du Pérou Cape gooseberry, Chinese lantern

Coques à petits fours Shell-shaped iced petits fours

Coquetier Egg cup; Wholesale egg seller

Coquillage Shellfish; Shell (of shellfish)

Coquille Shell; Shell-shaped; Scallop(-shape); Dish of creamy fish served in a scallop shell

Coquille Saint-Jacques Scallop

Coquillettes Small macaroni pasta

Coquilleur à beurre Butter curl

Corail Coral; Roe of scallop/*coquille Saint-Jacques*

Corb, Corvine Mediterranean fish

Corbeille Basket (for serving/presentation) (See also *Panier*)

Corbeille à pain Bread basket

Corbeille à papier Waste-paper basket

Corbières Full-bodied (mostly) red wine of Languedoc

Corde Cord, Rope, Line

Corde à linge Clothesline

Cordée [*twisted*] (terms) Pastry gone tough (too much water) or potato purée gone sticky (over-beaten)

Cordon [*cord*] Band of sauce poured around food

Cordon bleu [*blue ribbon*] Orig.

award for culinary excellence, now denotes good cook/cooking; Classic stuffing of ham & Gruyère cheese

Coriace Tough, Leathery (meat)

Coriandre Coriander

Corme Sorb apple (resembles small pear)

Cormé Cider-like beverage made from *cormes*

Corne Horn, Antler

Corne à pâtisserie Cream horn tin/mould

Corne à sel Samphire *[salicorne]*

Corne de bélier *[ram's horn]* Old variety of potato

Cornes (gâteaux à ..) Cornets; Cream horns

Cornet Cone-shaped; Rolled & filled slice of ham/salmon

Cornette Variety of crisp bitter lettuce

Cornichon Gherkin

Cornouille Cornelian: sharp oval wild cherry

Cornue d'hiver Winter/acorn squash

Corossol Custard apple: tropical fruit

Corps / .. gras Body / Fat (lard, etc.)

Corriger to Correct; to Adjust, to Amend (seasoning, etc.)

Corsé, -e Robust, Full bodied, Spicy

CORSE (la ..) Corsica *[Ile de beauté]*: France's largest island *département* in the Med.

Corse (vins de ..) Corsican wines: mostly *vins de pays* made from Italian grapes

Corser to Spice, to Lace

Corvée Chore, Drudgery

Cosse Husk, Pod (of bean, etc.)

Costaud Hefty, Husky, Tough, Beefy

Costières Table wine of Languedoc

Côte Rib, Chop; Coast; River bank, Side of hill

Côté / A .. Side / Beside, Next to, On/to one side

COTE d'AZUR The Riviera: Med. coastal resort in the South of France

COTE d'OR (Lit. golden hillside) In the heart of Burgundy, a long strip of superior wine growing country

COTE du RHÔNE Wine growing region of the Rhône Valley in the SE

Côte/Coteaux/Côtes de/du ... Denotes a wine's region of origin

Coteau Hillock, Small hill, Slope

Côte-Chalonnaise Red wine of Burgundy (around Chalon-sur-Saône)

Côte-de-Beaune Red & white wine from the region around Beaune in the Côte d'Or

Côte-de-Nuits (mostly) Red wine of Burgundy

Côtelé, -e Ribbed

Côtelette Cutlet

Côte-Rotie Red Côtes-du-Rhône wine from the banks opposite Vienne

Côtes-du-Luberon Fruity red, white & rosé wine of Provence

Côtes-du-Roussillon Robust deep red, rosé & white wine of Roussillon

Cotignac Quince paste (orig. sp. of Orléans)

Coton Cotton; Cotton wool

Cotonné, -e Woolly (fruit); Fruit covered with down

Côtoyer to Turn a joint during roasting

Cotriade Fish, onion & potato soup of Brittany

Cou Neck [col]

Cou d'oie/canard farci Stuffed boned neck of goose/duck, sp. of the SW

Couche Bed, Layer, Base

Coucher to Lie something down; (term) to Pipe cream, etc. through a piping bag [poche à douille]

Coucoulelli Diamond-shaped cake made with white wine & olive oil, sp. of Nice & Corsica

Coude / Coudé, -e Elbow / Elbow-shaped, Bent at an angle

Couder to Bend

Couenne Rind; Pork skin

Coufidou Rustic beef stew of the Massif Central

Coulemelle Parasol mushroom

Couler to Run, to Flow; (term) to Pour aspic into pie hole

Coulibiac, Koulibiak Russian-type pasty filled with fish/chicken

Coulis Sauce of puréed vegetables/fruit/shellfish

Coulommiers Cow's-milk cheese of the North similar to Brie

Coup de feu [shot] Last minute browning/charring (of meat, etc.); (term) When all the pots are on the stove; Last-minute preparations in the kitchen

Coup de feu de midi Lunchtime rush (in a restaurant)

Coup de fusil [gun-shot] (fam.) Outrageous price

Coup de main Helping hand

Coupage Blending (of wine); Diluting wine with water

Coupe Cut; Ice cream sundae; Sundae glass; Glass of/for champagne; Glass bowl

Coupe (à la ..) Freshly sliced (not pre-packed)

Coupe-faim Appetite suppressant

Coupe-frites Chip cutter

Coupe-jambon Bacon slicer

Coupelle Small bowl for desserts/fruit, etc.

Coupe-pizza Circular rolling cutter

Couper to Cut, to Slice, to Carve, to Chop; to Dilute

Couper (se ..) to Cut oneself

Couper en menu to Cut very small/finely

Couper en morceaux to Cut into pieces

Couperet Meat chopper, Cleaver

Couque, Couke, Koucke Flemish *brioche* cake

Courabiés Small gâteau with sour-cherry jam

Courant, -e Current, Average, Everyday; Running (water)

Courbe / Courber Curved, Curve / to Bend (something)

Courbine Fish similar to bass

Courge Marrow, Squash, Gourd

Courgette Summer squash, Zucchini

Couronne (en ..) Shaped into a ring (vegetables, rice, etc.) or crown (lamb cutlets, etc.)

Couronne [crown] Crown-shaped bread loaf

Couronne en gelée Ring mould of mixed ingredients (eggs, vegetables, ham, shrimps, etc.) set in aspic

Courquinoise Fish soup with eels, etc. of the North

Court-bouillon Seasoned stock used for poaching fish, shellfish & white meat

Courte [short] (term) Thick/concentrated sauce etc.

Courtier Broker: official interme-diary between (esp. wine) seller & buyer, paid commission by both

Couscous Processed semolina grains; N. African dish prepared with couscous

Couscoussier Domed dish for cooking couscous

Cousina, Cousinat Chestnut soup of the Auvergne; Ham stew of the Pays Basque

Cousinette Green vegetable soup poured over bread, sp. of Béarn

Cousinière Mosquito net

Coussinet Whortleberry, Bilberry [myrtille]

Coût Cost, Price [prix]

Couteau Knife

Couteauà découper Carving knife

Couteauà jambon Long thin-bladed ham knife

Couteaud'office General kitchen

Couteauà tomate Serrated tomato knife

Couteau-courbe Curved knife; Razor shell clam

Couteau-scie Serrated knife

Coutellerie / Coutelier Cutlery / Cutler

Couvage Hatching, Incubation

Couve Cake of the Dauphiné made in shape of a broody hen

Couvée Brood, Clutch

Couver to Sit on eggs; to Smoulder

Couvercle Lid, Bottle top, Screwtop

Couvert Cover; Table/place setting

Couvert, -e Covered

Couverts Cutlery; Number of seats/places in a restaurant

Couverture Covering, Coating; Blanket

Couveuse Incubator

Couvre-théière Tea-cosy

Couvrir to Cover

Crabe Crab

Cracher to Spit; to Spit out; to Splutter, to Crackle (fire)

Cramique Brioche of the North made with currants

Crapaud [toad] Nickname for monkfish [lotte]

Crapaudine (en ..) Spatch-cocked: preparation of small birds for grilling (split &

flattened out, they resemble toads/*crapauds*)

Crapiau Thick rustic sweet/savoury pancake with regional variations

Craquelé, -e Cracked (skin, crust, etc.)

Craquelin Cracknel: small light crunchy cake/biscuit

Craquelot Bloater: lightly smoked young herring, sp. of Boulogne-sur-Mer

Craterelle Horn of Plenty mushroom

Créât Sturgeon [*esturgeon*]

Crèche [*crib*] Plate-rack

Crécy (à la ..) Dish that includes carrots

Créer to Create

Crémaillère Chimney hook (for the cooking pot)

Crémaillère (pendaison de la ..) House-warming party (trad. when chimney hook is put in place)

Crémant [*creaming*] Sparkling wine (that can no longer be called *champagne*) of various regions, esp. Alsace, Burgundy, Cramant & the Loire

Crème Cream; Cream soup; Cream dessert; Sweet liqueur (*cassis*, etc.); Cream-coloured. (to Cream = *travailler*)

Crème (à la ..) Dish with cream or a cream sauce

Crème (un ..) Abb. for a small coffee with cream

Crème aigre Sour cream

Crème anglaise Custard

Crème au beurre French butter cream

Crème au caramel Caramel cream (used as garnish)

Crème brûlée Cream dessert with burnt sugar topping

Crème caramel Baked caramel custard [*crème renversée*]

Crème Chantilly Cream whipped to consistency of a mousse, sweetened (& often flavoured)

Crème d'amandes Almond cream: mix of ground almonds, butter, sugar & eggs used in confectionary

Crème de blé Semolina pudding

Crème de Gruyère Cheese spread

Crème de marrons Chestnut cream: sweetened chestnut purée used for iced desserts, etc.

Crème de tartre Cream of tartar (used in baking)

Crème épaisse Thick cream

Crème fleurette Light liquid cream to pour/whip

Crème fouettée Whipped cream

Crème fraîche Lightly soured cream ideal for cooking

Crème frite *Crème pâtissière* that is rolled, sliced & fried

Crème glacée Rich ice cream made with eggs & cream

Crème légère Low-fat cream

Crème liquide Liquid/running cream

Crème pâtissière Confectioner's custard, French pastry cream

Crème renversée Baked egg custard, Caramel custard

Crémer to Add fresh cream

Crèmerie Dairy (shop)

Crémet Light cream-cheese dessert

Crémeux, crémeuse Creamy

Crémier, crémière Dairy-man/woman

Crémière Cream jug

Créole (à la ..) Caribbean-style: often with rice/fruit/rum

Crêpe Pancake

Crêpe dentelle *[lace pancake]* Thin batter biscuit of Brittany

Crêperie Restaurant/shop specialising in pancakes

Crêpière Pancake pan (thin, shallow & smooth)

Crépine Caul: fatty membrane used as sausage skin

Crépinette Small flat sausage wrapped in *crépine*

Crépitement (à ..) When the fat starts to spatter

Crépiter to Sizzle, to Crackle, to Sputter

Cresson [de fontaine] Watercress

Cresson alénois Garden cress

Cresson de terre/jardin Garden cress

Cressonnière (à la ..) Dish containing watercress

Crête de coq Cock's comb

Cretonnée de pois Old recipe of puréed green peas with breadcrumbs, ginger & cooked chicken

Creuser to Hollow out

Creux, creuse Hollow; Shallow

Creux (avoir un petit ..) to Have an empty stomach

Crevasses Cracks, Fissures (in fruit, etc.)

Crever to Burst, to Split

Crever (faire ..) to Remove starch from rice by pre-boiling

Crever de faim to be Hungry, to be Starving

Crevette / .. rouge Shrimp/prawn / N. Atlantic red prawn

Crevette bouquet/rose Prawn

Crevette grise Common/brown shrimp *[boucaud]*

Crevette rose / .. tropicale Sword shrimp / Senegal prawn

Criée (la ..) Auction (esp. of fish)

Crique, Criquette Potato pancake (often made with local cheese)

Crisser to Crunch, to Crackle, to Rasp

Cristal, cristaux Crystal-clear; Crystalware

Cristalliser to Crystallise (fruit, flowers, etc.); to Form crystals

Cristaux (de soude) Washing soda

Crocher / Crochet to Hook / Hook

Croisillon Lattice pattern

Croissance Growth, Development

Croissant normal/pur beurre Croissant made with margarine/butter

Croissanterie Speciality cake shop

Croître to Grow *[grandir]* (See also *Cultiver*)

C

Cromesqui Kromesky; type of *croquette* of Poland

Croquandise Small crispy biscuit

Croquant, -e Crunchy, Crispy

Croquants Little crispy biscuits

Croque au sel (à la ..) Eaten raw with salt (celery, radishes, etc.)

Croque-madame Toasted cheese & ham sandwich with a fried egg

Croquembouche Pyramid of candied profiteroles esp. for weddings & first communions

Croque-monsieur Toasted cheese & ham sandwich

Croquer to Eat; to Crunch

Croquet Small dry stick-shaped petit four, Parkin

Croquette Shaped salpicon rolled in egg & breadcrumbs & deep-fried

Croquignole Small light crisp cake covered with icing

Crosne Chinese artichoke: small twisted tuber (sweeter than Jerusalem artichoke) *[artichaut japonais]*

Crottes de chocolat Chocolates, Chocolate drops (*crottes* = droppings)

Crottin *[horse dung]* Small round goat's-milk cheese

Croupion Parson's nose: rump of fowl, bearing tail feathers

Croustade Crust; Small case/basket made of bread/potato/rice/pastry

Croustillant Crispy, Crunchy

Croustille / Croustilles Thinly sliced fried potato / Game chips

Croustiller to Crunch (one's

food); to Be crunchy/crispy/crusty

Croûte / En .. Crust, Rind / Cooked in pastry/bread case

Croûte dorée *[golden crust]* French toast *[pain perdu]* of Savoie

Croûter, Croûtonner to Garnish with cubes of aspic

Croûtes [à potage] Toasted/fried bread garnish for soups & salads, etc.

Croûton Fried/toasted bread morsels; Knob end of *baguette*; Aspic cut into shapes

Crozets, Crousets Poached *quenelles gratinées*, sp. of the Dauphiné for Christmas Eve; Noodles of Savoie

Cru Locality in which vines are grown; (wine term) Specific vine 'growth'

Cru, -e Raw, Uncooked, Unpasteurized

Cruchade Cornmeal biscuits, trad. in the SW

Cruche Pitcher, Large jug

Cruchon Small jug; Stoneware bottle

Crucifères Sweet rocket

Crudités Dish of raw fresh fruit/vegetables

Crumble Various dishes with a crumble topping

Crustacés Shellfish, Crustaceans

Cucurbitacées Collective word for squash, gourd & marrow plants (some edible, some decorative)

Cueillette Picking, Crop

Cueillir to Pick, to Gather (flowers, etc.); to Pick up

Cuillère, Cuiller / Petite .. Spoon / Teaspoon

Cuillère (à la ..) Food (esp. meat & poultry) cooked well enough to eat with a spoon

Cuillère (biscuit à la ..) Sponge finger

Cuillère à café Teaspoon

Cuillère à glace Ice cream scoop

Cuillère à moka Coffee spoon

Cuillère à soupe Tablespoon, Spoon for soup

Cuillère de table Dessert spoon

Cuillère en bois Wooden spoon

Cuillère Parisienne Round-bowled [double-ended] spoon for melon/vegetable balls, etc.

Cuillerée Spoonful

Cuilleron Bowl (section) of spoon

Cuir Skin, Hide, Leather

Cuire / .. au four to Cook / to Bake, to Cook in the oven

Cuire à blanc to Blind bake (pastry, etc.); to Cook food (onions, etc.) without browning

Cuire à feu doux to Cook gently (on low heat)

Cuire à l'eau to Boil

Cuire à l'étouffée [smother] to Braise: cook slowly with very little liquid in a sealed container

Cuire à la broche to Spit-roast

Cuire à la poêle to Fry

Cuire à la vapeur to Steam

Cuire à petit feu to Simmer

Cuire au gril to Grill

Cuire sur le gril to Griddle

Cuiseur vapeur Steamer pan

Cuisine Kitchen, Galley; Cooking, Cookery, Food

Cuisine (faire la ..) to Do the cooking

Cuisine (fille de ..) Kitchen maid

Cuisine (grande ..) Top-class traditional cooking

Cuisine (haute ..) High-class cooking

Cuisine (la ..) Kitchen staff

Cuisine (nouvelle ..) Mode of light cooking of the 1970s

Cuisine américaine American-style kitchen

Cuisine calendaire Festive cookery, Party food

Cuisine familiale/bourgeoise Family-style home cooking

Cuisine française French cooking/food

Cuisine intégrée Fitted kitchen

Cuisine minceur Low-fat/calorie food/cooking

Cuisine paysanne Country-style cooking

Cuisine régionale Regional cooking using local ingredients

Cuisiner to Cook

Cuisines Kitchens (of restaurant, hospital, school, etc.)

Cuisinette Kitchenette

Cuisinier Male cook/chef

Cuisinier Gascon Anonymous cookbook of 1740 thought to have been written by Louis XIV's grandson

Cuisinière Female cook/chef; Cooker, Stove

Cuisse Thigh

Cuisseau Leg of veal

Cuisses de grenouilles Frogs' legs

Cuisson Cooking, Baking, Roasting; Cooking time

Cuissot Haunch of venison *[gigue]*

Cuistot (fam.) Cook *[cuisinier]*

Cuit, -e / Bien .. / Trop .. Cooked, Stewed, Baked / Well done (meat, etc.) / Overdone (meat, etc.)

Cuite Batch baking

Cuiter (se ..) (fam.) to Get plastered/drunk

Cuit-vapeur Steamer pan/basket

Cuivre Copper

Cul Bottom, Base, End contents

Cul de bouteille Base of bottle; Last of the bottle

Cul-de-poule Metal basin for whisking eggs, etc.

Culinaire Culinary: to do with cooking

Culot Base (of bottle)

Culotte *[pair of pants]* (cut of beef) Rump

Cul-sec! / Faire .. (fam.) Bottoms up! / to Down it in one

Cul-terreux (fam.) Peasant (who has his backside/*cul* in the earth)

Cultivable Arable (land)

Cultivateur Cereal farmer; Cultivator, Light plough

Cultivateur (potage ..) Vegetable soup

Cultiver to Grow, to Cultivate

Cumin Caraway seed, Cumin

Curaçao Orange-flavoured liqueur

Curcuma Turmeric

Cure Health cure

Cure-dents Toothpick

Curi (au ..) Curried dish

Curi de ... Dish of diced meat in curry-flavoured sauce

Cuve / .. close Wine vat / Sealed vat/tank

Cuvée Contents of a vat/*cuve* (& so, by extension, the vintage/blend of a wine)

Cuvée du patron House wine (choice of the proprietor)

Cuver / .. son vin to Ferment / (fam.) to Sleep it off!

Cuvette Washbasin, Bowl, Basin

Cuvier Tub

Cynorhodon Rosehip *[gratte-cul]*

D

Daguenelle Small dried [tapée] pear of Burgundy

Daguet Brocket: young stag

Daikon Japanese radish

Dail Piddock: shellfish of the Atlantic coast [pholade]

Daim Fallow deer

Dalle [flagstone] Thin slice/escalope of fish (Thick slice = darne)

Dalle (crever la ..) (fam.) to Be ravenous

Dalle (se rincer la ..) (fam.) to Drink

Damas [Damascus] Damson (plum); Damask (linen)

Dame blanche Various desserts using white ingredients (vanilla ice cream, meringue, etc.)

Dame-Jeanne Demijohn: vessel holding 50 ltrs, often encased in basketwork

Damier Rum-flavoured Genoese cake with chequer-board pattern; Check (pattern)

Danablu Danish Blue cheese

Danicheff Salad of white vegetables; Rich pineapple gâteau; Praline parfait

Danlas Variety of white dessert grape

Darblay Potato soup with a julienne of vegetables & thickened with egg yolks or cream

Dariole Small flower-pot-shaped mould; Any preparation cooked in a dariole mould

Darne Thick steak/slice of large fish (salmon, etc.)

Darphin Potato cake (fried & then browned in the oven)

Dartois Puff pastry hors d'œuvre with sweet/savoury filling; Various preparations named after the Comte d'Artois

Dattes Dates

Daube Classic stew cooked in wine

Daubière Heavy, covered cooking pot

DAUPHINE Region in the SE (between Savoie & Provence) with a cuisine rich in dairy produce, fruit, nuts, game & mountain fish

Dauphine (pommes ..) Deep-fried balls of potato purée & choux paste

Dauphinoise Pork & cabbage pâté, sp. of Dauphiné

Dauphinoise (à la ..) Dauphiné-style: most often a gratin

Daurade Sea bream [dorade]

Daurade royale Gilthead (sea bream family)

DCR: date de consommation recommandée Recommended date by which produce should be consumed

Dé à coudre [thimble] Thimbleful (measure)

Débarrasser to Clear away; to Transfer (to serving dish, etc.)

Débauche Orgy

Déborder to Overflow

Debout Standing, Upright

Débrancher to Unplug, to Disconnect

Débrider to Remove truss from poultry

Début / Débuter Start, Beginning / to Start with

Déca (abbr.) Decaffeinated coffee

Décanter to Decant (wine, etc.); to Clarify

Décapsuleur Bottle-opener

Décharné, -e Fleshless (bones, etc.), Bony

Déchets Waste, Refuse

Déchirer to Tear [off/up]

Décoction Decoction: to reduce/concentrate by boiling; Brew

Décongeler to Defrost

Décoratif, décorative Decorative, Ornamental (N.B: may mean 'non-edible')

Décortiquer to Shell, to Husk

Découenner to Remove skin from pork

Découpage Carving, Slicing

Découpe (à la ..) Cut, Ready sliced

Découpé, -e Cut, Sliced

Découpe-pâte Pastry roller cutter

Découper to Carve, to Cut, to Slice

Découpes Remnants, Cut-off bits

Découpoir Conical-shaped steel cutter for truffles, tomatoes, etc.

Découvert, -e Uncovered, Bare

Découverte Discoverery

Décrasser to Scrub, to Get something clean

Décuire (term) to Reduce cooking temperature by adding cold water

Dedans Inside

Deffarde, Défarde Spiced stew of tripe, sp. of the SE

Déficeler to Untie

Dégeler to Thaw

Dégermer to Remove seeds/sprouts/eyes, etc.

Dégivrer to Defrost (refrigerator/freezer) (See also *Décongeler*)

Déglacer to Deglaze pan with liquid

Dégorger to Purify (by soaking); to Sweat (cucumber, etc.) with salt

Dégoutant, -e, Dégueulasse Disgusting

Dégraisser to Remove fat/grease

Dégraissis Fat skimmed from stock, sauce, etc.

Dégriser (fam.) to Sober up

Dégustation Tasting, Appraisal of food/wine

Déguster to Savour, to Relish; to Taste, to Sample; to Sip

Déjeuner / Petit .. Lunch; to Have lunch / Breakfast

Délai Delay; Respite, Time allowed

Délayer to Thin; to Mix

Délicat Delicate, Refined; Subtle

Délicatement Delicately

Délicatesse Delicacy, Fine (opp. of coarse)

Délices *[delights]* Fancy cakes

Délicieux Delicious; Various cakes & desserts

Démarrer to Get started, to Start

Demi, -e Half

Demi (un ..) (fam.) Large glass of beer (25 cl); Half litre of wine

Demi-bouteille Half-bottle (measure of 37.5 cl)

Demi-deuil *[half-mourning]* Dish of contrasting dark & pale food

Demidof Chicken dish (named after Russian prince married to Napoleon's niece)

Demie (la ..) Second half of the hour

Demi-glace (sauce ..) Rich brown sauce made with *sauce espagnole* & stock

Demi-sec (wine term) Semi-sweet sparkling wine (sugar has been added); Sweet champagne

Demi-sel Partially salted (ham, butter, etc.); (brand name) Cream cheese

Demi-tasse Small/espresso coffee

Demoiselle de Cherbourg Small lobster of Normandy

Démouler / Démoulage to Turn out / Turning out

Dénaturer to Spoil, to Affect, to Alter (the taste, etc.)

Dénerver to Remove tendons, etc. from meat/poultry

Dénouer to Untie

Dénoyauter/ Dénoyauteur to Stone (fruit, etc.) / Cherry/olive stoner

Denrée alimentaire Foodstuff, Produce

Denté, Denti Dentex: Large Med. member of sea bream family

Dentelé, -e Jagged, Serrated, Perforated, Pinked

Dentelle/ En/de .. Lace / Lacy

Dents / Manger à belles .. Teeth / (term) to Eat with relish

Dents-de-lion *[lion's teeth]* Dandelion (leaves used in salads) *[pissenlit]*

Dents-de-loup *[wolf's teeth]* Garnish of fried bread, pastry or aspic triangles

Dépaqueter to Unwrap

Dépeçage Jointing (of meat, poultry, etc.)

Dépecer to Joint (poultry, etc.)

Déplaire to Displease, Not to like

Dépôts Deposits, Sediment

Dépouillé, -e / Dépouiller Skinned / to Skin

Dépourvu, -e [de] Lacking in, Devoid of, Deprived of

Dérober *[to steal]* (term) to Remove thin skin of potatoes, broad beans, tomatoes, almonds, etc.

Derval Garnish of sautéed artichokes for beef *tournedos* & *noisettes* of lamb

Dés Dice, Cubes

Déshydraté Dehydrated

Désormais Henceforth, From now on, In future

Désossée Boned

Dessalage De-salting by soaking

Dessécher to Dry off (by very gentle heating)

Dessert Dessert, Sweet course

Desserte Leftover food used in another dish; Sideboard; Trolley; Dumb waiter

Desservir to Clear the table

Dessous de plat/verre/bouteille
Trivet, Coaster, Mat

Détacher to Detach, to Remove

Détail Detail (minutia)

Détail (au ..) / Détaillant, -e
Retail (sale) / Retailer

Détailler to Cut meat/vegetables
into shapes

Détendre *[to relax]* (term) to
Soften or thin with liquid, etc.

Détendre (faire ..) to Allow
dough to 'relax'

Détonant, -e Explosive; Bursting
(with flavour)

Détrempe Flour & water paste

Détrempé, -e Soggy

Détremper to Lightly knead
dough with fingertips

Dévisser to Unscrew

Diable *[devil]* Double earthenware pot that can be reversed
during cooking

Diable (à la ..) Devilled (spiced)
dish

Diable de mer *[sea devil]* Nickname for monkfish *[lotte]*

Diablotin *[imp]* Thin rounds of
toast with grated cheese; Small
spoon; Christmas cracker

Diabolo Non-alcoholic drink
made of lemonade & fruit
syrup (usually mint/grenadine)

Diane (à la ..) Meat/game with
highly peppered sauce

Dictame Dittany: herb with
orange scent used for potpourri
& teas

Dieppoise (à la ..) Dieppe-style:
with shellfish garnish

Dieppoise (marmite ..) Fish &
shellfish soup/stew with cream,
sp. of Dieppe

Diète (à la ..) to Be on a health
diet (Diet = *régime*)

Diététique Dietetics: the study
of diet

Diffuseur Heat diffuser mat

Digeste Digestible, Easy to
digest

Digestif Digestive:
liqueur/spirit taken after a
meal

Dijonnaise (à la ..) Dijon-style:
with Dijon mustard or
blackcurrants

Dijonnaise (poire belle ..)
Dessert of pears with
blackcurrants

Diluer to Dilute, to Make
thinner

Dinde, Dindette Turkey
(strictly a hen turkey = *poule
d'Inde*)

Dindon / Dindonneau Cock
turkey / Young turkey

Dîner to Dine; Dinner; Dinner
Party

Dîner d'une soupe to Have
soup for dinner

Dînette Light meal; Doll's tea
set

Diot Fresh/dried pork sausage
of Savoie

Diplomate Diplomat pudding:
cold dessert of layered sponge
fingers or *brioche*, crystallized
fruit & cream/custard

Diplomate (à la ..) Rich
dish/sauce of lobster &
truffles

Dippelapes lorrain Potato
pancakes with stewed apple,
sp. of Lorraine

Discrétion (à ..) Unlimited *[à
volonté]*

Disette Famine, Food shortage

Disperser to Spread around, to Scatter

Disponible / Disponibilité Available / Availability

Disposer / .. de to Arrange / to Have; to Use

Dissoudre to Dissolve

Divers Various

DLC: date limite de consommation Date by which produce must be consumed

DLUO: date limite d'utilisation optimale Optimum date by which produce must be used

DLV: date limite de vente Sell-by date

Dodine Dish of boned stuffed braised meat/poultry

Doigts-de-morts [*dead man's fingers*] Salsify (in Lyon region)

Domaine Estate (esp. of vineyards), Property, Domain

Domestique Domestic; Household servant

Dorade Sea bream [*daurade*]

Dorer [*to gild*] to Brown (under grill or in fat); (term) to Glaze pastry/cake with egg yolk, milk, etc.

Doria Various classic dishes using colours of the Italian flag (green, white & red)

Dorine Creamy chestnut tartlet

Dorloter to Pamper, to Coddle, to Cosset

Dormeur [*sleeper*] Large crab [*tourteau*]

Dorsch Small Baltic cod

Dorure Glaze of milk or egg yolk (for pastry, etc.)

Dos Back

Dosage Quantity, Amount (of)

Doser / Doseur to Measure / Measuring glass

Doter to Provide, to Equip

Douberre Butternut squash

Douille / Poche à .. Socket; Piping shape / Piping bag

Douillet, douillette Cosy, Snug

Douillon, Douille Stuffed apple/pear in pastry, sp. of Normandy

Doux, douce Sweet, Soft, Smooth, Mild, Unsalted

Douzaine Dozen

Dragées Sugared almonds

Draguer to Dredge

Drap / Draper Sheet; Cloth / to Drape, to Cover

Drêche Draff: lees after brewing/distilling; Hog's-wash

Dresser to Dress/garnish a dish; to Set/lay the table; to Prepare; to Adjust, to Arrange

Dressoir Dresser, Sideboard

Droit, -e Straight, Right, Sound (correct)

Droit de banvin Right of a landlord to sell his own wine during a set period prior to its general sale

Droitier, droitière Right-handed (Left-handed = *gaucher*)

Dru, -e Vigorous, Strong, Thick, Heavy

Du Barry With cauliflower (favourite vegetable of Louis XV; Mme du Barry was his mistress)

Duc *[duke]* Title used for various 'noble' products

Ducasse Fair in the North *[kermesse]*

Duchesse *[duchess]* Sweet/savoury choux buns; Small items sandwiched with butter cream; Dessert using *Duchesse* variety of winter pear

Duchesse (à la ..) Dish served with *pommes duchesse*

Duchesse (pommes ..) Duchess potatoes: puréed with egg yolk & butter, piped & baked

Dugléré (à la ..) Light butter sauce for fish

Duo Duet

Dur, -e / Oeuf dur Hard / Hard-boiled egg

Durcir to Harden, to Set

Duvet Down (of duck/swan & of apricot skin)

Duxelles Classic mixture of sautéed mushrooms, onions, shallots & parsley

Duxelles (à la ..) Dish with *duxelles* as garnish/filling

LIMES

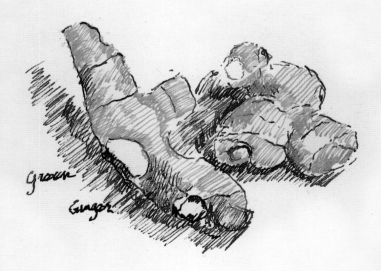

Green
Ginger

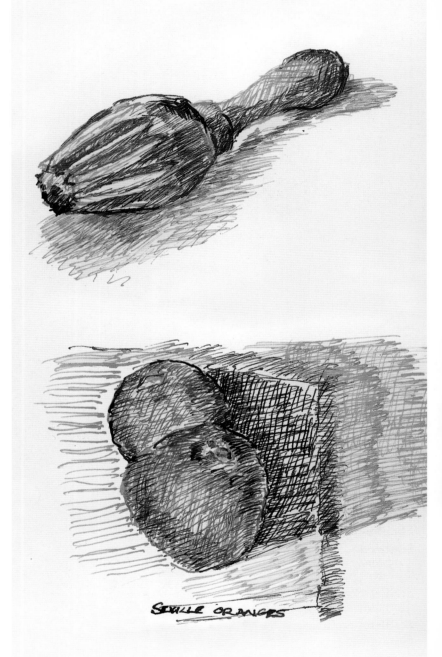

SEVILLE ORANGES

Eau / .. courante / .. douce Water / Running water / Fresh water

Eau bénite Holy water

Eau de Javel Bleach (chloride)

Eau de source Spring water

Eau des Carmes Melissa cordial

Eau minérale (plate/gazeuse) Mineral water (still/sparkling)

Eau naturelle/du robinet Tap water

Eau vinaigrée Water with a dash of vinegar (for cleaning)

Eau-de-vie General term for brandy & *alcool blanc* (spirit distilled from fruit/herbs)

Eau-de-vie-de-vin Liqueur brandy *[marc]*

Eaux Waters

Ebarber to Remove fins from fish; (term) to Trim poached eggs

Ebosser to Separate grain from the chaff

Ebossoir Sausage-making funnel

Ebouer / Eboueur to Scavenge / Rubbish collector

Ebouillanter to Scald; to Plunge fruit, etc. into boiling water for easier peeling

Ebrécher to Chip, to Notch, to Make a hole in something

Ebullition Boiling

Ecailler to De-scale fish; to Open oysters; Man who opens oysters; Shellfish stall

Ecailles Scales (of fish); Shells (of oysters, etc.)

Ecailleux, écailleuse Scaly, Flaky

Ecale Shell, Pod, Husk, Hull, Shuck

Ecaler to Shell (nuts, eggs, etc.), to Hull, to Shuck

Ecarlate Scarlet

Ecarlate (à l'..) (term) to Pickle pork/ox tongue (it turns red)

Ecart (à l'..) On one side; Set aside

Ecarter to Separate, to Part, to Spread/open out

Echafauder to Pile/heap/stack up (*échafaud* = scaffolding)

Echalote Shallot

Echantillon Sample, Specimen

Echaudé Classic light poached biscuit

Echauder / Echaudure to Scald / Scald

Echauffant Heating; Binding (of food)

Echauffer to Overheat (something)

Echine Chine (pork joint)

Echiré (beurre ..) *AOC* butter of Poitou-Charentes

Eclaboussure Splash, Splatter, Spot

Eclade, Eglade Smoked mussels, sp. of Charentes

Eclair *[flash]* Classic cream cake—eaten in a flash!

Eclater to Burst, to Shatter

Ecœurant, -e Sickening, Disgusting, Nauseating

Econome Double-bladed peeler (for potatoes, etc.)

Ecorce Peel, Skin (of chestnut, etc.),

Ecorcer to Peel, to Scrape, to Husk

Ecorcher to Skin (an animal)

Ecorses d'orange Candied [chocolate covered] orange peel

Ecossaise (à l'..) Scottish-style: often with salmon

Ecossaise (sauce ..) Sauce made with scotch-broth ingredients

Ecossaise (soupe à l'..) Scotch broth

Ecosser to Pod, to Hull, to Shell

Ecot (payer son ..) to Pay one's share (of a meal, etc.)

Ecraser to Crush, to Pound

Ecrémé / Demi-.. Skimmed / Semi-skimmed

Ecrémer to Cream; to Skim (milk, etc.)

Ecrevisse (fresh water) Crayfish

Ecrin Casing

Ecroûter to Remove crust/rind of cheese, etc.

Ecuelle / Ecuellée Small bowl, Porringer / Bowlful

Ecumer / Ecume to Skim [off]; to Froth / Foam, Scum

Ecumoire Skimming ladle, Skimmer spoon

Ecureuil Squirrel

Ecurie Stable (*Etable* = cowshed); (fam.) Place that 'looks like a pigsty'

Edulcorant, -e Sweetening, Sweetener

Edulcorer to Sweeten

Effeuiller to Remove leaves (from stalk) or petals (from flower)

Effilé [stream lined] Poultry with only the intestines removed

Effiler / S'.. to Flake (almonds), to Shred; to Thin out; (term) to String (green beans) / to Fray

Effilocher / S'.. to Slice, to Tear apart / to Fray, to Unravel

Effluve Fragrance, Smell

Effriter (s'..) to Crumble, to Flake

Eglantine Wild/briar rose

Eglefin Haddock [aiglefin]

Egoutter to Drain, to Strain

Egouttoir Drainer, Draining board

Egrener to Remove seeds/grains, to Shell (peas, etc.)

Egrugeoir Small wooden mortar for crushing seed & grains, etc.

Eierkückas [egg cake] Rich pancake, sp. of Alsace

Elaborer / Elaboré, -e to Put together / Sophisticated

Elan Elk, Moose; Momentum, Impetuous, Impulse

Electroménager Electrical household appliance

Elément Ingredient, Component

Elevage / D'élevage.. Livestock farming, Breeding / Farmed (fish, oysters, etc.)

Eleveur, éleveuse Breeder

Email Enamel

Emballage Wrapping, Packaging

Emballer to Pack, to Wrap up; (term) to Put into a mould

Embaumer to Smell of, to be Fragrant

Embellir to Embellish

Embeurrée Cooked/tossed/served in butter

Embeurrée de chou Dish of cabbage cooked in butter, sp. of Poitou

Embossoir Special funnel for filling sausage skins

Embrocher to Skewer, to Broach: put meat, etc. on spit

Emietter to Crumble (*miette* = crumb)

Emincer to Slice (into thin rounds/strips); to Shred

Emincés de ... Thin slices of meat/poultry

Emmagasiner to Store, to Stock up

Emmenthal Hard cow's-milk cheese with holes made in France & Switzerland

Emonder to Trim, to Prune (often incorrectly used for *monder*)

Emoussé, -e Dull, Blunt (knife)

Emoustiller to Rouse, to Kindle (the senses, etc.)

Empêcher to Prevent, to Hinder

Empereur Emperor bream (fish)

Empiffrer (s'..) to Guzzle, to Stuff oneself

Empiler to Stack, to Pile up

Emplettes / Faire ses .. Purchases / to Go shopping

Emplir to Fill (something) up (See also *Remplir*)

Emporte-piece Pastry cutter; Spoon, etc. to make shapes

Empreinte Print cut-out, Stamp (marker)

Emulsifiant, -e Emulsifier: additive (often egg yolk) used to stabilize *emulsions*

Emulsion Binding of two liquids (oil & water) with an emulsifier

(without which they remain separate)

Emulsionner to Emulsify: bind two liquids with an emulsifier

En plein air [*in the open air*] Alfresco, Outdoors

En train de ... In the process/making of ...

Encaquer to Barrel (herrings, etc.)

Encart Insert, Inset

En-cas Snack (in case of hunger!)

Enchaud Rolled (& often stuffed) pork fillet, sp. of Périgord

Encombrer to Encumber, to Glut, to Overstock

Encornet Squid [*calamar*]

Encre Ink (of squid, etc.)

Endaubage Mix of ingredients (bacon/onion/carrots/wine/peppercorns, etc.) used for braising

Endimanché, -e Dressed in one's Sunday best

Endive Chicory, Belgian endive [*witloof*]

Enduire to Coat, to Cover (with), to Smear

Enduit Coating

Enflammer to Ignite, to Set alight

Enflé, -e Swollen

Enfoncer to Plunge/sink (something) into

Enfouir / Enfoui, -e to Bury, to Embed / Buried, Embedded

Enfourner to Put in the oven

Enlever to Remove, to Take off/away

Enrober to Coat, to Cover, to Wrap

Enrouler to Roll up

Ensilage Silage

Entailler to Nick, to Cut into

Entame First slice (of bread/meat, etc.)

Entamer to Cut into; to Start eating; to Open up

Entasser to Pile/heap up

Enterrement [burial] (fam.) Hot Dog

Entier, entière Whole, Complete, Full (milk, etc.)

Entonnoir Funnel

Entortiller to Twist, to Wind, to Twine

Entraîner to Train; to Wash away/down

Entrecôte [between ribs] Sirloin steak

Entrée [entrance] Starter/first course of meal

Entremets [between dishes] Dessert, Sweet course; Side dish (of vegetables, etc.)

Entreposer to Store, to Bond

Entrepôt Warehouse, Stockroom

Environ About, Or so, Roughly (amount)

Epais, épaisse / Epaisseur Thick / Thickness, Depth

Epaule Shoulder; Cooked [chopped] ham

Epeautre Spelt: ancient variety of chaffy wheat

Epée de mer Swordfish [espadon]

Epépiner to De-pip (grapes, etc.)

Eperlan Smelt: tiny fish of salmon family, used in friture

Ephémère Short-lived, Fleeting

Epi Ear (of wheat, etc.); Bread stick with spikes

Epi de maïs Corncob

Epicer / Epicé, -e to Spice / Spicy, Highly spiced

Epicerie / Epicier, épicière Groceries; Grocer's shop / Grocer

Epicerie fine Delicatessen

Epices / Pain d'épice Spices / Gingerbread

Epicurien, épicurienne Epicure: one who enjoys & appreciates good food

Epigramme Lamb dish of fried breaded cutlets & slices of breast

Epinard[s] Spinach

Epine-vinette Barberry: prickly shrub with sour berries used in jellies, etc.

Epinoche Stickleback fish

Eplucher / Eplucheuse to Peel, to Pare / Peeling machine

Epluchures Peelings (of potatoes, etc.)

Epoisses Rich cow's-milk cheese of Burgundy

Eponge / Eponger Sponge / to Mop up

Epouvantail Scarecrow

Equeuter to Remove stalk/stem/tail

Equilibre Balance, Stability

Equille Sand eel [lançon]

Erable (sirop d'..) Maple syrup

Ersatz Substitute

Eructer to Belch, to Burp

Escabèche Spicy marinade, esp. for small fish

Escalope Thin slice of white meat, poultry or fish fillet

Escaloper to Slice thinly (meat/fish/mushrooms, etc.)

Escargot de mer Sea snail *[bigorneau]*

Escargotière Grooved dish for cooking & serving snails; Snail farm

Escargots Snails: eaten fresh/tinned/frozen all over France but collected under strict controls (See also *Petit gris*)

Escargots de Bourgogne/vigne Large snails of Burgundy

Escargue (fam.) Snail

Escarole Scarole: variety of curly endive

Escauton Spicy ham & vegetable stock of Gascony

Escuedella Festive stew of Catalan

Espacer to Space (out)

Espadon Swordfish *[épée de mer]*

Espagnole (à l'..) Spanish-style: with tomato, garlic, peppers & Madeira

Espagnole (sauce ..) Classic brown sauce base of a dark *roux* with tomato purée

Esprot Sprat

Esquimau *[Eskimo]* (brand name) Choc-ice

Essai Trial, Test

Essayer to Try

Essence de ... Concentrated aromatic liquid, Extract *[extrait]*

Essor / En plein .. Development / Booming

Essorer to Spin, to Wring, to Squeeze dry

Essoreuse / .. à salade Spin-drier / Salad spinner

Essuie-mains Hand towel

Essuie-tout Kitchen paper/roll

Essuyer to Wipe

Estaminet Small café/bistro of the North

Estamper to Engrave, to Print; to Rip (somebody) off

Estampillé, -e Stamped [with], Marked, Trade-marked

Estival, -e, estivaux Summery, Summer *[été]*

Estives Summer pastures

Estofinado, Estoficado Provençal name for salt cod stew *[stoficado]*

Estomac Stomach

Estomper to Become blurred (flavour, etc.)

Estouffade Stew of the SW; Clear brown stock

Estouffat Various regional stews, esp. pork & bean stew of Languedoc

Estragon Tarragon

Esturgeon Sturgeon

Etable Cowshed (Stable = *écurie*)

Etager to Layer

Etagère Shelf

Etain Tin; Pewter

Etal / Etalage Stall, Stand / Display (of goods)

Etal du boucher Butcher's block

Etalagiste Window dresser

Etaler to Spread, to Spread out, to Press flat

Etalon *[stallion]* Standard (measure); Yardstick

Etalonner to Test, to Verify, to Calibrate

Etamer to Tin (pots & pans, etc.)

Etamine Cheesecloth, Butter muslin

Etanche / .. à l'air Water-tight / Air-tight

Etancher to Make watertight; to Stem flow of liquid; to Quench one's thirst

Etang Pond, Pool, Mere

Etape Stage (of journey); Stopping place

Eteindre to Turn/switch off (heat/light); to Blow out (candles)

Eteint Out, Off, Extinct

Etendre to Spead out; to Roll out; to Dilute

Eternuer to Sneeze

Etêter to Remove head (of fish, etc.)

Etier Salt-marsh

Etincelles Sparks

Etiquette / Etiqueter Label, Price tag; Etiquette / to Label

Etirer to Stretch, to Draw out

Etoffe Material, Stuff, Substance

Etoffer / S'.. to Fill out; to Expand / to Put on weight

Etoile Star; Star-shaped

Etorki Cheese of the Pays Basque

Etouffe-chrétien Stodgy (cake, etc.)

Etouffée (à l'..) Braised: food cooked in sealed pan with very little liquid (*étouffer* = to smother)

Etouffer (s'..) to Choke, to Suffocate

Etourdissant *[deafening]* Stunning

Etrille Small crab

Etriper to Gut (an animal, etc.)

Etroit, -e Narrow

Etui Case, Box, Cover

Etuve Industrial steam oven; Incubator; Humidified cellar

Etuvé (term) Cheese (esp. Dutch) matured in humidified cellar for 5-9 months (*Demi-étuvé* = 2-5 months)

Etuvée (à l'..) Braised: cooked with very little liquid in sealed pan

Etuver to Sweat (onions, etc.) in sealed pan

Evaser to Widen, to Open (out)

Eveiller to Awaken; to Stimulate (the appetite)

Eventail Fan; Fan-shaped; Range (of options)

Eventaire Stall or flat tray/basket (of street trader)

Eventé Musty, Stale

Eventer (s'..) to Pass its best; to Go flat; to Go stale

Evide-pomme Apple corer *[colonne]*

Evider to Core, to Hollow out, to Scoop out

Evier Sink, Kitchen sink

Eviscéré Drawn (poultry, etc.), Cleaned fish (entrails, etc. removed) (= Ready-to-cook)

Eviter to Avoid

Excelsior Soft cow's-milk cheese of Normandy; Various

sophisticated dishes & garnishes

Exotique Exotic; Tropical (fruit, etc.)

Expert, -e Expert, Specialist

Exploitant agricole Farmer *[agriculteur]*

Exprès Deliberately, Intentionally

Express Express; Quick; (abbr.) Espresso coffee

Exprimer to Squeeze [out]

Extra Extra special/strong/fine; Additional

Extrait Extract; Concentrated aromatic liquid *[essence]*

Fabriquer to Make, to Manufacture

Face Face, Front, Side

Facile Easy

Façon Style, Fashion, Manner

Façonner to Shape, to Mould

Facultatif, faculative Optional

Fade Tasteless; Flat (non-gassy) drink

Fagot Faggot: ball of minced pork, liver, onion, breadcrumbs & herbs wrapped in caul fat

Faïence Earthenware/pottery with tin glaze

Faim (tromper sa ..) to Stave off one's hunger

Faim / Avoir .. Hunger / to Be hungry

Faim de loup (avoir une ..) to Be ravenous

Faine Beechnut

Faire to Make; to Do

Faire (se ..) to Make (something) for oneself; to Become; (term) to Ripen (of cheese), to Mature (of wine)

Faire maigre to Fast (See also *Maigre*)

Faisan / Faisane Cock pheasant / Hen pheasant

Faisandage Hanging of meat/game (to allow it to become tender & flavoursome)

Faisandeau Young pheasant

Faisander / Faisandé, -e to Rot, to Fester / Gamy, High (game, etc.)

Faiseur (bon ..) Good maker/manufacturer/supplier

Faisselle Basket or pierced container for draining fresh cheese [*fromage frais*]; Fresh cheese in a *faisselle*

Fait maison Homemade

Fait-tout, Faitout [*do everything*] Stockpot: heavy pan with tight-fitting lid

Fallue Rich brioche trad. at Epiphany (6 Jan.)

Fanchette, Fanchonnette Puff pastry tart covered with meringue balls

Faner to Wilt, to Wither, to Fade; to Make hay

Fanes Leaf-tops of carrot/beet/celery, etc.

Fanfreluches Frills & flounces

Fantaisie Fun, Fantasy, Novelty, 'a Little something'

Fantaisiste Unreliable, Far-fetched, Eccentric

FAO: Food & Agriculture Organisation The FAO

Faon Fawn

Far [breton] Baked flan (trad. with prunes), sp. of Brittany

Faramineux, faramineuse Colossal, Staggering (price, etc.)

Farce Stuffing; Forcemeat: finely chopped & seasoned vegetables/meat/fish used for stuffing, sausages, etc.

Farcement Festive cake of potato, prunes & dried pears made in mould lined with bacon, sp. of Savoie

Farci Stuffed cabbage of Périgord; Stuffed tomato of Provence

Farcidure Dish with stuffing balls, of various regions

Farcir / Farci, -e to Stuff / Stuffed, Filled with

Farçon Rich potato purée dish of Savoie; Fat saveloy/*cervelas* sausage of the Dauphiné

Farigoule Thyme (in Provence)

Farinade Floury omelette/pancake of various regions, esp. Corsica

Farinage Rolling/coating (meat, etc.) in flour

Farine Flour

Farine à gâteau Self-raising flour

Farine à pâtisserie supérieure/suprême (type 45) Fine white flour

Farine avec levure Self-raising flour

Farine blanche White flour

Farine d'avoine Oatmeal

Farine de blé / .. complète Wheat flour / Whole wheat flour

Farine de châtaigne Chestnut flour

Farine de gruau Whole wheat flour

Farine de maïs Cornflour (often called by brand name *Maïzena*)

Farine de matzo Matzoh meal

Farine de sarrasin Buckwheat flour, Saracen corn (for *galettes*, etc.)

Farine fluide/extra fluide Fine/extra fine flour (for creams, pancakes & sauces, etc.)

Farine ménagère (type 55) Plain, less fine, flour

Farine ordinaire Plain flour

Farine panifiable Bread flour: wheat flour with gluten

Fariner to Flour, to Lightly cover (food/mould, etc.) with flour

Farinette Floury omelette/pancake of various regions

Farineux, farineuse Farinaceous, Floury, Starchy

Faséole Kidney bean

Fatiguer *[to tire]* (term) to Toss (salad, etc.)

Fausse soupe à la tortue Mock turtle soup (made with calf's head)

Faux Scythe

Faux, fausse False, Incorrect, Inaccurate

Faux-filet Cut of beef sirloin (second-grade fillet)

Favori, favorite Favourite

Favouille Small crab *[étrille]* in Provence

Fayots (fam.) Beans *[haricots]*

Feche, Fetge Dried pork liver, sp. of Toulouse region

Féchun Dish of stuffed cabbage cooked in vegetables, sp. of Franche-Comté

Fécond, -e Fertile

Fécule / .. de maïs Starch, Potato flour / Cornflour

Féculent, -e Starchy (food, etc.)

Fela, Fiela Conger eel of the Med.

Fêlé, -e Cracked, Split

Fenaison Haymaking

Fendant Swiss name for *Chasselas* grape

Fendiller to Crack, to Craze, to Chap

Fendre to Chop, to Split, to Crack

Fenouil Fennel

Fente Crack, Split, Cut, Groove

Fenugrec Fenugreek: bitter Med. aromatic plant

Fer / .. de fonte / .. blanc Iron / Cast iron / Tin plate

Fer à cheval Horseshoe

Fer à repasser Iron (for pressing clothes)

Féra Prized mountain trout esp. of Lakes Annecy & Geneva

Ferblanterie Tinware; Ironmonger's

Férié (jour ..) Public holiday

Fermage Tenant farming, Farm tennancy

Ferme / Fermette Firm, Stiff, Solid; Farm, Farmhouse / Small farmhouse, Farmhouse-style cottage

Ferment / Fermenter Ferment, Leaven / to Ferment

Fermer / Fermé, -e to Close / Closed

Fermeté Firmness

Fermeture Closing (of shop, etc.); Closure; Fastening

Fermier, fermière Farmer; Farm fresh; Farm-style; Free-range

Fermière (à la ..) Farmer's-wife style: braised meat/fish/poultry served with buttered vegetables

Festin / Faire un .. Feast / to Have a party

Festonner [festoon] to Arrange items decoratively on dish

Festoyer to Feast

Fête Party, Celebration, Festival, Saint's day

Fête de bienfaisance Fund-raising event/party

Fête des rois/mages Twelfth Night, Epiphany (6 Jan.)

Fête foraine Fair, Funfair

Fête nationale French National holiday (Bastille Day: 14 July)

Fêter / .. quelqu'un to Celebrate / to Wine & dine (someone)

Fétiche Something lucky; Mascot

Fétide Foul-smelling (of mould, etc.)

Feu / .. doux/vif Fire, Heat / Low/high heat

Feuille Leaf; Sheet (of paper etc.)

Feuille de Dreux Semi-skimmed cow's-milk cheese

Feuilleté Puff pastry cocktail snack or small *entrée*; Pasty

Feuilleté, -e [foliated] With puff pastry (as garnish/casing/topping)

Feuilletée (pâte ..) Puff pastry

Feuilletée (pâte demi-..) Rough puff pastry

Feuilleter [to leaf] (term) to Roll & fold pastry

Feuilleton Sliced veal/pork layered with forcemeat

Feutre / Feutrine Felt (material) / Baize

Fève Broad bean; Lucky charm found in *galette des rois*; General name for flat bean

Fiadone Corsican cake made with *Broccio* cheese & lemon peel

Fiasque Straw-covered flask/bottle

Fibre / Fibreux Fibre / Fibrous, Sinewy

Ficeler : Ficelé, -e to Tie with string / Tied with string, String of …

Ficelle String; Thin bread stick

Ficelle picarde Ham rolled in a pancake, filled with chopped mushrooms & covered in cheese sauce, sp. of the North

Fichu (fam.) Done for, Nasty, Rotten, Dreadful

Fidés Type of flat pasta, orig. from N. Africa

Fiefs-Vendéens White & rosé wine of the Vendée

Fiel Bile; Venom (of snake)

Fier, fière / Fierté Proud / Pride

Fièvre aphteuse Foot-&-mouth disease

Figer to Congeal, to Thicken

Fignoler to Put the finishing touch; to Fuss over

Figue / Figuier Fig / Fig tree

Figue de Barbarie Prickly pear (species of cactus fruit)

Figue de mer Sea squirt *[violet]*

Fil Thread; Wire; Grain (of meat); String (of bean); Edge (of blade)

Fil à fromage Cheese wire/cutter

Fil dentaire Dental floss

Filandreux, filandreuse Stringy (meat, cooked cheese, etc.)

Filet Fillet (of meat/fish); Breast (of poultry); Trickle, Dash (of lemon); Net; String bag

Fileter to Fillet fish; to Trickle, to Dribble

Filière Course, Field; Official (channel, line, etc.)

Fillette *[little girl]* Trad. name in SW for 1/3 litre bottle of wine

Film [étirable] Clingfilm

Filo, Fillah (pâte à ..) Filo pastry

Filtre / Filtrer Filter / to Filter, to Strain

Filtre à café / Café filtre Coffee filter / Filtered coffee

Fin End, Termination

Fin du fin The ultimate, Best of the best

Fin, -e Delicate; Fine; Quality; Thin

Financier Petit four made with almond paste & egg whites

Financière (à la ..) Sauce/garnish with truffles & Madeira

Fine Brandy

Fine champagne Cognac brandy of the Charente region

Fine de claire Oyster of Marennes (raised in *claires*)

Fine gueule *[delicate mouth]* (fam.) Goumet, Epicure

Fines herbes Mix of herbs (parsley, chervil, tarragon & chives)

Finesse Thinness; Delicacy, Fineness

Finir / Finition to Complete/finish / Finishing touch

Fiole Flask

Fistuline hépatique Beefsteak fungus, Ox Tongue mushroom

Fitou Red *AOC* wine of Languedoc

Fixe Fixed (price, etc.)

Flageolet Pale green haricot bean

Flairer to Smell, to Sniff (something)

Flamande (à la ..) Flemish-style: often with cabbage, turnips, boiled potatoes [à l'anglaise], bacon & sausage

Flambage Singeing (of feathers, etc.)

Flambant neuf Brand new

Flambé, -e Flamed with warmed spirits (brandy, etc.)

Flamber to Add alcohol/spirits for 'flaming'

Flamiche, Flamique Trad. leek & cheese tart of the North

Flamme / Flammèche Flame / Spark

Flammenküche Flame cake of Alsace: onion & bacon tart

Flamri, Flamery Baked semolina pudding made with white wine

Flamusse Apple pudding of Burgundy & Nivernais

Flan Sweet/savoury baked tart; Custard/cream tart

Flanchet Flank of beef [bavette]

Flandre, Flondre Flounder fish [flet]

FLANDRE[S] Flanders: region in the NW (part in Belgium)

Flanière Flan dish

Flaquer to Slit fish (trout, etc.) to remove backbone

Flèche [arrow] Flitch (of bacon): salted & cured side of pork; (term) Steak cut from fish (esp. halibut)

Flet Flounder

Flétan Halibut

Flétries Stains, Blemishes

Flétrir to Wilt, to Fade

Flétrissure Mark, Crack, Wrinkle, Blemish

Fleur Flower, Blossom; Fine powder on dried sausages, etc.

Fleur d'oranger Orange blossom; Orange flower water

Fleur de ... Finest/top quality (flour, salt, etc.)

Fleur de courge Courgette flower

Fleur de maïs Cornflour

Fleur des champs Wild flower

Fleurer to Flour, to Lightly cover (food, mould, etc.) with flour

Fleurette (crème ..) Whipping cream

Fleuri, -e In bloom; With flowers, Flowery

Fleurie AOC Beaujolais wine with a flowery bouquet

Fleurir to Flower; to Decorate with flowers; to Spring up

Fleuron Floret; Flower/leaf motif made of puff pastry; 'Jewel in the crown': the best

Fleurs (à ..) Flowery

Flion Wedge-shell clam

Floc Aperitif of Armagnac & grape juice

Floc de Gascogne White & rosé fortified wine, trad. drunk to celebrate the end of the grape harvest

Flocons Flakes

Flognarde, Flagnarde Fruit cake/flan of Limousin & Périgord

Flône Little cheesy tartlet of Rouergue

Floralies Flower show

Flore Flora; Yeast that 'flowers' on surface of some wines (esp. sherry) in the barrel

Florentine (à la ..) Florence-style: fish, white meat or egg dish with spinach & Mornay sauce

Floutes Potato dumplings of Alsace *[pflutters]*

Fluide Fluid, Runny

Flûte Thin bread stick; Glass for/of champagne

Foie Liver (*Crise de foie* = indigestion)

Foie de volaille Duck/goose/turkey (but usually) chicken liver

Foie gras (d'oie/de canard) Preparation of rich goose/duck liver that has been enlarged by force-feeding

Foie gras (parfait/bloc de ..) Processed *foie gras*

Foie gras (pâté de ..) Pâté made with *foie gras*

Foie gras (terrine de ..) Terrine made with *foie gras*

Foie gras avec morceaux Processed *foie gras* containing whole pieces of liver

Foie gras cru/mi-cuit Raw/lightly-cooked *foie gras*

Foie gras en conserve Pasteurized *foie gras* in jar/tin

Foie gras entier Whole *foie gras*

Foie gras frais Fresh raw/cooked *foie gras*

Foie gras truffé *Foie gras* containing morsels of truffle

Foin Hay; Feathery 'choke' of artichoke

Foire Fair, Country show (Funfair = *fête foraine*)

Foison (à ..) Plenty, Profusion, Abundance

Foisonner to Abound; to Swell, to Expand

Folie / .. douce Madness, Extravagance / Utter madness

Foncer (term) to Line dish/mould with pastry, bacon, fat, etc.

Fond Base, Bottom (of pan, glass, etc.) (*Base* = basic); Heart (of artichoke); Stock

Fond de veau Veal stock (available powdered, in cubes, etc.)

Fondant Soft icing paste of sugar syrup & glucose; Melting

Fond-de-culotte *[seat of the pants]* (fam.) Cocktail mix of *Suze* & *Cassis*

Fondre to Melt, to Dissolve; Vegetables 'sweated' in fat

Fondu creusois Dish of melted cheese with fried/puréed potatoes, sp. of Limousin

Fondu, -e Melted

Fondue Vegetables cooked to a pulp; Dish of small/cubed items cooked at the table in hot oil/cheese/syrup

Fondue bourguignonne Cubed meat cooked in oil & dipped into various sauces

Fondue comtoise Rich cheese fondue of Franche-Comté

Fondue normande Cubed bread dipped into mix of hot Normandy cheeses, cream, *Calvados* & shallots

Fondue Savoyarde Cubed bread dipped into mix of hot *Beaufort* cheese, white wine & Kirsch

Fongique Pertaining to mushrooms

Fontaine / .. à thé Fountain, Spring / Tea-urn

Fontaine (faire une ..) (term) to Make a hollow in flour during pastry/bread making

Fontainebleau Rich fresh cow's-milk cheese; Garnish of diced vegetables in a potato case

Fonte Melting; Cast iron

Fontenelle (à la ..) Asparagus with butter & a soft-boiled egg

Forain / Forains Stall holder / Fairground people

Forestière (à la ..) Dish with mushrooms

Forêt-noire Black Forest gâteau: rich chocolate cake with cream & cherries

Forme Shape, Form; Figure

Formé, -e Formed, Full-grown, Set (fruit)

Former / Se .. to Form, to Make, to Create / to Acquire

Formule Formula; Choice of combinations on a menu

Fort, -e Strong, Intense, Concentrated

Fortune / Fortuné, -e Fortune, Luck / Fortunate, Successful

Fortune du pot (à la ..) Pot luck: a meal of what is available

Fortuné, -e Wealthy, Rich (Fortunately = *heureusement*)

Fou, fol, folle Mad, Excessive, Amazing

Foudre Hogshead, Large cask/barrel [*fût*]

Foudroyant, -e Instant, Sudden (*foudre* = lightning)

Fouet / Fouetter Whisk / to Whisk, to Whip

Fougasse, Fouace Flat latticed bread baked with herbs & olives, sp. of Provence & trad. at Christmas

Fougassette Small *fougasse*, sp. of Nice

Fouler to Press, to Crush

Four / .. à catalyse/pyrolyse Oven / Self-cleaning oven

Four à chaleur tournante Fan-assisted oven

Four à micro-ondes Microwave oven

Fourchette / A la .. Fork / Fork meal, Buffet

Fourchette à spaghetti Spaghetti rake

Fourme d'Ambert Mild blue cow's-milk cheese of the Auvergne

Fourmis Ants

Fourneau [*furnace*] Kitchen range, Cooker, Stove

Fournée Batch (of loaves, etc.)

Fournil Bakehouse

Fourniment Clutter

Fournitures Supplies, Equipment

Fourrage / .. sec Forage / Fodder

Fourré, -e Filled/stuffed (with)

Fourrer (term) to Fill, to Stuff, to Line

Frai Fish/frog spawn; Fish fry; Spawning season

Fraîcheur Freshness, Coolness

Frais, fraîche Fresh; Cool, Chilled

Frais (tenir au ..) to Keep (something) cool

Fraise / .. des bois [*woodland*] Strawberry / Wild strawberry; Liqueur made with wild strawberries

Fraise [de veau] Mesentery: membrane covering animal's intestines

Fraiser, Fraser to Knead

Fraisier Strawberry-plant; Genoese sponge cake with Kirsch & strawberries

Framboise Raspberry; Raspberry liqueur, sp. of Alsace

Franc, franche Frank, Straightforward

Française (à la ..) French-style: often with braised lettuce, asparagus tips & cauliflower florets

Franc-Comtoise (à la ..) Franche-Comté-style: hearty dishes containing pork, cabbage & potato

Francillon Potato salad with mussels & celery (named after a Dumas play)

Francillon (bombe ..) Champagne-flavoured *bombe* coated with coffee ice cream

Frangipane Type of soft marzipan; Classic paste [*panade*] used for binding stuffings, etc.

Franquette (à la bonne ..) (term) to Have an informal meal

Frappé, -e Iced, Chilled, On ice, With crushed ice

Frelon Hornet

Frémir to Simmer

Frémissement Quivering, Simmering

Fressure Pluck: heart, spleen, liver & lungs

Fretin Fish fry [*alevin*] (See also *Menu fretin*)

Friable Crumbly, Flaky

Friand Snack food, Tit-bit

Friandise Fondness for delicacies; Favourite food/dish

Friandises Sweetmeats, Petits fours, Fancy cakes

Fribourg French name for Swiss Gruyère cheese

Fricadelle Meatball/burger served in [spicy] sauce

Fricandeau Rough pork pâté of the SW; Dish of larded veal; Braised fillet of fish (tuna, etc.)

Fricassée [*medley*] Pan-cooked mix of ingredients in a sauce

Fricassée périgoudine Vegetables taken out of a *pot-au-feu* & fried, sp. of the SW

Fricasseur [*squanderer*] (fam.) Indifferent cook

Friche Waste land

Frichti (fam.) Snack (from German *frühstück* = breakfast)

Fricot / Fricoter (fam) Stew, Food, Grub / to Stew, to Cook

Frigo Fridge

Fringale Hunger pangs, Starving hungry

Fripé, -e Crumpled, Wrinkled

Frire to Fry

Frisée Curly endive (salad green)

Friser to Curl, to Wave

Frisons Trimmings, Shavings (that curl up)

Frissonner [to shudder] to Simmer

Fritelle Sweet fritter of Corsica

Friterie Chip shop/stall

Frites Chips, French fried potatoes, French fries

Friteuse Deep-fat fryer

Friton Fatty pork paste [rillette]

Fritons Crispy pork fat pieces [grattons]

Fritots Hors d'œuvre fritters made from various small items (leftovers, vegetables, frogs' legs, shellfish, etc.)

Friture Frying oil; Deep fat frying; Dish of deep-fried food (esp. small fish)

Froid Cold

Froisser to Crush, to Crumple

Frôler to Skim, to Scrape off

Fromage Cheese

Fromage à pâte filée/molle/persillée/pressée 'Stringy'/soft/blue/hard cheese

Fromage à raclette Semi-hard, quick-melting cheese (orig. from Savoie, cut in half & the melting cheese removed with a scraper/raclette), trad. eaten with boiled potatoes

Fromage à tartiner Cheese spread

Fromage allégé Low-fat cheese

Fromage artisanal Cheese made by a small producer using local milk

Fromage au lait cru Cheese made from unpasteurized/raw milk

Fromage blanc Quark: fresh cream cheese

Fromage de brebis Ewe's-milk cheese

Fromage de chèvre Goat's-milk cheese

Fromage de lactosérum Type of cottage cheese

Fromage de soja Tofu: diced soybean preparation, Bean curd

Fromage de tête Brawn

Fromage de vache Cow's-milk cheese

Fromage double-crème Cream cheese

Fromage fermier Cheese made from the farm's own milk

Fromage fondu Processed cheese

Fromage fort Strong cheese steeped in wine & matured in jars, sp. of Lyon region

Fromage frais Fresh (neither cooked/matured) cheese

Fromage frais au petit-lait Cottage/curd cheese

Fromage industriel Factory-made cheese

Fromage laitier/de fruitier Cheese made in a co-op dairy

Fromage maigre Low-fat cheese

Fromage triple-crème Rich cream cheese

Fromager, fromagère of Cheese; Cheesemaker; Cheese seller

Fromagerie Cheese shop/stall/counter

Froment Quality wheat [blé]

Frometon (fam.) Cheese

Frotter to Rub, to Scratch, to Scrape

Fruit de la passion Passion fruit

Fruit givré Hollowed-out fruit filled with ice cream or sorbet

Fruité, -e Fruity; Tasty (cheese, wine, etc.)

Fruitier Cold store for fruit; Fruit seller; Greengrocer

Fruitière Cheesemaker in Franche-Comté & the Jura

Fruits (pâte de ..) Fruit paste used as a confectionery base

Fruits à l'eau-de-vie Fruit preserved in alcohol

Fruits confits Crystallized fruit

Fruits de mer Seafood

Fruits déguisés *[disguised]* Fresh, dried/crystallized fruit in marzipan & coated with caramel /icing

Fruits exotiques Tropical fruit

Fruits rafraîchis Fruit salad *[salade de fruits]*

Fruits rouges Soft fruit (esp. red berries & currants)

Fruits secs Dried fruit (currants, raisins, nuts, etc.)

Fruits tombés Windfalls (apples, etc.)

Fumé, -e Smoked, Cured

Fumet Concentrated fish/mushroom stock; Smell, Aroma

Fumier Manure

Fumoir *[smoking room]* Smokehouse; Home smoking kit

Funérailles (repas de ..) Meal following a funeral (Wake = *veillée*)

Fur et à mesure (au ..) Progressively, As needed

Fuseau *[spindle]* Thin dried sausage

Fusil *[gun]* Steel, Sharpener

Fût / Futaille Cask, Barrel; Tree trunk / Large barrel

Futé, -e Sharp; Cunning, Crafty

Fuxéenne (à la ..) Foix-style: rich dishes with goose, game, mountain fish & mushrooms

Gabelle Ancient salt-tax (imposed from the C14th-18th)

Gâche Yeast cake; Type of sweet bread with regional variations

Gâcher / Gâchis to Waste, to Squander / Waste, Mess

Gaillac *AOC* red, white & rosé wines of the Tarn valley in the SW

Galabart Large black pudding of the SW

Galantine Pressed meat/fish/poultry/game in/with gelatine

Galbé Curved

Galère Galley; Prawn of the Camargue

Galette Small round cake/biscuit of various regions

Galette de pain azyme Rice paper

Galette des rois Twelfth Night cake (trad. puff pastry filled with frangipane) sold with a paper crown & lucky charm/*fève*

Galicien Pistachio-flavoured sponge cake with green icing

Galimafrée Peasant feast (now, often meaning unappetizing)

Gallinacé Gallinaceous: of fowl (chickens, pheasants, etc.)

Galon Braid, Ribbon

Galopin *[urchin]* Stuffed apple/pear in pastry, sp. of Orléans; Small measure (of beer)

Gamay Grape variety used esp. for Beaujolais wine

Gamba King prawn

Gamelle Lunchbox, Billycan; Tin dish; Pet's bowl

Gamme Range (of products, etc.)

Ganache Classic chocolate cream used for fillings & desserts

Ganga Pin-tailed grouse

Gant de cuisine Oven glove *[manique]*

Gaperon Low-fat cheese of the Auvergne (where *gape* = buttermilk)

Garbure Stew/soup with cabbage & goose *confit*, sp. of Béarn

Garde-manger Larder, Pantry, Meat-safe; (orig. Chef in charge of cold foods)

Garder to Keep, to Retain

Gardon Roach

Garenne Wild rabbit; Rabbit warren

Gargantuesque Gargantuan

Gargote (fam.) Cheap restaurant

Gargouillau Dessert of sliced pears in batter, sp. of Limousin & Bourbonnais

Gargouillou Rustic vegetable stew of the Auvergne

Gargoulette Drinking vessel with handle & special spout (to use without touching the lips)

Gariguette Prized variety of strawberry

Garnir / Garni, -e to Garnish / Garnished (with vegetables, salad, etc.)

Garniture Garnish, Trimmings

Garrigue Scrubland (in the South)

GASCOGNE Gascony: region south of Bordeaux

Gaspillage Waste, Wasteful

Gastrique Sauce base of boiled vinegar & sugar

Gastronomade Traveller who enjoys regional dishes

Gastronome Connoisseur & judge of gastronomy

Gastronomie Gastronomy: the art & science of good eating

Gâtais de la mariée Brioche [wedding] cake of the Vendée

Gâté, -e / Gâter Spoiled, Spoilt (food, child, etc.) / to Spoil

Gâteau / .. d'anniversaire / .. marbré Cake, Gâteau / Birthday cake / Marble cake

Gâteau à la broche Cone-shaped celebration cake of the Pyrenees, trad. hung from the spit/*broche* in the chimney

Gâteau apéritif/sec Cocktail biscuit, Cracker

Gâteau Basque Sponge cake of the Pays Basque

Gâteau battu Rich cake of the North

Gâteau Breton Heavy fruit cake of Brittany

Gâteau brioché Cake made with *brioche* dough

Gâteau de riz/semoule Rice/semolina pudding

Gâteau de Savoie Light biscuit-cake of Savoie

Gâteau flamand/à la bière Moist sponge cake of the North

Gâterie Titbit; Little treat

Gâte-sauce [*sauce-spoiler*] (fam.) Young kitchen apprentice (orig. *gars de sauce* = lad in charge of sauces)

Gatis Cheese-filled *brioche* of the SW

Gauche Left (side); Awkward, Clumsy

Gaucher, gauchère Right-handed (Left-handed = *droitier*)

Gaudes Cornmeal porridge with regional variations

Gaufre Waffle; Honeycomb

Gaufrer to Crinkle; to Emboss

Gaufrettes Wafers; Very fine potato chips

Gaufreuse Pastry wheel

Gaufrier Waffle iron

Gauler to Knock nuts/fruit out of a tree

Gauloise (à la ..) Dish with cock's comb & kidneys; Garnish of mushroom tartlet with truffles

Gavage Force-feeding (of ducks/geese to be used for *foie gras*)

Gaver (se ..) to Stuff oneself, to Guzzle

Gayotte Faggot

Gaz / .. de ville Gas / Mains gas

Gaze Gauze

Gazeux, gazeuse Fizzy (drink, etc.)

Gazinière Gas stove/cooker

Gelée Jelly

Gélifiant Gelling agent (pectin, starch, agar-agar, etc.)

Géline Old word for hen; Chicken (esp. in Touraine)

Gélinotte Hazel/wood-grouse

Gendarme *[policeman]* (fam.) Pickled herring; Small flat smoked sausage (orig. of Switzerland)

Génépi Alpine wormwood: bitter herb used for teas & liqueurs

Gênes (pain de ..) Genoa cake: ground almond sponge made in fluted mould

Genevoise (à la ..) Fish with butter & red wine sauce

Genièvre Juniper; Dutch gin

Génisse Heifer: young cow that has not yet calved

Génisson Bullock: castrated bull

Génoise Genoese sponge cake; Classic sponge cake mix

Génoise (à la ..) Genoa-style: with tomatoes

Gentiane Gentian: mountain plant used in various aperitifs, notably *gentiane*

Gerbe Sheaf of corn; Bouquet/wreath of flowers; Spray of water

Germe Seed, Germ, Shoot, Sprout/eye (of potato)

Germe de blé Wheat germ

Germe de soja Bean sprout

Germiny (potage ..) Sorrel soup (named after Bank of France governor)

Germon Albacore, White tuna

Gésier Gizzard

Gevrey-Chambertin *AOC* red Burgundy wine from the Côte-de-Nuits

Gewurztraminer Grape variety & 'spicy' white wine of Alsace

Gibassie, Gibassier Crown-shaped brioche of Provence made at Christmas-time

Gibecière Game bag; Satchel

Gibelotte Rabbit stew with wine & mushrooms

Gibier / .. à poil / .. à plumes / .. d'eau Game / Furred game / Game birds / Water fowl

Gigolette Turkey joint (thigh & drumstick); Rabbit joint (front legs & abdomen, separated from the saddle/*rable*)

Gigondas *AOC* red & rosé Rhône wine

Gigorit *Ragoût* of pork offal in red wine, sp. of Poitou-Charentes

Gigot Leg of lamb; Poultry drumstick & leg tied together

Gigot de mer Dish of monkfish (that looks like a leg of lamb/*gigot*) in tomato & wine

Gigue *[jig]* Haunch (of venison)

Gimblette Small crown-shaped biscuit, sp. of Albi

Gin tonic Gin & tonic

Gingembre/ .. confit Ginger / Stem ginger

Giraumon turban Turban squash

Girelle Girella: small Med. fish used in *bouillabaisse*

Girofle (clous de ..) Cloves

Girolle Girolle/Chanterelle mushroom

Gitan, -e Gypsy

Gîte *[shelter]* Place to stay for the night (now a classified holiday lodging)

Gîte à la noix Topside, Silverside of beef

Gîte-gîte Shin of beef

Givré (fruit ..) Hollowed-out citrus fruit filled with ice cream, sorbet or iced soufflé

Givré, -e Frosted; Tipsy

Glaçage Glazing (with butter, aspic, jam, egg yolk, etc.); Icing (with sugar)

Glace Ice, Ice cream

Glace de cuisine Glaze (of concentrated cooking juices)

Glace de sucre / .. royale Icing / Royal icing

Glacé, -e Ice-cold, Iced, Crystallized, Glazed

Glacer to Ice; to Glaze

Glacier Ice cream maker; Ice cream parlour

Glacière Coolbox

Glaçon Ice cube; Block of ice

Glaire Glair: white of egg used as varnish

Gland [du chêne] Acorn

Glane / Glaner Rope/string (of onions), Cluster / to Glean: gather up

Glauque Murky (water/colour)

Glisser to Slide, to Slip

Glouglou Gurgle; Gobble (of turkey)

Gloussement [chuckle] Clucking (of chicken)

Glouton, glutonne Glutton, Voracious

Gloutonnerie Gluttony

Gluant Sticky

Glucide Carbohydrate

Glutamate de sodium MSG: monosodium glutamate

Gnocchi Small dumpling of flour/semolina/potato/choux paste

Gnole (fam.) Brandy

Gobelet Goblet, Tumbler

Gober to Swallow, to Gulp down (whole egg, oyster, etc.)

Gobie Goby: small sea fish [goujon de mer]

Godard Elaborate garnish for meat, poultry & sweetbreads

Godelé, -e Grooved (carving board, etc.)

Godet Small goblet, (term) a Drink; Pot; Wooden bowl

Godiveau Forcemeat of veal/fish/poultry used for quenelles

Gogue Black pudding [boudin] of Anjou

Goguette (en ..) Spree, Frolic; Tipsy

Goinfre / Goinfrer (se ..) Guzzler, Greedy-guts / to Make a pig of oneself, to Stuff oneself (with food)

Gombo Okra, Ladies' fingers: tropical plant with edible pods used in Caribbean cuisine

Gomme Gum (for stabilizers, thickeners, chewing gum, etc.)

Gonfler to Swell, to Puff out, to Blow up

Goret Piglet

Gorge, Gosier Throat, Gullet

Gorgée / Petite .. Mouthful; Gulp / Sip

Gorger / Se .. to Stuff, to Gorge / to Over-eat

Gouère, Gouerre, Gouéron Cake of various regions made with fruit/cheese

Gougère Cheese-flavoured choux bun

Goujon Gudgeon: small fresh-water fish

Goujon de mer *[gobie]* Goby: small sea fish

Goujonettes Fillets of fish (sole, etc.) cut into strips & fried

Goulache Goulash: Hungarian beef stew

Goulot / Boire au .. Neck of a bottle / to Drink from the bottle

Goulu, -e Glutton, Gluttonous, Greedy

Goulûment Greedily

Goupillon Bottle brush

Gourde Gourd, Flask

Gourgane Variety of small bean

Gourmand, -e Greedy person, Good eater

Gourmandises Sweets; Sweetmeats

Gourmet Connoisseur, Epicure: lover of good food

Gourmet (sauce ..) Sauce made with *beurre de homard* & used to coat sliced eel

Gousse Pod, Husk, Shell

Gousse d'ail Clove of garlic; Small cut of beef from fillet end of leg *[noix]*

Goût Taste, Flavour, Palate

Goût (avoir bon/mauvais) to Have [a] good/bad taste

Goût (une affaire de ..) A matter of taste

Goûté, Goûter Snack, High tea

Goûter to Taste (something), to Snack

Goûter d'enfants Children's party

Goûteur [official] Taster (of wine, tea, coffee, etc.)

Goûteux Tasty

Goutte Drop, Dash, Drip; Sip; (term) Tot of *eau-de-vie*

Gouttelette Droplet, Globule

Goyave Guava: tropical fruit

Goyère Rich tart made with *Maroilles* cheese, sp. of the North

Graillon (fam.) Smell of stale fat/grease

Grain(au ..) Corn-fed

Grain / .. de café / .. de poivre / .. de moutarde Grain / Coffee bean / Peppercorn / Mustard seed

Grain de raisin a Grape

Graine Seed; (fam.) Grub, Nosh

Grainer (terms) to Overheat sugar (that crystallizes) or to Over-whisk egg whites (that separate); (fam) to Eat

Graisse / .. de lard Grease, Fat(s) / Dripping, Lard *[saindoux]*

Graisse de [rognon de] bœuf Suet *[suif]*

Graisse normande Superior cooking fat, sp. of Normandy

Graisser to Grease a tin/mould to prevent sticking

Graisseux, graisseuse Greasy, Fatty

Grand, -e Large, Big, Plenty, Important, High, Tall

Grand cru *[great growth]* (term) Excellent, Better; Superior vintage (of wine)

Grand magasin Department store

Grand Marnier Orange-flavoured liqueur (used in soufflés, etc.)

Grand veneur Game served with *sauce grand veneur* & chestnut purée

Grand veneur (sauce ..) *Sauce poivrade* made with redcurrant jelly, cream & juice of game it accompanies

Grand verre à Xérès Sherry schooner

Grand-duc Various dishes with asparagus tips & truffles

Grande marque High quality; Well-known brand

Grande surface Supermarket [*supermarché*]

Grand-mère [*grandmother*] Traditional-style: often with bacon, onions & mushrooms

Grand-Roussillon *AOC vins doux naturels* from the Perpignan area in the SW

Granité Gritty sorbet (often served between courses)

Granule / Granulé, -e Granule / Granulated

Granuleux, granuleuse Grainy, Gritty

Grappa Italian *eau-de-vie*

Grappe Bunch, Cluster

Gras, grasse Fat, Fatty, Full fat (products), Oily (fish), Greasy

Gras (au ..) Dish with meat (opp. of *au maigre*)

Gras-double Tripe: ox stomach; Dish of tripe

Gratin / Le .. Golden crust formed by cooking *au gratin* / (fam.) The upper crust (of society)

Gratin (au ..) Covered with breadcrumbs, grated cheese or white sauce & browned under grill

Gratinée Classic onion soup topped with bread & grated cheese browned under grill

Gratiner / Gratiné, -e to Brown under grill / Browned under grill or in hot oven

Gratte-cul Rose-hip (Rose-hip syrup = *sirop d'églantine*)

Gratter to Scrape, to Scratch

Grattons, Gratterons Cracklings: residue of melted pork & goose fat

Gratuit, -e Free, Complimentary (See also *Libre*)

Gravenche Rare Alpine fish of salmon family

Graves Red & white *AOC* wines of Bordeaux

Gré Liking, Taste, Accord

Grec, Grecque (à la ..) Greek-style: with olive oil or spicy marinade (similar to Med. cuisine)

Grège Oatmeal (colour: grey-beige)

Grêle [*hail*] Skinny, Thin

Grêlé, -e Pockmarked

Grelots [*tiny bells*] Dwarf varieties (button onions, cherry tomatoes, etc.)

Grenade Pomegranate

Grenadier Grenadier fish

Grenadille Passion fruit

Grenadin Small slice of veal fillet cut from the loin

Grenadine Sweet drink made with grenadine syrup

Grenaille [*lead shot*] Dwarf variety (esp. potato)

Grenier Granary, Grain store; Attic, Loft

Grenobloise (à la ..) Grenoble-style: fish *à la meunière* with capers & lemon slices

Grenouilles / Cuisses de .. Frogs / Frogs' legs

Grès Stoneware (pottery)

Grésiller / Grésillement to Sizzle, to Sputter / Sizzling

Gressin Italian bread stick (grissini)

Gribiche (sauce ..) Thick sauce made with mayonnaise, hard-boiled egg & capers

Griffe *[claw]* Cut of beef (between neck & shoulder) used for stews & soups

Grignoter to Nibble

Gril / Grillade Grill / Grilling; Grilled dish; Mixed grill

Grille Oven shelf; Cooling rack; Drain

Grillé, -e Grilled, Toasted

Grille-pain Toaster

Griller to Grill; to Toast; to Roast (almonds, etc.)

Grilloir Griddle pan

Grimolle Apple cake cooked in cabbage leaves, sp. of Poitou

Grincer des dents to Grind one's teeth

Griotte Morello: variety of sweet cherry

Gris, -e / Grisâtre Grey / Greyish

Gris (petits ..) Variety of snail

Gris de Lille Strong soft cow's-milk cheese of Flanders

Griser / Se .. to Get someone tipsy / to Get tipsy

Grisons (viande des ..) Dried salt beef, orig. of Switzerland

Grisot Sea bream

Grive Thrush (used in pâtés, etc.)

Grog Hot toddy

Groin Snout (of pig, etc.)

Grondin *[grunter]* Gurnard, Red gurnet (similar to red mullet)

Gros, grosse Big, Large, Thick, Coarse

Gros bonnet *[big wig]* (fam.) Head chef

Gros gibier Big game; (fam.) Brain box *[gros poisson]*

Gros pain Extra-large loaf of bread

Gros Plant Grape variety *[Folle blanche]* & AOC white wine of the Pays Nantais region in the Loire Valley

Gros sel Coarse/cooking salt

Groseille à maquereau Gooseberry

Groseille de Chine Kiwi fruit *[kiwi]*

Groseille rouge/blanche Red/white currant (Blackcurrant = *cassis*)

Grossier, grossière *[crude]* Coarse, Rough

Grossiste Wholesaler

Gruau Fine wheat flour; Husk (of cereal); Gruel

Gruau d'avoine Oatmeal, Groats

Grue Crane (bird)

Grugeoir (utensil) Pound, Cutter, Crusher

Gruger to Crunch, to Crumble

Grumeau, -x / Grumeler Curd; Lumps / to Curdle, to Clot

Grumeleux, grumeleuse
Curdled, Clotted; Lumpy;
Granular; Gritty (pear, etc.)

Gruyère Firm cow's-milk cheese
with holes, orig. of Switzerland
made in eastern France (Swiss
Gruyère = *Fribourg*) (See also
Beaufort)

Gruyère (crème de ..) Cheese
spread

Guèpe Wasp

Guère Barely, Hardly

Guéridon Pedestal table

Gueule (fam.) Face, Mouth (See
also *Fine-gueule*)

Gueule de bois (fam.)
Hangover

Gueuleton (fam.) Blow-out, Big
feed

Gueuletonner (fam.) to Feast

Gui Mistletoe

Guigne Gean: variety of cherry

Guignolet Cherry liqueur of
Anjou

Guimauve [*mallow*]
Marshmallow

Guinguette Tavern with music;
Pleasure garden

Guirlande Garland, Paper
chain, Bunting

Gustatif, gustative Gustative,
of Gustation: (sense of) tasting

GUYENNE (la ..) Old name for
Aquitaine region in the SW

Gyrocéphale roussâtre Gyro-
cephalus Rufus mushroom

Habillage 'Dressing' of fish, game & poultry

Habiller [to dress] (terms) to Prepare poultry (for cooking) & fish (for serving)

Habit (en..) [in a costume] In its skin (potato, etc.)

Hacher / Haché, -e to Chop up, to Mince / Minced

Hachis Mince, Minced meat, Finely chopped vegetable, Hash

Hachis Parmentier Cottage/shepherd's pie (Parmentier promoted the potato in France)

Hachoir Chopper, Mincing machine; Chopping board

Hachoir berceuse Chopper with rolling blade (berceuse = rocking chair)

Hachua Basque stew with ham

Haddock Smoked haddock (Fresh haddock = églefin)

Halicot Mutton/Irish stew [haricot de mouton]

Halle / les Halles Market hall / Covered market

Hampe Fibrous strip of beef used for steaks

Hanap Tankard

Hanneton May bug

Hareng Herring

Hareng 'gendarme' Pickled herring (salted & smoked)

Hareng roulé Rollmop

Hareng salé Herring preserved in salt/brine

Hareng saur/fumé Kipper: smoked herring

Haricot Haricot bean (fresh/dried)

Haricot 'Chevrier' Flageolet bean: small pale-green haricot bean of Brittany

Haricot 'Cornille' Black-eyed bean

Haricot aiguille Dwarf French bean

Haricot beurre Yellow snap bean

Haricot blanc Small white haricot bean

Haricot coco de Paimpol AOC haricot bean of Brittany

Haricot d'espagne Runner bean

Haricot de Lima Lima bean (large pale green)

Haricot de maïs Sweet corn grain

Haricot de mouton Mutton/Irish stew [halicot]

Haricot de Soissons Large white bean of Picardy

Haricot filet Dwarf French bean

Haricot flageolet Flageolet: small pale green bean

Haricot lingot Lingot: large creamy-white bean

Haricot mange-tout Green snap bean

Haricot mungo, Soja vert Mung bean, Bean Sprout

Haricot noir Black bean

Haricot pinto Pinto bean

Haricot rouge Red kidney bean

Haricot tarbais Very white haricot bean grown around

Tarbes in the SW, esp. used in *cassoulets*

Haricot vert French/green bean

Haricot violet Long thin green & purple French bean

Haricot-de-mer Wedge-shell

Haricots panachés Mix of green & white haricot beans

Harissa Spicy purée of N. African cuisine

Hase Doe: female hare

Hâtelet Small decorative skewer

Hâter (se ..) to Hasten, to Hurry

Hâtereau Dish of cold pork liver meatballs, sp. of Burgundy

Hâtier Spit-rack

Hâtif, hâtive *[hasty]* Early (potatoes, etc.)

Hausse Increase, Rise (in price, etc.)

Haut, -e High, Tall/long, Above, Top, Upper, Raised

Haut (le ..) The top, The summit, The upper reaches

Haute (la ..) Top society, 'The upper crust'

Hebdomadaire Weekly

Henons Cockles (in Picardy)

Herbe / Herbage Grass / Pasture *[pâturage]*

Herbes (aromatiques) Herbs (orig. green, not root, vegetables)

Herbes (fines ..) Mix of finely chopped herbs (parsley, chives, chervil & tarragon) used in omelettes, etc.

Herbes à soupe Root vegetable tops used to flavour soups & stews

Herbes à tortue Mix of herbs (basil, marjoram, chervil, savory & fennel) esp. for turtle soup/sauce

Herbes de Provence Mix of Provençal herbs (esp. sweet marjoram, rosemary, savory, basil & thyme)

Herbes Vénitiennes *[Venetian]* Mix of herbs (tarragon, parsley, chervil & sorrel) in kneaded butter

Herbicide Weed killer, Herbicide

Herboriste Herbalist

Hère Young stag

Hérissé Spiky; Bristling; Ruffled

Hérisson Hedgehog

Hermitage Red & white *AOC* Côtes-du-Rhône wine

Heures (le dix/quatre ..) Two of the five daily meals trad. taken by workers (at ten/four o'clock)

Historier *[to embellish]* Vandyke: garnish of tomatoes, lemons, etc. with zig-zag-cut (as a Van Dyke ruff); Basket-shaped garnish; Decorative mould

Hiver / Hivernal, -e, hivernaux Winter / Wintry, of Winter

Hochepot Hotchpotch: classic Flemish (oxtail) stew

Hogget [d'agneau] Cut of meat used in Irish stew

Hollandais, -e Dutch

Hollandaise (à la ..) Dutch-style or with *sauce hollandaise*

Hollandaise (sauce ..) Classic warm butter & egg yolk sauce

Hollande Holland *[Pays Bas]*; (abbr. for) Dutch cheese

Homard Lobster

Homogène Homogeneous

Hongrie / Hongrois, -e Hungary / Hungarian

Hoqueter / Avoir le hoquet to Hiccup / to Have hiccups

Horde Horde (of people), Pack (of animals)

Hors [de] service Out of order

Hors du feu Off the heat

Hors-d'œuvre *[not part of the main work]* Various hot/cold small dishes served after/instead of soup

Hors-d'œuvre à la russe Small items served before a meal

Horticole / Horticulture Horticultural / Horticulture

Horticulteur, horticultrice Horticulturist

Hortillons (soupe des ..) Vegetable soup of market gardeners who work the canal-allotments *[hortillonnages]* of Amiens in the North

Hôte / Hôtesse Host, Landlord; Guest / Hostess, Landlady, Receptionist

Hôtel / .. particulier Hotel / Town house

Hôtel de ville/des vents Town hall / Salesroom

Hôtelier, hôtelière Hotel management

Hôtelière (à l'..) Grilled meat/fish served with *beurre hôtelière*

Hôtelière (beurre ..) Softened butter with parsley, lemon juice & *duxelles*

Hotte Hood of cooker; Grape picker's basket

Houblons / Jets de .. Hops / Hop shoots

Houille / .. blanche Coal *[charbon]* / Hydro-electric power

Houlette Shepherd's crook; Crozier; Trowel

Hoummos Hummus: chickpea purée

Housse Cover, Protective bag, Dust cover

Houx / Baies de .. Holly / Holly berries

HT: hors taxes Tax not included

Huche Bread bin; Hopper

Huile / Huiler Oil / to Oil

Huile blanche Poppy seed oil

Huile d'arachide Peanut oil

Huile d'olive Olive oil

Huile de colza Rapeseed oil

Huile de foie de morue Cod-liver oil

Huile de girofle Oil of cloves

Huile de maïs Corn oil

Huile de noix Walnut oil

Huile de soja Soya bean oil

Huile de tournesol Sunflower oil

Huile végétale Vegetable oil

Huilier Oil & vinegar cruet stand *[burette]*

Huître / .. plate/creuse Oyster / Flat/concave oyster

Huîtrière Oyster bed/farm

Humecter to Moisten

Humer to Sniff (something)

Humide Damp

Huppe Crest (of bird)

Hure Type of brawn [*fromage de tête*]; Head of pig/wild boar; Jowl of pike/salmon

Hydne Hydnum species of mushroom

Hydrolyse Decomposition of a compound in water

Hydromel Mead: drink made with honey & water

Hydrophile Absorbent (material)

Hygrophore Hygrophorus species of mushroom

Hypocras Hippocras: home-made mulled wine

Hysope Hyssop: Med. plant used in liqueurs

Icaque Coco, Icaco plum

Idem Ditto, Same as …

If *[yew]* Spiked rack for storing empty bottles

Igname Yam (similar to sweet potato)

IGP: indication géographique protégée Denotes product comes from a named region (less strictly regulated than *AOC*)

Ile de Beauté Corsica

ILE de FRANCE Region that includes Paris & where some of the world's greatest chefs work & where the finest fruit & vegetables are still grown; numerous dishes & specialities bear the names of Argenteuil, Bercy, Chartres, Meaux, Poissy, Saint-Germain, etc.

Ile flottante Floating island: dessert of lightly baked egg white in egg custard

Imbiber to Steep: saturate with syrup/alcohol/liqueur

Imbrucciata Pastries with *broccio* cheese, sp. of Corsica

Imbuvable Undrinkable

Immangeable Inedible

Immonde / Immondices Filthy, Revolting / Refuse

Impératrice (à l'..) Various rich dishes; Dessert of rice, crystallized fruit & Bavarian cream

Impériale Bottle size (8 btls)

Impériale (à l'..) Various complex dishes using cocks' combs, sliced truffles & kidneys, etc.

Imprévu Unexpected

Inciser to Make incisions in meat/fish before grilling

Inclus, -e Included, Inclusive

Incolore Colourless, Clear

Incomber to Be the responsibility of someone

Inconditionnel, inconditionnelle Unconditional, Absolute, Wholehearted, (fam.) Mad about …

Incontournable Essential

Incorporer to Incorporate, to Add ingredients during cooking

Indice Indication, Clue, Sign

Indienne (à l'..) Indian-style: with curry flavours

Indigeste / Indigestion Indigestible / Indigestion

Indigotine Indigo carmine (E132): blue food colouring

Industriel, industrielle Industrial, Factory-made

Inégal, -e Uneven, Unequal, Changeable

Infect, -e Foul, Revolting (smell, etc.)

Infusion Infusion: steep in boiling liquid; Herbal tea

Ingrédients Ingredients; Components

Inox Stainless steel

Inoxydable Rustproof

Insecte Insect

Intercalaire Divider

Intercaler to Insert, to Layer

Intestin Bowel, Intestine

Intoxication alimentaire Food poisoning

86

Intoxiquer to Poison

Introduire to Insert

Inutile Useless, Needless, Unnecessary

Irouléguy *AOC* red, rosé & white wine of the Pays Basque

Isard Izard: Pyrenean mountain goat *[chamois]*

Isolant, -e Insulated

Isotherme Refrigerated; Protective cooling material

Issu, -e (être .. de) to Come/originate (from), to Result (from)

Issue/ .. de secours / Sans .. Way Out, Exit / Emergency Exit / No Exit

Issues (term) Inedible parts of animal carcass; Flour by-products (bran, etc.)

Italia Variety of white dessert grape

Italienne (à l'..) Italian-style: with macaroni or *sauce italienne*; Pasta with artichoke hearts

Italienne (sauce ..) Button mushrooms, shallots, olive oil, tomato purée, parsley & chopped ham

Ivoire Ivory

Ivoire (à l'..) Veal or poached chicken with *sauce à l'ivoire*

Ivoire (sauce à l'..) *Sauce suprême* with white stock

Ivraie Rye grass

Ivre / Ivresse Drunk / Drunkenness, Intoxication

Ivrogne Drunkard

Izarra Liqueur of the Pays Basque

Jabot Crop (of bird)

Jacque Apple pancake of Périgord

Jadis Formerly, Of old, In former times [*autrefois*]

Jaffer / Jaffe (fam.) to Eat / Food; Prisoners word for soup

Jailles Stew of pork & apples, trad. in the Alps

Jalousie [*venetian blind*] *Frangipane* cake with slatted pastry topping

Jambe de bois [*wooden leg*] Shin of beef on the bone used in *pot-au-feu*; Soup using leg of beef, sp. of the Lyonnais

Jambon / .. blanc/cuit Ham / Cooked ham

Jambon au torchon [*in a cloth*] Superior ham (with implication that it has been cooked in the traditional way)

Jambon cru Raw, dried ham, often smoked

Jambon d'York English-style ham: cooked on the bone

Jambon de Bayonne Salted & dried ham of the Pays Basque

Jambon de campagne Local, regional ham (often smoked)

Jambon de Paris Lightly salted, cooked ham, block-moulded

Jambon de Parme Salted & dried Italian ham

Jambon de Prague Lightly smoked, sweetened cooked ham

Jambon de Reims Cooked, pressed ham rolled in breadcrumbs

Jambon San Danielle Dried & salted Italian ham

Jambonneau Ham knuckle; Leg of pork; Stuffed leg of chicken

Jambonnette Chopped pork & bacon re-moulded into ham shape

Jambonnière Ham-shaped cooking pot for large joint

Japon / Japonais Japan / Japanese

Japonais (artichaut ..) Chinese artichoke: tiny twisted tuber with sweet flavour [*crosne*]

Japonaise Peach ice cream *bombe* filled with tea mousse

Japonaise (à la ..) Dish containing *artichauts japonais*

Jaque Jackfruit: knobbly tropical fruit used as vegetable

Jardin / .. anglais / .. à la française / .. public Garden / Landscape garden / Formal garden / Park

Jardin d'enfants Kindergarten

Jardin d'hiver [*winter garden*] Conservatory

Jardin potager Vegetable garden

Jardinier, jardinière Garden (produce, etc.); Gardener

Jardinière Garnish of lightly cooked garden vegetables

Jardins d'acclimatation/agrément Pleasure gardens

Jardins ouvriers Allotments

Jarre Large wide-mouthed earthenware jar (for olives, anchovies, etc.)

Jarret Knuckle, Shin

Jarretière [*garter*] Scabbard fish

Jars Gander: male goose

Jasmin Jasmine (essence is made from the flowers)

Jasnières *AOC* white wine of Touraine

Jaspage, Jaspure Marbled, Mottled, Sprinkled

Jasserie Trad. name for a dairy in the Forez region

Jatte Shallow bowl, Milk-pan, Small basin

Jau, Jaud Cockerel (in central France)

Jaune / Jaunâtre Yellow / Yellowish

Jaune d'œuf Egg yolk

Jaunir / Faire .. to Go yellow, to Fade / to Lightly brown (in fat)

Javel (eau de ..) Bleach (chloride)

Javeliser to Chlorinate

Jean-doré John Dory (fish) *[Saint-Pierre]*

Jéroboam Champagne bottle size (4 btls/3 ltrs)

Jessica Garnish of artichokes & morel mushrooms on potato cakes; Omelette filled with morels & asparagus tips

Jésuite Small iced puff pastry cake; Turkey (in some regions)

Jésus Large coarse sausage of various regions

Jetable Disposable

Jets de houblons Hop shoots

Jeu de sets de table Set of place mats

Jeun (à ..) On an empty stomach; (fam.) Sober

Jeûne / Jeûner Fasting / to Fast (*Déjeuner* = to break fast)

Jointoyer *[to point]* (term) to Smooth surface of cakes, etc.

Joli, -e, / Joliment Pretty, Nice, Lovely / Prettily, Nicely

Jonc (bull) Rush

Jonchée Fresh cream cheese with regional variations

Jonquille Daffodil; Daffodil-yellow (colour)

Joue Cheek, Jowl

Jouer (pour ..) to Make the best [use] of something

Jour de l'an New Year's Day

Judru Small thick dry pork sausage of Burgundy

Juive (à la ..) Jewish-style; Carp dish; Artichokes stuffed with mint

Jujube Jujube: Chinese/'red' date

Jules-Verne Garnish of stuffed potatoes & turnips; Author (1828-1905) of 'Around the World in 80 Days'

Juliénas *AOC* red wine of Beaujolais

Julienne Ingredients (esp. vegetables) cut into thin strips; Ling, Sea burbot; Rocket

Julienne (couteau à ..) Special vegetable shredding device

Julienne (potage ..) Soup with finely sliced fresh vegetables

Jumeler *[to twin]* to Arrange in pairs

JURA Mountainous *département* in the east, bordering Switzerland, renowned for its cattle, *Vin Jaune* & Arbois wine

Jurançon Semi-sweet & dry white wine from the Pyrenees

Jurassiene (à la ..) Jura-style:
often with cheese/bacon

Jus / .. de cuisson Juice; Stock /
Gravy, Pan juices

Jus (au ..) Served with gravy

Jussière Garnish of stuffed
onions, braised lettuce &
château potatoes

Juteux, juteuse Juicy

Kaki *[khaki]* Persimmon: orange tomato-like fruit

Kangourou Kangaroo

Kari Curry *[cari]*

Karité (beurre de ..) Shea butter: made from tropical fruit seed

Kascher Kosher *[cascher]*

Keftedes Kefta: spicy Greek hamburger

Képhir Kefir: fermented-milk drink of the Middle East

Kermesse Fête, Village fair (from the Flemish *kermis*)

Ketchup Spiced tomato & vinegar condiment

Kiev (à la ..) Deep-fried chicken breasts stuffed with garlic butter & herbs

Kilo, kg. Abbr. for *kilogramme* (1000 g/2.2 lb)

Kipper Kipper: smoked herring

Kir Aperitif of white wine (trad. *Aligoté*) & blackcurrant liqueur *[cassis]*. (Canon Félix Kir was a French Resistance hero & mayor of Dijon)

Kir communard Red wine with *cassis [rince cochon]*

Kir royal *Kir* made with champagne or sparkling white wine

Kirsch Brandy distilled from cherries

Kissel Russian dessert of red fruit purée with cream

Kiwano Horned cucumber/melon (tropical fruit)

Kiwi Kiwi fruit; Kiwi bird

Knackwurst Alsace version of Frankfurter sausage

Knepfle Small dumpling of Alsace

Koeckbotteram Butter cake: *brioche* cake of Dunkirk

Kouglof, Kougelhof, Kugelhopf Stale yeast cake of Alsace

Kouing-aman *[cake & butter]* Rich cake made with bread dough, butter & sugar, sp. of Brittany

Koulibiac Russian-style fish pie with hard-boiled eggs

Koulitch Kulich: trad. tower-shaped Russian Easter cake

Krapfen Hot doughnut filled with jam or almond paste

Krassens Dumplings of Brittany

Kummel Liqueur flavoured with caraway seeds

Kumquat Small orange-like fruit with sweet rind & sour flesh

Kyrielle de ... A lot/string/host of …

Label Mark of quality (& giving specific characteristics)

Label rouge Official mark of quality, esp. for meat & poultry

Labre Wrasse [*vieille*]

Lac Lake

Lactaire délicieux Saffron Milk Cap mushroom

Lacté, -e Milky

Laisser to Leave, to Put aside

Lait / .. frais / .. entier Milk / Fresh milk / Full cream milk

Lait (petit ..), Lait clair Whey

Lait battu Milk shake

Lait caillé / .. sucré Curd / Curds & whey

Lait concentré/condensé Condensed milk

Lait cru Unpasteurized/raw milk

Lait d'amandes Almond milk: blancmange base; Almond cake

Lait de baratte/de beurre Buttermilk

Lait de coco Coconut milk

Lait de poule Eggnog: sweet milk drink with egg & alcohol

Lait de soja Soya milk

Lait écrémé/demi-écrémé Skimmed/semi-skimmed milk

Lait en poudre Powdered milk

Lait fermenté Slightly soured milk

Lait ribot Churned milk; Liquid yoghurt

Lait stérilisé/pasteurisé U.H.T., Longlife milk

Lait tourné Sour milk

Laitage Dairy produce

Laitance, Laite Milt, Soft roe (of male fish)

Laité Soft-roed fish

Laiterie Dairy

Laiteron Sow thistle, Milkweed: bitter lettuce with white sap

Laiteux, laiteuse Milky; Milk-white (colour)

Laitier, laitière Milk/dairy (product); Dairyman, Milkmaid

Laiton Brass

Laitue / .. pommée Lettuce / Hearty lettuce

Laitue de mer Sea lettuce (algae)

Laitue romaine Cos lettuce

Lame (d'un couteau) Blade (of a knife)

Lamelles Thin strips, Slivers; Gills (of mushroom)

Lamproie Lamprey (eel-like fish)

Lançon Sand eel [*équille*]

Landaise (à la ..) Landes-style: ham, *confit*, mushrooms & potatoes

Langouste Crawfish: clawless lobster

Langoustine Scampi

Langres Strong cow's-milk cheese of Champagne

Langue Tongue

Langue de bœuf Ox tongue; (fam.) Beefsteak mushroom

Langue de chat [*cat's tongue*] Thin dry biscuit

Languedocienne (à la ..) Languedoc-style: with

tomatoes, aubergines & mushrooms

LANGUEDOC-ROUSSILLON Large region in the south curving round the western end of the Med. coast with a varied cuisine as well as a notable & extensive selection of wines

Languette Long thin strip (of bread, material, foil, etc.)

Lanières Thin strips, Thin ribbons

Lapereau Young rabbit

Lapin / Lapine Rabbit / Doe: female rabbit

Lapin de clapier *[hutch]* Domestic rabbit

Lapin de garenne/des champs Wild rabbit

Laqué, -e Glazed

Lard Fatty pork/bacon; Side of bacon (Lard = *saindoux*)

Larder to Lard, Larding

Lardoire Larding needle *[aiguille à larder]*

Lardons Diced fatty bacon (for omelettes, salads, etc.)

Large / Largeur Wide, Broad / Width, Breadth

Lasagnes, Lazagnes Lasagne: flat ribbon pasta, sp. in Savoie

Lasser (se ..) / Finir par .. to Get tired of something / to Cloy

Laurier (feuille de ..) Bay leaf

Laurier-sauce Bay laurel tree, Bay tree

Lavabo Wash-hand basin

Lavandière Washer woman

Lavaret Mountain trout found in the Lac du Bourget of Savoie

Lavasse (fam.) Thin as dishwater

Lave-linge Washing machine

Laver to Wash

Lavette Dishcloth

Lave-vaisselle Dishwasher

Lavignon 'False clam': mollusc with peppery flavour

Lavoir Wash house

Lèchefrite Dripping-pan under grill/spit to catch juices

Lécher to Lick

Lèche-vitrines *[window-licking]* Window-shopping

Légère / Légèrement Light, Thin, Weak / Lightly, Gently

Légume / .. de mer Vegetable / Seaweed

Légumier Vegetable dish: serving dish with cover

Légumineuses Pulses: seeds used as a vegetable

Léman (lac ..) Lake Geneva

Lentilles / .. du Puy Lentils / AOC lentils of the Auvergne

Lentillons de Champagne Pink lentils of Champagne

Lépiote Family of mushrooms (including *Coulemelle*)

Lessive Washing powder/liquid; the Washing/laundry

Lest Weight[s]

Levain Leaven: small ball of bread dough retained for the next batch

Lever to Rise (of pastry, etc.)

Levraut Leveret: young hare

Lèvre Lip, Rim

Levure / .. chimique Yeast / Baking powder

Levure de boulanger/bière Baker's/brewer's yeast

Liaison *[link]* Thickening/binding agent

Liant, -e *[affable]* Binding, Thickening

Librairie Bookshop (Library = *bibliotèque*)

Libre Free (availability/access), Vacant (Free of charge = *gratuit*)

Librement Freely

Libre-service Self-service

Lie de vin Lees: sediment left in wine cask after racking; (fam.) Dregs

Lie-de-vin Wine(-coloured)

Liège Cork (of tree) (A cork = *bouchon*)

Liégeoise (à la ..) Liège-style (Belgium): with gin/juniper berries (*Café liégeois* = coffee cream dessert)

Lier to Bind, to Tie up, (term) to Thicken

Liesse / En .. Jubilation / Jubilant

Lieu noir/jaune Black/yellow pollack (large sea fish related to whiting)

Lièvre Hare

Ligne Line; Figure, Shape

Limaçon Small snail *[escargot]*

Limande / .. sole Dab / Lemon sole

Limandelle Megrim: flat sea fish

Lime Sweet lime (citrus fruit) (Lime = *citron vert*)

Limon Sour lime (citrus fruit); Topsoil; Silt

Limonade Lemonade

Limonadier Bottle/can opener; Soft drinks' supplier

Limoner (term) to Wash (fish, brains, etc.) under running water (to remove silt/*limon*); to Remove fish scales; to Open oysters *[écailler]*

LIMOUSIN Livestock country in the west-centre of France that also provides game, plums, cherries & chestnuts

Limousine (à la ..) Limousin-style: often with red cabbage

Limousine (race ..) Small red-brown beef cattle of Limousin

Limpide / Limpidité Clear, Pure, Transparent / Clarity

Lin / Grain de .. Flax; Linen / Linseed

Linge / .. sale Laundry; Linen; Cloth / Dirty washing

Lingot (haricot ..) Lingot bean: large creamy-white bean

Lingue Ling, Sea burbot *[julienne]*

Linzertorte à confiture Latticed jam & cinnamon tart of Austria

Lipides Lipids: group of fatty substances found in foods

Liquéfier to Liquefy (sauces, etc.)

Liqueur Liqueur, Distilled alcohol

Liqueur de Fécamp Another name for *Bénédictine* liqueur

Liquide Liquid, Runny

Liquoreux, liquoreuse Thick, sweet & sticky

Lirac Red, white & rosé wine from the Côtes-du-Rhône

Lisette Small mackerel, sp. of Dieppe

Lisse Smooth

Lisser to Make smooth; to Smooth out; (term) to Coat (with sugar, etc.)

Listériose Listeria: bacteria found esp. in milk products

Listrac Red Bordeaux wine from the Haut-Médoc

Lit Bed (of lettuce, etc.); Base, Bottom layer

Litchi Lychee (tropical fruit)

Littoral Seashore

Livarot Strong soft cow's-milk cheese of Normandy

Livèche Lovage (herb)

Loche Loach: freshwater fish with long slimy body

Loir Dormouse

Loire (vins de la ..) Wine from both sides of this great river that runs into the Atlantic at Nantes (Touraine, Anjou, Pays Nantais, Saumurois, etc.)

Lolo Child's word for milk *[lait]*

Lompe Lumpfish *[lump]*

Long, longue Long; (long) Time; Length *[longueur]*

Longane Longan: tropical fruit, similar to lychee, with smooth skin

Longe Loin

Longeole Sausage of Savoie (& Switzerland) made with green vegetables, pork fat & pluck

Longuement For a long time, At length

Longuet Long-lasting dry bread made with fat & sugar

Longueur / Longuet, longuette Length, Long / Longish, Slender

Lorette Garnish with asparagus; Salad with celeriac & beetroot

LORRAINE Region in the NE known for its *quiche*, Moselle wines & Vosges mountains

Lorraine (à la ..) Lorraine-style: often with red cabbage

Lorraine (quiche ..) Classic egg & bacon tart, orig. of Lorraine

Losange Diamond-shape, Lozenge

Lots Batches, Lots

Lotte Monkfish *[baudroie]*

Lotte de rivière Burbot: freshwater fish with prized liver

Loubine, Louvine Grey mullet

Louche Ladle

Loukoum Turkish delight

Loup / Louve / Louveteau Wolf / She-wolf / Wolf-cub

Loup de mer *[sea wolf]* Sea bass in Provence *[bar]*

Loupiac Sweet *AOC* white wine of Bordeaux

Louquenka Spicy sausage of the Pays Basque, trad. eaten with oysters

Lourd, -e Heavy

Louvine Sea bass *[bar]* in the Pays Basque

Lu (brand name) Biscuits of Nantes

Lucullus Various rich dishes named after this Roman general (renowned for his sumptuous feasts), notably smoked tongue, quail & pheasant (all prepared with *foie gras*)

Luisant, -e Shiny

Lumas *Petit-gris* snails in Aunis (region of La Rochelle)

Lump Lumpfish

Lunel *Vin doux naturel* of the Languedoc, made from Muscat grapes

Lut Lute: paste of flour & water used to seal casserole lid

Luter to Seal with lute

Luzerne Lucerne, Purple medick: fodder-plant *[alfalfa]*

LYON France's third city (after Paris & Marseille), founded by the Romans on the confluence of the Rhône & the Saône; its cuisine is considered one of the finest in France & its third river is said to be the Beaujolais!

Lyonnaise (à la ..) Lyon-style: with onions or *sauce lyonnaise*

Lyonnaise (sauce ..) Onion sauce with vinegar & white wine

Lyophilisé Freeze-dried

Lyre à foie gras Wire cutter for block of *foie gras*

Macaron Macaroon

Macaronis Macaroni pasta tubes

Macédoine Mixture/salad of diced fruit/vegetables

Macérer to Macerate: soak (fruit etc.) in liquid (alcohol, wine, etc.)

Mâche Lamb's lettuce

Mâcher to Chew

Machine à café Commercial coffee machine (See also *Cafetière*)

Machine à pain Home bread-making machine

Mâchon Trad. snack (usually pork sausage & potatoes) served with Beaujolais wine; Celebration following the wine harvest in Burgundy

Mâchure Bruise (on fruit, etc.)

Macis Mace: shell of nutmeg

Mâcon Red, white & rosé *AOC* wine from the region between the Côte-de-Beaune & Beaujolais

Mâconnaise (à la ..) Dish cooked with Mâcon wine

Macre, Madi Water chestnut

Macreuse Cut of beef shoulder; Scoter: large sea duck

Macvin Sweet spiced wine of the Jura

Madeleine Small rich sponge cake

Madeleines (moule à ..) Special mould with shell shapes

Madère Madeira: fortified wine from this Portuguese island

Madérisé White wine that has become oxidized & takes on colour & smell of Madeira

Madiran *AOC* red wine of Béarn in the SW

Madrilène (à la ..) Madrid-style: with tomatoes; Consommé with tomato pulp

Magasin / Grand .. / En .. Shop / Department store / In stock

Magasin d'alimentation Food shop

Magasins spélialisés Specialist shops

Magazine Magazine; Magazine programme

Magistère Rich & nourishing consommé soup

Magnificat Rich cream soup of mushroom, lettuce & hazelnuts

Magnum Bottle size (2 btls/1.5 ltrs)

Magret Breast of duck that has been force-fed for *foie gras*

Maigre Lean, Low fat; Lean part of meat; Meagre (Med. fish); Sparce, Thin, Skinny, Meagre, Frugal

Maigre (au ..) Dish without meat (with meat = *au gras*)

Maigre (repas/jour ..) Meal without meat / Fast-day

Maigrir to Slim, to Lose weight

Maillot Garnish with Madeira

Maïs Maize, Sweetcorn

Maïs en épi Corn on the cob, Corncob

Maison *[house]* Should mean homemade or, at least, a speciality of the establishment (but not always!)

Maître d'hôtel Head waiter; Butler *[majordome]*; Various dishes with *beurre maître d'hôtel*

Maître d'hôtel (beurre ..) Seasoned butter with parsley

Maître de chai Wine cellarman

Maître-queux Master chef (*queux* is old word for *coq* = cook); (term) A very good cook

Maîtriser to Master (something), to Bring under control

Maïzena (brand name) Cornflour

Majordome Butler (orig. in charge of the wine & plate, etc. of a household) (See also *Bouteillerie*)

Malakoff Various rich cream cakes with nuts & coffee

Malaxer to Mix, to Knead, to Cream

Malbec Pale black grape variety used (often blended) in red wines (esp. Cahors) of the SW [*Auxerrois, Côt*]

Malin Crafty, Nifty, Clever

Malouin, -e of Saint-Malo in Brittany

Malsat, Melsat *Boudin blanc* sausage of the SW, esp. Albi

Maltais Iced petit four made with crystallized orange

Maltaise (à la ..) Dish with [Maltese blood] oranges

Mancelle (à la ..) Le Mans-style: often with poultry/wild rabbit

Manche Handle; Sleeve; (term) Protruding bone of leg of lamb/*gigot*

Manche à gigot Meat-carving tongs

Manchette [*cuff*] Paper frill for protruding bones of chops, etc.

Manchon [*muff*] Knuckle joint of poultry; Cigarette-shaped petit four filled with butter cream

Mandarine Mandarin orange, Tangerine

Mandoline Vegetable/egg slicer shaped like the musical instrument; Slicing machine

Manège à couverts Circular cutlery holder (*manège* = merry-go-round)

Manette Control button/switch

Mangeable Edible [*comestible*]

Mangeaille Soft food, Feed (for chickens)

Mangeoir Manger, Feeding trough

Manger / A .. to Eat, to Have a meal / Food; Edible

Manger (donner à ..) to Provide a meal

Manger (faire ..) / Se .. to Feed (someone) / to Be eaten alive (by mosquitoes, etc.)

Manger (faire à ..) to Cook, to Do the cooking

Manger à la cuillère Denotes well-cooked meat/poultry (tender enough to eat with a spoon!)

Manger à sa faim to Have enough to eat

Manger froid to Have something cold (to eat)

Manger sur le pouce [*off the thumb*] to Have a quick snack

Mange-tout [*eat all*] Pea/bean eaten whole without podding; Snow pea

Mangoustan Mangosteen: tough red-skinned fruit whose white flesh is eaten fresh or used in jams

Mangue / Manguier Mango / Mango tree

Manière (à la .. de) In the style/fashion of ...

Manières / Faire des .. Manners / to Stand on ceremony

Manioc Root of tropical cassava plant (producing tapioca)

Manique, Manicle Pan holder, Oven glove/mitten

Maniveau Basket/tray esp. used for mushrooms

Manivelle Handle

Manne / Mannequin Hamper, Crate / Small hamper

Manouls Tripe dish, sp. of the Languedoc

Manqué Speciality sponge-biscuit cake of Paris

Maquereau Mackerel

Maquis Scrubland of Corsica

Maraîchère (à la ..) Market-garden-style: with fresh vegetables

Marais Marshland (often used for market-gardens)

Marais salant Salt marsh: land flooded by seawater

Marandella Traditional Corsican Easter Monday picnic

Marasquin Maraschino: cherry liqueur

Marauder / Maraudeur, maraudeuse to Pilfer / Petty thief

Marbrade Pork brawn, sp. of the SW

Marbre / Marbré Marble; Striped bream / Marbled, Veined

Marc de .. Residue (after wine-making) from which

brandy/*marc* is made in various regions

Marc de café Coffee grounds

Marcassin Young wild boar

Marcelin Pastry-based cake with strawberry jam & ground almonds

Marchand, -e Shopkeeper, Stallholder; Dealer

Marchand de vin (au ..) Dish cooked with red wine & shallots

Marchand de vin/de fruits/de couleurs Wine merchant / Greengrocer / Ironmonger

Marchand en gros Wholesaler

Marchander to Haggle over (price, etc.)

Marchandise Goods, Merchandise

Marché / .. aux fleurs / .. aux puces Market / Flower market / Flea market (Covered market = *les halles*)

Marché (faire son ..) to Shop at the market

Marché commun The Common Market

Marché noir Black market

Mardi gras [*fat Tuesday*] Shrove Tuesday: day before start of Lent

Maréchale (à la ..) Various classic dishes of small cuts of meat coated in breadcrumbs & sautéed

Marée [*tide*] Collective term for fish/shellfish from the sea

Marengo Sautéed chicken/veal with white wine, tomato & garlic

Marennes Green (due to algae)

oysters of the Marennes region on the west coast

Mareyage / Mareyeur Fish trade / Fishmonger

Margaux *AOC* wine from the Médoc region of Bordeaux

Marge, Margelle Edge, Rim, Border

Mariage Wedding; Marriage (of flavours, etc.)

Marie-salope *[slut]* Bloody Mary cocktail: vodka & tomato juice

Marignan Savarin with apricot jam & meringue, decorated with angelica

Marin, -e Of the sea

Marin / Marine The Navy / Marine blue (colour)

Marinade Seasoned liquid used to marinate meat/game, etc.

Mariner to Marinate, to Pickle

Marinette Small puff pastry filled with apple purée & raisins

Marinière (à la ..) Marine-style: shellfish (esp. mussels) cooked in wine

Marivaux Garnish of mixed vegetable nests

Marjolaine Sweet marjoram

Marmelade Thick sweet fruit purée/*compote* (Marmalade = *confiture d'orange*)

Marmite Heavy lidded cooking pot; Dish cooked in a *marmite*

Marmite dieppoise Fish soup of Normandy with mussels

Marmite mongole Saucepan of stacking units for steaming

Marmite norvégienne Type of double slow-cook saucepan

Marmiton Chef's young assistant *[commis de cuisine]*

Marmotte Variety of cherry

Marocaine (à la ..) Morocco-style: lamb with rice & courgettes

Maroilles Strong-smelling *AOC* cow's-milk cheese of the North used in a classic tart

Marque Brand, Make, Mark, Sign

Marque déposée Registered trademark

Marquise Various smooth rich chocolate mousse desserts

Marron Sweet chestnut with single fruit in the husk (*châtaigne* has twin fruits); Brown

Marron d'Inde Horse chestnut

Marron glacé Chestnut preserved in sugar syrup

Marrons chauds Roasted chestnuts

Marseillaise (à la ..) Marseille-style: with tomatoes, garlic, onions, olives & anchovies

Mascotte Rich praline-coated Genoese sponge cake soaked in alcohol

Mascotte (à la ..) Garnish of potato, artichoke heart, [tomato] & truffle

Masquer to Mask, to Coat (with sauce, cream, etc.)

Massacanat Traditional Easter omelette of the South

Masse Mass, Bulk; Mixed preparation (term esp. in cake making) *[appareil]*

Massepain Marzipan; Marzipan petit four

Masser to Massage, to Rub

Massif, massive Solid (wood, etc.), Heavy, Massive

Mastiquer / Mastication to Chew / Chewing

Matafan, Matefaim Large thick pancake, sp. of the SE

Matelote Freshwater fish stew

Mathusalem Champagne bottle size (8 btls/6 ltrs)

Matières grasses Fat, Fat content, Fatty ingredients

Matignon Pulp [fondue] of vegetables used as coating/garnish

Matin / Matinal, -e, matinaux Morning / Morning (time), Early, Early riser

Matinée / Faire la grasse .. All morning / to Have a lie-in

Matois, -e Sly, Wily

Matzo Matzoh: unleavened crisp-bread of Jewish cuisine

Maury Fortified sweet wine served as an aperitif

Maussade Dull, Sad

Mauve Mallow (used in salads)

Maximal, -e, maximaux Maximum

Mayonnaise Cold sauce of seasoned egg yolks & oil

Mazagran Goblet for coffee & iced desserts; Savoury preparation in a case of duchess potatoes

Mazarin Meringue/Genoese gâteau with praline/fruit

Mazarine (à la ..) Small cuts of meat served with rice, mushrooms & stuffed artichoke hearts

Mechoui, Mechouia N. African festive dish of spit-roasted lamb

Médaillon Medallion-shaped (meat, etc.); Pat of butter

Médoc Wine-growing region of the SW, running along the Gironde from Bordeaux to the Atlantic

Meilleur, -e/ Le .. Better / the Best (See also *Mieux*)

Mélange / Mélanger Mixture, Blend / to Mix, to Blend

Mélangeur électrique Electric hand mixer

Mélasse Molasses, Black treacle

Melba Peach & ice cream dessert; Stuffed tomato garnish

Mêler to Mix, to Blend, to Combine

Mélilot Melilot, Sweet clover

Méli-mélo Hotchpotch, Mix of ingredients

Mélisse Lemon balm, Melissa

Mélochie Melokhia: type of mallow used like spinach

Melon Melon (French varieties include *canteloup charentais, cavaillon, sucrin & galia*)

Melon brodé Rough-skinned variety of melon

Melon d'Espagne Honeydew melon

Ménage Household; Housekeeping

Ménager to Save, to be Economic

Ménagère Canteen of cutlery; Domestic; Housewife

Ménagère (à la ..) Housewife-style: simple economic dish

Mendiant French toast with apples, sp. of Alsace

Mendiants [beggars] Mix of

fruit, trad. at Christmas (almonds, figs, hazelnuts & raisins), representing the habits of the 5 mendicant orders: Dominicans, Franciscans, Carmelites & Augustinians

Mensonge Lie, Fib, Untruth

Menthe / .. poivrée Mint / Peppermint

Menthe à l'eau Peppermint cordial

Mentonnaise (à la ..) Menton-style: with vegetables of the South

Menu Menu (edible) (Menu card = *carte*), Set meal

Menu fretin (fam.) Small fry [*fretin*], Insignificant

Menu, -e Small, Finely (cut); Slight (build, etc.)

Menu-droit Strips of poultry fillets marinated in cream & grilled

Mer / Bord de .. / Eau de .. Sea, Seaside; Tide [*marée*] / By the sea / Sea water

Mercédès Garnish of tomato, mushroom, lettuce & potato; Chicken consommé with sherry, sliced kidney, cocks' combs & chervil

Mercerisé Treated material (cotton, etc.)

Mercurey Red & white wine from the Côte Chalonnaise in southern Burgundy

Mères Lyonnaises Name given (from the end of the C19th) to several renowned lady cooks of Lyon (& to their establishments)

Merguez Spicy sausage, orig. of N. Africa & Spain

Méridionale of the South; Southerner

Méridionale (à la ..) Midi-style: using ingredients of the South

Meringage Cake/dessert with meringue

Meringue cuite Egg whites & sugar whisked over heat & then baked as baskets & petits fours etc.

Meringue italienne Whisked egg whites with sugar syrup used for toppings, creams & icings, etc.

Meringue simple Whisked egg whites, sugar & pinch of salt used raw/baked for toppings, etc.

Meringue suisse Egg whites & sugar whisked in a bain-marie until firm & shiny for use as decoration

Meringué, -e Topped with meringue

Meringuer to Cover/decorate with meringue mixture

Merise Wild cherry

Merlan Whiting; Cut of beef used for steaks

Merlan en colère [*angry*] Whiting served with tail in its mouth

Merle Blackbird (used esp. in Corsican pâtés)

Merlot Black grape variety (often blended with Cabernet Sauvignon) used esp. in red wines of Bordeaux

Merlu / Merluche Hake [*colin*] / Hake; Dried hake [*stockfisch*]

Merluchon Small hake

Mérou Grouper: large fish of sea perch family

Merveilles [*little marvels*] Fritters in Montpellier

Mesclun Salad made with various (bitter) leaves

Mesure Measuring device (spoon, cup, etc.)

Mesurer to Measure [*doser*]

Métal Metal (aluminium, steel, copper, cast iron, etc.)

Méteil Flour obtained from mixture of wheat & rye

Méthode Method, Way, Formula

Métis, métisse Cross-breed; Mix (esp. of fabric)

Métisser to Mix

Mets Dish (of prepared food), Delicacy

Méture Porridge/bread made mainly with maize

Meule / Meuler Millstone; Shape of large cheeses / to Grind

Meunier / Meunière (à la ..) Miller / Miller's-wife-style: ingredients tossed in flour before being fried

Meurette Various (river fish, egg, veal & brains) dishes cooked in red wine sauce, sp. of Burgundy

Meursault Wine (mostly white) from the Côte-de-Beaune in Burgundy

Mexicaine (à la ..) Mexican-style: garnish of stuffed mushrooms

Meyerbeer Egg dish with lamb's kidney & *sauce Périgueux*

Mi-... Half-...; Medium-sized ...

Miam-miam! Yum-yum!

Miche [*buttock*] Round bread loaf (cob)

Michon Pancake with apple filling, sp. of Brittany

Micro-ondes Microwave

Midi Midday, 12 pm, Noon; South, Facing south

MIDI (le ..) The South of France

Mie / Pain de .. Soft interior of loaf / Sandwich loaf

Miel / .. mille/toutes fleurs / .. crémeux Honey / Blended honey / Thick (spreading) honey

Miel (rayon de ..) Honeycomb

Miel alfalfa Clover honey

Miel d'acacia/oranger Acacia flower/orange blossom honey

Miel de bruyère/châtaigner/citronnier Heather/chestnut/lime blossom honey

Miel de lavande/pin/romarin Lavender flower/pine/rosemary honey

Miel de sainfoin/sapin/thym Sainfoin (similar to clover)/pine/thyme honey

Miel de tournesol/trèfle Sunflower/clover honey

Miellé, -e In/with honey

Mielleux, mielleuse Cloying (like honey/*miel*)

Miette Crumb, Morsel, (fam.) Just a tiny bit

Mieux / Le .. Better / the Best (See also *Meilleur*)

Migaine Basic mix of eggs & cream (for flans, etc.)

Mignardise Delicacy, Sweetmeat, Petit four

Mignon (filet ..) Tender cut of beef/veal/pork from the fillet

Mignon [*dainty*] Dish of sweetbreads/small cuts of meat, sautéed & coated with Madeira sauce

Mignonnette Ground [white] pepper; Various elaborate dishes using small cuts of meat, etc.

Migourée Fish soup of the Vendée

Mijoter (faire ..) to Simmer food; to Put (ingredients) together

Mijoter / Mijoté, -e to Simmer, to Stew / Simmered, Stewed

Mijoteuse Electric casserole, Slow-cooker

Mikado Japanese-style: with rice, soy sauce, bean sprouts, etc.

Milanais Various small cakes & biscuits

Milanaise (à la ..) Milan-style: dipped in egg & breadcrumbs before frying or with pasta garnish

Mildiou Mildew; Brown rot (of vines)

Milieu, milieux Middle, Centre

Millas, Millasse, Millias Corn-meal porridge with regional variations & often eaten cold like bread

Millasou Type of soufflé made with fruit in the SW

Mille-feuille Puff pastry layers with sweet/savoury filling

Millésime Vintage (of wine); Year of manufacture

Millet Millet (cereal grain)

Mimolette Bright orange semi-hard cheese

Mimosa Garnish of sieved hard-boiled egg yolk

Minable Shabby, Seedy, Lousy, Crummy

Mince / Minceur Thin, Slender, Scant / Thinness

Mine / Avoir bonne/mauvaise .. Aspect, Appearance / to Look well/ill

Minéola Type of tangerine (crossed grapefruit & orange)

Minérale (eau ..) Mineral water

Minervois Red, white & rosé wine of Languedoc

Mingaux, Maingaux Froth taken from cream & beaten with bundle of twigs, sp. of Rennes

Minimal, -e, minimaux Minimum

Minoterie / Minotier Flour mill/milling / Miller

Minuscule Minute, Tiny

Minute *[60 seconds]* Steak, etc. cooked very quickly

Minuterie / Minuteur Time-switch / Timer

Mique Rich dumpling, sp. of Périgord

Mirabeau (à la ..) Garnish using anchovies

Mirabelle Small perfumed yellow plum (esp. of Lorraine)

Mirepoix Classic mix of chopped vegetables & diced ham

Mirliton *[toy flute]* Little almond pastry

Miroton, Mironton Cooked sliced beef in vinegar sauce with onions

Mise au point (term) to Make finishing touches to a dish

Mise en place *[put in place]* (term) to Prepare for a meal

Mise-en-bouche *[pop in the mouth]* (term) Bite-size snack

Mistelle Grape juice with spirits (base of vermouths, etc.)

Mitan Middle section of large fish (salmon, etc.)

Mite Moth

Mitonnée de ... Dish (stew, etc.) cooked by slow simmering

Mitonner to Cook slowly, to Simmer *[mijoter]*

Mitron Baker's boy

Mixer to Blend, to Liquidize

Mixeur Blender, Liquidizer

Mocovite (à la ..) Moscow-style: dish of Russian cuisine

Mode (à la .. de) In the style of ...

Mode (bœuf à la ..) Classic dish of boiled beef & carrots

Moelle / Os à .. Bone marrow / Marrowbone

Moelleux, moelleuse Soft, Mellow, Tender

Moisi, Moisissure Mould, Mildew

Moisson / Moissonner Harvest, Crop / to Reap, to Harvest, to Gather (crops, etc.)

Moite Moist, Clammy

Moitié / Moitié-moitié Half / Half-and-half

Mojettes, Mogettes Small white beans; Chocolate beans

Moka Mocha: variety of strong Arabian coffee; Various coffee-flavoured cakes & creams

Molette (d'éperon) Pastry cutter (*éperon* = spur)

Molle (See *Mou*)

Mollet / Œuf .. Soft / Soft-boiled egg

Mollir to Soften

Mombin Santa Rosa plum

Monbazillac Soft white dessert wine of the Dordogne

Mondé, -e Skinned, Blanched

Monder to Remove thin skin of nuts, etc. (esp. almonds)

Monopole Monopoly

Montagnard, -e Of/from the mountains

Montagne Mountain

MONTAGNE (Prosper) Famous chef & writer (1864-1948) who organised the allied army kitchens in WW1

Montbéliard Breed of red & white cattle, orig. of Franche-Comté; Sausage of the Jura

Mont-blanc Various cold desserts using chestnut purée, cream & meringue

MONT-BRY Pseudonym of chef & writer Prosper Montagné (1865-1948) & name of dishes created by him

Monte-charge Goods lift

Monte-plats Service lift, Dumbwaiter

Monter *[to go up]* (term) to Whisk, to Beat

Montmorency Variety of cherry; Dish with cherries

Moque Stoneware cup (trad. for cider)

Morbier Cow's-milk cheese of Franche-Comté, with strip of 'ash' that orig. separated evening from morning cheese

Morceau Piece, Bit, Slice, Lump (of sugar)

Morceaux du boucher (term) Butcher's bits: prize pieces of meat (trad. retained by the butcher!)

Morceler to Break up, to Parcel out

Mordiller to Nibble (at)

Mordre to Bite

Morgon Red Beaujolais wine with a flavour of cherries

Morille Morel mushroom

Mornay Dish with Mornay sauce & browned under grill

Mornay (sauce ..) Béchamel sauce made with egg yolks & grated cheese

Mortadelle Large Italian sausage (mortadella)

Morteau Smoked sausage of Franche-Comté

Mortes-eaux Neap tides

Mortier [et pilon] [pestle &] Mortar

Mortifier [*mortify*] to Hang game, etc.

Morue [salée] Dried salt cod (used in *brandade*)

Morue verte Salted (not dried) cod (= Portuguese *bacalao*)

Morvandelle (à la ..) Morvan-style: with raw Morvan ham

Mosaïque Mosaic: shapes cut from colourful fruit & vegetables to decorate cakes, pâtés, etc.

Moscovite Various cold creamy desserts made in a mould

Moselle White wine from this *département* in Lorraine

Motelle Rockling: Med. fish

Motte [*mound*] Block, Lump, Pat (of butter)

Mou Lights: lungs of slaughtered animal

Mou, mol, molle Soft, Flabby, Limp, Flat (wine, etc.)

Mouche / .. bleue/à viande Fly; Speck / Bluebottle, Blow-fly

Mouche à vinaigre Fruit fly

Moucheron Midge, Gnat

Moucheté, -e Spotted, Speckled, Flecked

Moucheur Candle snuffer

Mouclade Mussels in white wine with cream, sp. of Charentes

Moudre / Moulu to Mill, to Grind / Ground, Powdered

Mouflon Wild sheep

Mouiller to Wet, to Moisten, to Dampen

Mouillettes Sippets, 'Soldiers': fingers of bread/toast or asparagus for dipping into soft-boiled egg

Moulage Moulding, Casting

Moule Mould; Baking/cake tin; Mussel

Moulé (pain ..) Bread baked in a mould (giving it a different texture)

Moule à côtes Decorative mould (for cream desserts, etc.)

Moule à fond amovible Baking tin with detachable base

Moule à gâteau Sponge cake tin

Moule à génoise Swiss roll tin

Moule à kougelhopf Grooved ring mould for the sp. cake of Alsace (*kougelhopf*)

Moule à manqué Deep cake tin

Moule à pâtisserie Baking/cake tin

Moule à savarin Ring mould

Moule à soufflé Soufflé dish

Mouler to Mill; to Purée; to Mould

Moules à plat Mussels farmed like oysters

Moules de bouchot Mussels reared on poles

Moules de Bouzigues Large mussels of the South

Moules marinières Mussels cooked in white wine

Moules sur cordes Mussels reared on ropes (esp. in the Med.)

Mouli-légume Vegetable mill/press

Moulin / .. à café Mill, Grinder, Press / Coffee mill

Moulinette Small vegetable mill

Moult Much, Greatly

Moulu, -e Milled, Ground

Mourvèdre Black grape variety used (often blended) in red wines (esp. Bandol) of the South

Mousse [*moss*] Mousse; Froth; Blunt (knife)

Mousse d'Irlande Irish Moss, Carrageen

Mousseline Mousse-like, Light & creamy; Muslin

Mousseron Fairy Ring mushroom

Mousseux, mousseuse Frothy, Foamy, Whisked up

Moustique Mosquito

Moût Must: juice of grapes before yeast has converted sugar to alcohol in wine making

Moutarde / .. douce Mustard / French mustard

Moutarde germée Sprouting mustard

Moutardier Mustard pot

Mouton Sheep; Mutton

Mouvette Flat wooden spoon (for 'moving' sauces, etc.)

Moyen Means, Way (of doing)

Moyen (au .. de) By means of, By using …

Moyen, moyenne Medium(-sized), Moderate, Average, Middle

Muge Grey mullet

Muguet Lily of the Valley

Muid Large barrel; Hogshead

Muire Old French word for pickling brine

Mulard Variety of duck (cross of Rouen & Barbary)

Mulet Mule; Mullet (fish)

Mulet doré/lippu/porc Grey mullet

Multi-cuiseur Electric casserole

Munster Strong *AOC* mountain cheese of the Vosges

Mûr, -e / Mûrir Ripe, Mature / to Ripen

Mûre Blackberry, Mulberry (Bramble = *ronce*)

Murène Moray eel of the South

Musc Musk: strong-smelling substance from gland of musk deer & musk mallow, etc.

Muscade Nutmeg

Muscadet Dry white *AOC* wine of the Loire

Muscat de Hambourg Variety of black dessert grape

Muscat, Muscatel Grape variety & sweet white wine of Frontignan

Muscle Muscle: meat flesh

Museau Muzzle of animal

Museau de porc Type of brawn made with pig's muzzle

Muselet Muzzle: wire over champagne-style cork

Musette Lunch box; Haversack

Myrtille Bilberry, Blueberry (Myrtle = *myrte*)

Mystère [*mystery*] Ice cream coated with meringue & nuts

Mytiliculture Mussel farming

Nabuchodonosor Nebuchadnezzar: champagne bottle size (20 btls/1600 cl)

Nacre Mother-of-pearl

Nage (à la ..) *[swimming]* Shellfish served in its cooking liquid *[nage]* & cream

Nageoire Fin (of fish)

Nain, -e Dwarf (variety), Undersized

Naissain Embryo cultivated oyster/mussel

Najacois of Najac, in Rouergue, famous for its ham

Nanan Something nice (to eat, etc.)

Nantais Almond shortbread; Square curd cheese from Brittany

Nantaise (à la ..) Nantes-style: with white wine & butter sauce

Nantes (pain de ..) Iced lemon/orange cake surrounded with almonds

Nantua (à la ..) Dish with crayfish & truffles, sp. of Bugey

Napoléon Emperor of France (1804-1815); Term used for age of Cognac (7+ yrs.) & Calvados (5+ yrs.)

Napolitain Layered almond-pastry cake; Small chocolate

Napolitaine (à la ..) Naples-style: with spaghetti, cheese & tomato

Nappe Tablecloth

Napper to Coat, to Cover (with cream, sauce, etc.)

Napperon Mat, Place mat; Doily

Natte *[braid]* Plaited bread loaf

Nature, Naturel (au ..) Plain, Natural, Without garnish/sauce

Navaline Navel orange

Navarin Mutton/lamb stew; Dish with turnips/*navets*

Navarin printanier Stew with spring vegetables

Navet *[bad film/play]* Turnip

Navette *[shuttle]* Dry boat-shaped cake; Rape, Colza

Nectar Nectar (of honey & wine, etc.)

Nectarine Nectarine: variety of peach *[brugnon]*

Néfaste Harmful

Nèfle Medlar: acid pear-shaped fruit mostly used for compotes, etc.

Nèfle du Japon Loquat, Japanese medlar: small Med. fruit

Négociant Wine-shipper/-merchant who buys in wine from growers & bottles it for sale

Nègre en chemise *[negress in a shirt]* Chocolate dessert covered with Chantilly cream

Neige (œufs à la ..) Egg whites whisked to stiff peaks

Neige *[snow]* Sorbet of red fruit juice

Neige de Florence Feather-light flakes of pasta added to consommés & clear soups

Nélusko Iced cherry filled with redcurrant jelly; Curacao-flavoured chocolate ice bombe

Nemours Garnish, fish dish & soup (named after the town)

Nerto Liqueur made from essence of myrtle leaves

Nes. (fam.) Abbr. for Nescafé®, Instant coffee

Nesselrode Dish/pastry containing chestnut purée

Net, nette Clean, Tidy, Clear

Nettoyer to Clean

Neufchatel *AOC* cow's-milk cheese of Normandy, often heart-shaped

Newburg Various lobster dishes (usually sautéed in cream)

NF: norme française French manufacturing standard & official stamp of *AFNOR* (French trading standards authority)

Niçoise (à la ..) Nice-style: with olives, sardines, anchovies, tomatoes & French beans

Nid / .. d'oiseau Nest / Wire scoop spoon

Nids d'hirondelles Swallows' nests (used in Chinese cuisine)

Niflette Puff pastry filled with frangipane cream, sp. of Brie

Nigelle Nigella, Fennel flower, Allspice

Nîmoise of Nîmes in the Gard

Niniche de Bordeaux Type of chocolate fudge of Bordeaux

Niolo Sharp-flavoured farmhouse cheese of Corsica

Niveau (au .. de) Up to the level of …

NIVERNAIS Old province, between Burgundy & the Auvergne, famous for Charolais beef cattle

Nivernaise (à la ..) Nevers/Nivernais-style: with carrots, turnips, braised lettuce, onions & boiled potatoes

Noce (faire la ..) Go on the spree, Live riotously

Noces / .. d'argent/or Wedding celebrations / Silver/golden wedding anniversary

Noël Christmas

Nœud Knot (to Tie a knot = *nouer*)

Nœuds d'amour *[love-knots]* Ribbon-shaped fritters

Noir, -e / Noirâtre Black / Blackish, Darkish

Noir (petit ..) (fam.) Small cup of black coffee

Noircir to Go/turn black, to Darken, to Blacken

Noisette Hazelnut; Nut-shape; Nut-brown; 'Eye' of lamb cutlet; Slice from fillet of beef; Small knob of butter

Noisette (beurre ..) Butter heated until nut-brown in colour; Hazelnut-flavoured butter

Noisette (sauce ..) Hollandaise sauce with *beurre noisette*

Noix Nut(s); Walnut(s) (Peanuts = *cacahouètes*)

Noix de beurre Knob of butter

Noix de cacao Cocoa bean (origin of chocolate)

Noix de cajou Cashew nut

Noix de coco Coconut

Noix de macadam Macadamia nut

Noix de muscade Nutmeg

Noix de pecan Pecan nut

Noix de Saint-Jacques Shelled scallops

Noix de veau Cut of veal from upper fillet end of leg

Noix du Brésil Brazil nut

Nombril Navel, Belly button

Nonnat Mix of small white fish used for frying

Nonnette *[young nun]* Small iced gingerbread cake

Non-pareilles Capers in vinegar; 'Hundreds & thousands' sugar decoration

Noque Small rich dumpling served in soup or with custard, sp. of Alsace

Normande (à la ..) Normandy-style: often with shellfish, cream & apples/cider

NORMANDIE Normandy: region in the NW producing much of France's dairy produce

Nouer to Tie up, to Knot

Nouet Little muslin bag for herbs, *bouquet garni*, etc.

Nougat [blanc] White nougat (with 15% nut content)

Nougat de Provence Nougat made with caramelized sugar syrup, honey & 30% nut content

Nougatine Paste of sugar syrup & almonds, used for moulding & cake decoration

Nouilles Noodles

Nouveau, nouvel, nouvelle, nouveaux New, Novel, Fresh *[frais]*, Young *[jeune]* (*Nouvelles* = news)

Nouvel An New Year

Nouvelle cuisine Style of 'light' cooking established in 1972

Noyau, noyaux Kernel, Stone (of fruit, etc.); Liqueurs based on fruit kernels

Nu, -e (à ..) Naked, Bare, Without garnish/embellishment

Nuance Shade, Tone, Hue

Nul, nulle Useless, Valueless

Occidental, -e, occidentaux Western, Occidental

Occitane (à l'..) Pays d'Oc-style: with garlic & goose fat

Ocre Ochre (yellow colour)

Odorant Odorous, Sweet-smelling

Odorat Smell, Sense of smell

OECE: organisation européenne de co-opération économique Organisation of European economic co-operation

Œillet / .. de fleuriste Pink /Clove pink

Œillette / Huile d'.. Opium poppy / Poppy seed oil

Œnologie Œnology: science/study of wines

Œnologue Wine expert, Wine writer

Œuf / .. coque Egg / Egg in its shell

Œuf daté Dated egg (stamped with date of laying)

Œuf de caille Quail's egg

Œuf de cane Duck's egg

Œuf de pigeon Pigeon's egg

Œuf de poule Chicken's egg

Œuf du jour New laid egg

Œuf extra-frais Egg laid within 24 hours of date stamp

Œuf frais Fresh egg (not quite as fresh as *extra-frais*)

Œufrier Egg-holder (for boiling); Egg-stand (for storing)

Œufs à la Bénédictine Poached eggs on salt cod purée *[morue]* & covered with a cream sauce

Œufs à la bûcheronne Fried eggs on baked potato halves

Œufs à la coque Boiled eggs

Œufs à la coquille Soft-boiled eggs

Œufs à la crème Baked egg custard

Œufs à la genevoise Cheese custard

Œufs à la gitane *[gypsy]* Baked eggs set in mixed vegetables, chopped ham & sausage

Œufs à la neige Floating islands: poached egg whites in custard *[îles flottantes]*

Œufs à la tripe Sliced hard-boiled eggs with onions in béchamel sauce

Œufs au lait Baked egg custard

Œufs au miroir Fried eggs basted with fat (so they shine) or baked in very hot fat

Œufs au plat Shirred eggs (cooked in cool oven); Fried eggs

Œufs au vinaigre Pickled eggs

Œufs brouillés Scrambled eggs

Œufs cuits au four Eggs baked in the oven

Œufs de cabillaud Cod's roe

Œufs de lump Lumpfish roe

Œufs de poisson Hard roe (of female fish) (Soft roe = *laitance*)

Œufs de saumon Salmon roe

Œufs déguisés Scotch eggs; Egg shells filled with chocolate

Œufs durs Hard-boiled eggs

Œufs en chocolat Chocolate eggs, Easter eggs

Œufs en cocotte Baked eggs

Œufs en gelée Eggs in aspic

Œufs en meurette Eggs cooked in red wine sauce, sp. of Burgundy

Œufs en nids *[in nests]* Eggs broken into hollow of cooked potatoes & baked

Œufs farcis Stuffed eggs

Œufs filés Egg threads (used to garnish soups)

Œufs frits Fried eggs

Œufs mimosa Eggs mimosa: garnish of finely chopped hard-boiled white & yolk of egg

Œufs mollets Soft-boiled eggs

Œufs moulés Eggs baked in a mould

Œufs pochés Poached eggs

Œufs sur le plat Shirred eggs (cooked in cool oven); Fried eggs

Office Functional, Duty (knife, etc.); Pantry, Serving area; Servant's hall

OGN: Organisme génétiquement modifié Genetically modified (crop): GM

Oie / Oison Goose / Gosling

Oignon / .. nouveau/blanc Onion / Spring onion

Oignons grelots Button onions

Oille Old word (orig. Spanish) for a type of stew

Oiseau sans tête *[headless bird]* Slice of stuffed rolled meat cooked in sauce *[paupiette]*

Oiselet / Oisillon Small bird / Fledgling

Oléagineux, oléagineuse Oily, Oil-yielding

Oléiculture Olive-oil industry

Olivacé Olive-green colour

Olive Bitter fruit of the Med. region that is picked unripe (green) or ripe (black) & pickled or pressed for oil

Oliveraie Olive-grove

Olives cachado Cracked olives; Pickled olives of the Midi

Olives de cailleter Little black olives of Nice

Olives de Nyons Black olives of the Drôme & Vaucluse

Olives lucques Green olives of Hérault

Olives picholines Green olives of the South

Olives salonenques Green olives of Provence

Olivette Plum tomato

Olivier / Oliverie Olive tree / Olive-oil factory

Omble chevalier Char: type of mountain lake salmon *[ombre]*

Omble commun Grayling (fish)

Ombrine Fish (similar to bass) from the Med. & Bay of Biscay

Omelette (en ..) Mixed/beaten as for an omelette

Omelette à la dijonnaise Omelette with cream, macaroons & blackcurrants

Omelette à la jardinière Omelette with lightly cooked mixed vegetables

Omelette à la paysanne Omelette with sorrel & potatoes

Omelette à la portugaise Omelette with spicy tomato purée

Omelette à la verdurière
Omelette with sorrel & lettuce

Omelette Argenteuil Omelette
with asparagus tips

Omelette au boudin Omelette
with black pudding

Omelette aux fines herbes
Omelette with chopped parsley, chervil, tarragon & chives

Omelette de Pâques Sausage &
artichoke omelette served on
Easter Monday in Roussillon

Omelette Diane Omelette filled
with salpicon of game &
truffles

Omelette Du Barry Omelette
with cauliflower florets

Omelette du Curé Omelette
with tuna & soft-roe

Omelette espagnole Spanish
omelette: with potatoes &
sweet peppers

Omelette Feydeau Creamy
omelette filled with mushroom
duxelles & topped with
Mornay sauce

Omelette flambée Sweet
omelette sprinkled with warm
liqueur & set alight

Omelette Mistral Egg & tomato
mixture poured over fried
aubergine

Omelette mousseline Type of
light pancake made with stiff
egg whites, yolks & cream

Omelette nature Plain omelette

Omelette novégienne Baked
Alaska: dessert of ice cream
enclosed in flamed meringue

Omelette Parmentier Omelette
with diced potato & parsley

Omelette pascale Easter
omelette: trad. made with eggs
laid on Good Friday

Omelette plate Flat omelette

Omelette soufflée Omelette
made with soufflé mixture

Omelette surprise Baked
Alaska with liqueur & fruit

Onctueux, onctueuse Rich,
Smooth, Creamy

Onglet Flank of beef; Groove,
Nick

Opéra Garnish for *noisettes* &
tournedos; Cream dessert with
meringue & strawberries

Orange / .. givré Orange /
Sorbet in a hollowed-out
orange

Orangeat Disc-shaped almond
& orange peel petit four

Orangeat perlé Boiled sweet
containing orange peel

Oranger (fleur d'..) Orange
blossom

Orangeraie / Orangerie Orange
grove / Orangery

Ordinaire Ordinary, Common,
Not special

Oreillard Hare *[lièvre]*

**Oreille de mer, Ormeau,
Ormier** Abalone, Ear shell,
Ormer: single-shelled mollusc
that clings to rocks

Oreilles *[ears]* Small handles on
casserole pots, etc.

Oreillettes *[earflaps]* Fritters of
Montpellier

Oreillons d'abricots Apricot
halves (resembling ears) (*oreillons* = mumps)

Orge / .. perlé Barley / Pearl
barley

Orgeat (sirop d'..) Barley water

Orgie Orgy: feast of eating,
drinking & debauchery

Orient / Oriental, -e, orientaux
The East / Oriental

Orientale (a l'..) Usually dish of
Turkish/Balkan cuisine

Orientale (sauce ..) Tomato &
sweet pepper mayonnaise

Origan Oregano, Wild marjoram

Orléanaise (à l'..) Orléans-style:
garnish of braised endives &
maitre d'hôtel potatoes

Orléans Poached egg tartlets;
Rolled poached sole fillets

Orloff Stuffed loin of veal glazed
with cheese; Garnish of braised
celery, potato & lettuce

Orly Whole/filleted fish dipped
in egg & bread-crumbs, fried &
served with tomato sauce

Oronge Caesar's mushroom

Orphie Garfish, Sea-snipe

Orratza Conger eel in Gascony

Ortie Nettle

Ortolan Ortolan: small (now
protected) species of bunting

Os / A l'.. Bone / On the bone

Oseille *[dough, dosh]* Sorrel

Oseille de Guinée Roselle,
Jamaica sorrel

Oser to Dare

Osier Wicker (basket ware)

Osso-bucco Italian (Milanese)
dish of braised veal knuckle

Osssau-Iraty Ewe's-milk cheese
of the Pyrenees

Ostréiculture Oyster farming

Oter to Remove, to Take
out/away

Ouailles Flock (of sheep)

Oublie Very old type of wafer
[gaufrette]

Oublyeurs Street-sellers of
oublies in the Middle Ages

Ouïes Gills (of fish) *[branchies]*

Ouillade, Ouillat, Oulade Rich
rustic soup/stew from various
regions cooked in an *oule*

Oule, Oille Large trad. copper
cooking pot

Ours / Ourse / Ouson Bear /
She-bear / Bear cub

Ours en peluche Teddy bear (!)

Oursin Sea urchin

Outre (en ..) Besides, In addition to, Furthermore

Outre passer to Override, to
Disregard, to Ignore

Outre-mer Overseas

Ouvert, -e / Ouverture Open /
Opening

Ouvre-boîtes Tin opener

Ouvrir to Open

Ovale Oval

Ovins Sheep

Ovipare Egg-laying animal

Oxtail Oxtail soup

Oyonnade Goose stew, trad. in
the Bourbonnais

squash

SPICE MORTAR.

Pacane Pecan-nut

Pachade Thick pancake with prunes or soft fruit

Pagre, Pageot Mediterranean sea bream

Païen, païenne Pagan, Heathen

Paillasson [*door mat*] Ingredients shaped into a thick slab

Paille / Paillette Straw; Drinking straw / Cheese straw

Pailleter to Spangle: describes ice cream/sorbet that crystallizes in the making

Paillis Mulch

Pain Bread; Loaf. (French bread is trad. sold by weight & the classic 'stick' has several regional names including: *baguette, bâton, ficelle, flûte, gros/petit pain*)

Pain (miettes de ..) Crumbs of bread, Breadcrumbs

Pain à chanter Unconsecrated wafer

Pain à la levure Bread made with fresh yeast

Pain au lait Milk bread

Pain au levain Bread made with leaven (small ball of dough reserved from previous batch which acts as a 'starter')

Pain au son Wholemeal bread with added bran

Pain aux bœufs Christmas cake of Berry

Pain aux lardons Bacon bread

Pain aux noix Walnut bread

Pain aux œufs Egg custard of the Jura

Pain aux raisins Currant bun

Pain azyme Unleavened bread

Pain bénit Consecrated bread/wafer

Pain bis/noir Brown (wholemeal) bread

Pain blanc White bread

Pain brié Hard bread of Normandy

Pain brioché Soft bread made with sweet *pâte à brioche*

Pain chapeau Heavy, two-tiered loaf of Finistère

Pain chocolat Croissant-like roll with chocolate filling

Pain complet/entier Wholemeal bread

Pain couronne French stick curled into a ring/crown

Pain d'épice [*spice bread*] Type of gingerbread, sp. of Dijon

Pain de campagne Farmhouse bread

Pain de cuisine Force-meat/vegetable loaf (hot or in aspic)

Pain de Gênes Genoa cake

Pain de la Mecque Mecca cake: choux bun sprinkled with sugar

Pain de légumes Vegetable loaf

Pain de méteil Round loaf made with mixed flours

Pain de mie Sandwich loaf; Soft white bread (*mie* = crumb, as opposed to crust)

Pain de Nantes Small iced orange/lemon-flavoured cake of Nantes

Pain de poisson Fish loaf

Pain de seigle Rye bread

Pain de sucre Sugar loaf: cone of sugar

Pain de viande Meat loaf

Pain épi French stick shaped with 'ears of corn'

Pain fendu Large rye stick with a deep cut down its length

Pain frais Fresh bread

Pain grillé Toast

Pain moisson Harvest loaf

Pain moulé Bread baked in a mould (giving it a different texture)

Pain perdu *[lost bread]* French toast

Pain polka Large loaf with heavy 'squared' crust

Pain rassis Stale bread

Pain salé Fried pork trimmings

Pain surprise Large round loaf crust refilled with bite-size sandwiches made from its cut-out centre

Pain Viennois Soft sweet bread (orig. of Vienna)

Paisible Peaceful, Quiet, Calm

Paître to Graze, to Feed (on)

Palais / Bon .. Palate / Good sense of taste

Palatinat Palatinate/Pfalz: wine region running along the Rhine in Germany, north of Alsace

Paleron Chuck (cut of beef); Shoulder blade, Blade-bone

Palet Disc-shape; Small crisp petit four of various flavours

Palets d'or Gold-topped/covered chocolates

Palette Butt/shoulder-blade (cut of pork); Spatula

Paleur Pallor, Paleness

Palmier Palm-tree; Sugared pastry/biscuit in the shape of palm leaf

Palois Layered nut meringue gâteau

Paloise (à la..) Pau-style: garnish for meat or with *sauce paloise*

Paloise (sauce ..) *Sauce béarnaise* made with mint instead of tarragon

Palombe Wood pigeon

Palourde Clam

Palud / Paludier Salt-marsh / Salt-marsh worker

Pamplemousse Grapefruit

Panaché *[variegated]* Mixed; Mixed ingredients; Shandy (drink)

Panacher to Mix (items/colours/textures, etc.)

Panade Panada: paste used to bind & thicken; Classic soup base of bread, stock & egg

Panais Parsnip

Pan-bagnat *[soaked bread]* Bread roll rubbed with garlic & filled with *salade niçoise*, sp. of Provence

Paner / Pané, -e to Coat with breadcrumbs / Coated with breadcrumbs

Paner à l'anglaise to Coat with flour, egg & breadcrumbs

Paner à la milanaise to Coat with egg & grated cheese mixed with breadcrumbs

Paner au beurre to Coat with melted butter & breadcrumbs

Panerée Basketful

Paneterie Pantry

Panetière Trad. bread
box/cupboard; Sideboard

Panetière (à la ..) Preparation
served in hollowed-out oven-
warmed loaf

Panette douce Raisin bread, sp.
of Corsica at Easter

Panettone Large dry Italian
[Christmas] cake with dried
fruit

Panier / .. à salade Basket,
Hamper / Wire salad basket

Panier à frites Deep-fryer basket

Panier à légumes Vegetable
basket

Panier vapeur Steamer basket

Panisse Provençal chick-
pea/cornmeal cake fried in oil

Panizze Chestnut flour *panisse*
cake of Corsica

Panne Fat under pork skin
(which, when melted, makes
lard/*saindoux*)

Panneauteur Poacher, Trapper
(*panneau* = trapper's net)

Pannequet Sweet/savoury filled
pancake browned under grill

Panse Belly, Paunch, Bulge

Pantelante *[twitching]* State of
butchered meat prior to rigor
mortis

Panure Fresh breadcrumbs
(Dried breadcrumbs =
chapelure)

Paon / Paonne Peacock / Peahen

Papaye Papaya, Papaw (tropical
fruit)

Papeton Dish of puréed aubergines, sp. of Avignon (once a
Papal city)

Papier absorbant Kitchen
towel/paper

Papier blanc/de cuisine
Greaseproof/waxed paper

Papier d'alu/étain Tinfoil

Papier sulfurisé Waxed paper,
Baking parchment

Papille [gustative] Taste bud

Papillon / .. de nuit Butterfly /
Moth

Papillotte Paper frill;
Buttered/oiled paper (for
cooking food in); Sweet in
shiny fringed paper; (Christmas) Cracker

Papillotte (en ..) Food cooked
in paper/foil

Papinette Wooden spoon

Paprika Ground sweet red
pepper spice

Pâques / Pâque Easter /
Passover

Paquet Packet

Parc Park; Pen (for animals),
Playpen; Oyster bed

Parcimonie (avec ..) Sparingly

Par-dessous Under, Beneath,
Underneath

Par-dessus Over, On top of, On

Pardessus *[overcoat]* Total
covering, Coating

Paré, -e Trimmed, Dressed

Pareil, pareille Similar, the
Same; Alike, No difference

Parer to Prepare, to Trim, to
Dress, to Adorn

Parfait *[perfect]* Fresh cream
iced dessert of various
flavours

Parfum Perfume, Flavour,
Fragrance, Aroma

Parier to Bet, to Gamble

Paris-Brest Rich choux pastry cake filled with praline cream

Parisien Lemon sponge with meringue topping; Paris variation of *baguette*

Parisienne (à la ..) Paris-style: numerous classic dishes of Parisian restaurants

Paris-Nice Similar to *Paris-Brest* but filled with Chantilly cream

Parme (jambon de ..) Parma ham (of northern Italy)

Parmentier Dish with potatoes (named after pharmacist who promoted the potato in France in the C18th)

Parmesan Hard cow's-milk cheese of northern Italy

Paroi Side/wall (of container, etc.)

Paroisse Parish

Parsemer de ... to Sprinkle with ...

Part / .. du lion Part, Portion, Share / Lion's share

Partager to Divide, to Share

Parure / .. de table Dress, Finery / Set of table linen

Parures Trimmings: fat, skin, fish heads, etc. (discarded before cooking)

Parvenir to Achieve; to Reach maturity

Pascade Pancake made with walnut oil, sp. of Rouergue

Pascal, -e Paschal, of Easter

Pascaline Dish of Easter lamb

Passarelle Variety of grape used for raisins

Passe l'an Cow's-milk cheese of Languedoc that takes one year to reach maturity

Passé, -e Past, Dated, Faded

Passe-bouillon / Passe-thé Soup strainer / Tea strainer

Passe-crassane Variety of pear

Passe-plats Serving hatch

Passer to Pass (round, etc.); to Strain, to Filter, to Purée

Passer (faire ..) to Make something pass/go through

Passer (se .. de) to Do/go without (something)

Passer à la poêle to Put into frying pan, to Fry

Passer à table to Come to the (dinner) table

Passer au four to Put (briefly) in the oven

Passe-tout-grains *AOC* red wine of Burgundy

Passette Tiny strainer

Passoire Strainer, Colander

Pastèque Water melon

Pasteurisé, -e Pasteurized

Pastilla Small item rolled/folded in *pâte à brik*, sp. of Morocco

Pastillage Icing sugar paste for decorative moulding

Pastille Small round sweet, Jujube, Lozenge

Pastilles de chocolat Chocolate buttons

Pastis Various pastries of the SW; Aniseed-flavoured alcoholic drink

Pastourelle (à la ..) Shepherdess-style: with lamb

Patate / .. douce (fam.) Potato, Spud / Sweet potato

Pâte Dough, Pastry, Batter; Paste; Substance of cheese

Pâté Pâté, Patty, Small pie: meat/fish/vegetables/fruit baked in a mould or in pastry. Some towns have specialities: Chartres (partridge); Pithiviers (lark); Pézenas (mutton), etc.

Pâte à biscuit Sponge cake mixture

Pâte à brik Wafer-thin pastry used for small 'parcels', etc.

Pâte à brioche Rich yeast dough

Pâte à choux Double-cooked choux pastry used for puffs & éclairs

Pâte à crêpes Batter

Pâte à filo/fillan Filo pastry: wafer-thin pastry used for small 'parcels', etc.

Pâte à foncer Lining pastry (for pâtés, etc.)

Pâte à frire/friture Batter

Pâte à levain Leaven dough (See *Levain*)

Pâte à modeler Plasticine® (not for eating!)

Pâte à pain Bread dough

Pâte à savarin Savarin/baba dough

Pâte à sel Flour & water paste (for modelling, etc.)

Pâte à tarte Pastry

Pâte briochée (See *Pâte à brioche*)

Pâte brisée Short crust pastry

Pâté de campagne Rough pork pâté with offal, onion, herbs & spices

Pâté de canard d'Amiens Boned duck stuffed with pâté, sp. of Amiens in Picardy

Pâté de foie Smooth pork liver pâté

Pâté de foie gras Rich smooth pâté made with fattened goose/duck liver *[foie gras]*

Pâte de fruits Fruit paste: fruit pulp, sugar & pectin

Pâté de Reims Hot/cold pork pâté made with champagne

Pâté de tête Brawn *[fromage de tête]*

Pâte demi-feuilletage Rough puff pastry

Pâté en croûte Rich meat, game/fish pâté cooked in mould lined with pastry

Pâté en terrine Pâté cooked in terrine dish lined with bacon

Pâte feuilletée Puff pastry

Pâte fraisée Little balls of dough rolled in palm of hand before rolling out (for very smooth pastry)

Pâte frite Fritter

Pâté impérial Spring roll (of Chinese cuisine)

Pâte levée Dough

Pâté pantin *Pâté en croûte* not cooked in a mould

Pâte sablée Rich sweetened shortcrust pastry

Pâte sucrée Sweetened short-crust pastry

Pâtée Dog/cat food

Patelle Limpet

Patère Hook, Peg; Shallow cup

Pâtes [alimentaires] / .. fraîches Pasta / Fresh pasta

Pâteux, pâteuse Stodgy, Doughy, Sticky

Patia Dish of potatoes cooked in milk, sp. of Auvergne

Patidou Sweet Dumpling: variety of pumpkin

Patience Dock (leaves used in soups)

Pâtis Pasture, Grazing-ground

Pâtisser to Make pastry & cakes

Pâtisserie Pastries & cakes; Pastry & cake making; Cake shop, Tea rooms

Pâtissier, pâtissière Confectioner; Pastry cook

Pâtisson Custard squash/marrow, Pattypan squash

Patois Provincial dialect, Jargon

Pâton Small ball of dough in bread making

Patranque, Patrenque Auvergne version of *pain perdu* made with Cantal cheese

Pâtre Old word for shepherd [*berger*]; Herdsman

Patron, patronne Manager; Boss; Proprietor; Patron saint

Patte Foot, Leg, Paw

Pâture / Pâturage Animal feed; Pasture / Grazing

Pauillac AOC red wine from this important *commune* of Bordeaux

Paulée de vendanges Feast held after the grape harvest in Burgundy

Paume Palm (of hand)

Paupiette Small rolled & stuffed slice of meat/fish/cabbage

Pause-café Coffee (or tea) break

Pavé [*paving stone*] Various square cheeses of Normandy; Square-shaped cake; Cold mousse in square mould; Thick prime beef steak

Pavie Clingstone peach

Pavot Poppy (Wild poppy = *coquelicot*)

Pays / Paysage Country, Land / Countryside, Landscape

PAYS BASQUE Basque country: region in the SW corner, bordering Spain, with the Atlantic & the Pyrenees. *Basquaise* cuisine is dominated by Bayonne ham, sweet peppers & garlic

PAYS d'OC Ancient region of southern France, which, because *langue d'oc* was spoken (as opposed to *langue d'oil* in the north), became Languedoc (See *Languedoc-Roussillon*)

PAYS de la LOIRE Region, east & south of Brittany, that straddles the Loire as it approaches the Atlantic at Nantes

Paysan, paysanne Peasant, Rustic, of the Land

Paysanne (à la ..) Country-style: usually with vegetables

PAYS-NANTAIS Wine growing region around Nantes in the western Loire Valley

Peau, peaux Skin, Peel (of fruit)

Peaufiner to Refine, to Put finishing touches to something

Pécharmant Red AOC wine from Bergerac region

Pêche Peach; Fishing; Catch (of fish)

Pêche (avoir la ..) to Be feeling great

Péché / .. mignon Sin / Little weakness (for something)

Pêche à la mouche Fly-fishing

Pêcher to Fish, to Go fishing;
Peach tree

Pêcheur / Pêcherie Fisherman /
Fish factory; Fishing ground

Pecorino Hard ewe's-milk
cheese of Italy

Pédoncule Stalk/stem (of tomato,
etc.)

Peine (à ..) Hardly, Barely, Just
(cooked, etc.)

Pélamide Pelamid, Bonito (type
of tuna)

Pélardon Goat's-milk cheese of
the Cévennes

Pêle-mêle Higgledy-piggledy

Peler to Peel

Pèlerine *[pilgrim]* Scallop *[coquille
Saint-Jacques]*

Pelle Various utensils for lifting
food (slice, scoop, etc.)

Pelle à gâteau/tarte Cake slice

Pelle à poussière Dustpan

Pelure Peel, Skin, Rind, Paring

Pelure d'oignon *[onion skin]*
(wine term) Specific colour of
some rosé wines

Pépinière Nursery (for plants,
etc.); Seed-bed

Pépiniériste Nurseryman, Nursery gardener

Pépins / Sans .. Pips / Seedless

Pépites / .. de chocolat Nuggets,
Tiny pieces / Chocolate chips

PERCHE Region of Normandy
famous for its horses
(*percherons*)

Perche / Perchot Perch / Small
perch

Perdreau, perdrix Partridge

Perdrix de neige Ptarmigan

Perforé, -e Perforated

PERIGORD Region in the SW
renowned for its rich cuisine
based on fine local ingredients
(poultry, *foie gras*, truffles,
chestnuts, mushrooms, etc.)

Périgourdine (à la ..) Périgord-
style: Dish with *sauce périgour-
dine/Périgueux*

Périgourdine (sauce ..) *Sauce
demi-glace* enriched with
purée of *foie gras* & sliced
truffles

Périgueux (sauce ..) Madeira
sauce with finely chopped
truffles

Périmé Lapsed, Expired, Out-
of-date

Perle / Perlé, -e Pearl, Bead /
Pearl (barley), Polished (rice)

Perle du nord *[pearl of the north]*
Variety of chicory *[endive]*
from the North

Perler to Bead: decorate with
tiny items

Perles du Japon Tapioca

Permis Permit, Licence;
Allowed, Permitted, Lawful

Pernod (brand name) Aniseed
aperitif *[pastis]*

Persane (à la ..) Persian-style:
often with aubergine garnish

Persil / .. plat/frisé Parsley /
Flat/curled parsley

Persil chinois Coriander
[coriandre]

Persil en branche Sprig of
parsley

Persillade Mixture of chopped
parsley & garlic

Persillé Blue-veining in cheese;
Beef flecked with fat

Persiller to Add parsley or
persillade

Peser to Weigh

Pétafine Farmhouse cheese of the Dauphiné made with oil & champagne

Pétales / .. de maïs Petals / Cornflakes

Pétasse Gooseberry in some regions [groseille à maquereau]

Péter to Break wind, to Fart; to Crackle; to Pop (a cork)

Pétéram Stew of ham, sheep's feet, tripe, calf's mesentery, bacon, potatoes & herbs in white wine, sp. of Haute-Garonne

Pétillant, -e Bubbly, Fizzy; Sparkling wine

Pétillement Fizziness; Crackling (of fire)

Pétiole Petiole: leaf stalk of plant

Petit déj (abbr. for petit déjeuner) Breakfast

Petit feu (à ..) On a low heat; to Cook gently

Petit four Sweet/savoury fancy cake/confectionery (orig. baked in cooled bread oven = à petit four)

Petit lait Whey

Petit noir (fam.) Small strong black coffee

Petit pain Bread roll

Petit pain natté Short plaited baguette loaf

Petit salé Salt pork: small joint steeped in brine/dry salt & must be soaked before cooking

Petit, -e Little, Small, Baby (variety, etc.)

Petit-beurre Small square buttery biscuit, sp. of Nantes

Petite marmite Little individual stew-pot

Petit-gris Variety of snail

Petits bateaux (term) Small fish caught in large fish nets

Petits pois Peas

Petits pois frais / .. à écosser Fresh peas / Peas in pods

Petit-suisse Small fresh cream cheese (orig. of Normandy)

Pétoncle Queen scallop

Pétrin Kneading machine

Pétrir / Pétrissage to Knead / Kneading

Pétrocorienne (à la ..) Périgueux-style: with foie gras, truffles, etc.

Pets-de-nonne [nun's farts] Little sugar-covered choux pastry fritters

Peu couteux, peu couteuse Inexpensive

Pezize Elf Cup fungus

Pflutters Potato dumplings of Alsace [floutes]

Pholade Piddock: burrowing shellfish of Atlantic coast

Pholiote [du peuplier] Pholiotte mushroom

Phylloxera Aphid that attacks vine roots

Piano (fam.) Range, Cooker (at which the master chef performs his masterpieces!)

Pibales Elvers in the Pays Basque

Picanchâgne Rich pastry dessert with pears, of Bourbonnais

Picarde (à la ..) Picardy-style: often with leeks/onions/cheese

PICARDIE Picardy: agricultural region in the North

Pichet / .. d'eau Pitcher, Jug of wine / Jug of water

Picholine Pickled olive

Picodon, Picadou Various tangy goat's-milk cheeses

Picon (Amer ..) (brand name) Bitter aperitif

Picorer to Forage; to Pilfer

Picoter to Tickle (the throat); to Sting (the eyes); to Peck (as a bird at food)

Picotin Ration; Peck

Picpoul Grape variety & red & white wine of the Midi

Picrate (fam.) Plonk, Cheap red wine

Pie rouge Breed of Swiss cow imported into the mountainous central region of France

Pièce montée Pyramid cake made (esp. for weddings, etc.) with choux buns [croquembouches]

Pied Foot, Trotter; Head (of celery, etc.); Stalk

Pied bleu Wood Blewit mushroom

Pied-de-cheval Variety of oyster from English Channel

Pied-de-mouton Wood Hedgehog mushroom

Pieds de cochon Pig's trotters

Pieds et paquets Dish of sheep's trotters & tripe, sp. of Marseille

Piémontaise (à l ..) Piedmont-style: with rice/cheese/truffles

Pierrade Stone-topped electric table grill

Pieuvre Octopus [poulpe]

Pigeon de Montauban Large pigeon of the SW

Pigeon ramier Wood pigeon

Pigeon, pigeonne / Pigeonneau Pigeon / Young pigeon

Pignons de pin, Pignoles Pine nuts/kernels

Pilaf, Pilau Spicy rice dish (orig. of Turkey)

Piler to Grind (nuts, etc.); to Crush (garlic); to Pound; (fam) to Eat

Pili-pili N. African hot spice (base of rougail)

Pilon Pestle; Drumstick (of poultry)

Pilon tamiseur Potato masher

Piment / .. doux Chilli pepper / Sweet pepper [poivron]

Piment d'Espelette Mild chilli pepper of the Pays Basque

Piment de Cayenne Cayenne pepper

Piment de la Jamaïque Allspice

Piment oiseau Bird pepper: very hot small chilli pepper

Pimenté, -e Spicy, Hot

Pimprenelle Salad burnet

Pin / Pomme de .. Pine (See also Pignons) / Pine/fir cone

Pinard (fam) Wine, Plonk

Pince à tarte Device to seal edge of tart/pie pastry

Pinceau à dorer/pâtisserie Pastry brush

Pincée Pinch (of salt, etc.)

Pincer to Pinch, to Nip; to Sprinkle (sauce, etc.)

Pinces Tongs; Claws (of lobster, etc.)

Pinces à escargots Special tongs for holding snails

Pinces à linge Clothes' pegs

Pineau des Charentes Sweet *AOC* aperitif made from grape juice with added Cognac

Pinot Grape variety, of which there is *blanc, noir, gris & meunier*, all used in wine making

Pintade / Pintadeau Guinea-fowl / Guinea-poult

Pinter to Drink a lot/too much, (fam.) to Get plastered

Pinton Small glass (orig. a monk's measure, probably a pint)

Piocher to Pick, to Dig; to Help yourself (at table); (fam.) to Dive in!

Piperade Spanish omelette; Rich tomato & sweet pepper stew, sp. of the Pays Basque

Piquage Interlarding: inserting thin strips of pork fat into lean meat to ensure constant basting

Piquant, -e Sharp, Spicy, Pungent

Pique Small stick (for cocktails); Pick; Swizzle stick

Piqué Sour (taste)

Pique-assiette Scrounger, Sponger, Free-loader

Pique-nique / Pique-niquer Picnic / to Have a Picnic

Piquer to Prick, to Sting, to Burn (with hot spice); to Prickle

Piqueter to Dot, to Speck

Piquette (fam.) Plonk, Vinegary wine

Pirot Dish of kid goat, sp. of Poitou

Pis Udder

Pisciculture Fish-farming

Pissaladière Type of pizza with onion, garlic, anchovy, olives & *pissalat*, sp. of Nice

Pissalat, Pissala Purée of anchovy, olive oil, herbs & spices

Pissenlit Dandelion (leaves used in salad)

Pistache Pistachio nut; Mutton dish with garlic cloves of Languedoc

Pistole Sun-dried prunes of the SW

Pistolet *[pistol]* Short white bread roll

Pistou (fam.) Basil in Provence; Paste of basil, garlic & Parmesan cheese (Italian *pesto*)

Pistou (soupe au ..) Vegetable & pasta soup with *pistou*

Pithiviers Large puff pastry pie filled with almond cream, sp. of the Orléanais; Soft cow's-milk cheese of Orléans

Placard Cupboard

Placard à provisions Store cupboard

Plan de travail Work surface

Planche / .. à pain Board / Bread board

Planche billot Chopping/block board

Plancher Wooden floor

Planchette Small board

Plaque Metal plate/sheet

Plaque à gâteau Baking tray

Plaque à rôtir Oven tin

Plaque chauffante Hot-plate

Plaque de cuisson Cooker ring

Plaque de marbre Marble slab

Plat Dish of/for food; Main course

Plat à alvéoles Grooved dish for snails

Plat à gâteau/cake/tarte Cake plate

Plat à rôtir Baking tin

Plat cuisiné/préparé Ready-cooked meal/food

Plat de cuisson Oven dish

Plat de résistance (term) Main course

Plat de service Serving dish

Plat du jour Dish of the day, 'Today's special'

Plat, -e Flat, Still (water); Bland, Insipid

Plat-de-côtes Flank of beef/pork

Plateau Tray, Platter

Plateau à fromage Cheese board

Plateau de fromages Selection of cheeses (on a board)

Plateau sécable Compartmented tray/dish

Plateau-repas Meal tray

Platée Plateful (of …)

Plates Flat variety of oyster (*belons*, etc.)

Plein Full (*Etre plein* = to Be drunk. N.B: I'm full = *je n'en peux plus*); Complete, Rounded

Plein à ras bord Full to the brim

Plein verre Glassful

Plein-air Outdoors, Open air

Pleinement Wholly, Fully, Entirely

Pleurote [en huître] Oyster mushroom

Plie Plaice *[carrelet]*

Plier to Fold up, to Bend

Plisson Very sweet, thick dessert cream, sp. of Poitou

Plombières Ice cream made with almond-flavoured milk, cream & crystallized fruit

Plonge (fam.) Washing-up

Plongeur *[diver]* (term) Restaurant washer-up

Pluches Pith (of fruit); Slivers (of truffles, etc.); Chopped/scissored herbs/leaves

Pluie (en ..) Sprinkling, Showering

Plume / Gibier à .. Feather / Game bird

Plumer to Pluck (fowl/game birds)

Plumet / Plumeau Plume / Feather duster

Pluvier Plover (Plover's eggs = *œufs de vanneau*)

Poche à douille Piping bag

Poche du fiel Gall-bladder

Pocher / Poché, -e to Poach / Poached

Pocheuse à œufs Egg poacher

Pochouse Dish of river fish cooked in white wine, sp. of Burgundy

Poêlage Pot-roasting

Poêle / Poêlé, -e Pan, Frying pan; Heating stove / Pan-fried

Poêlon Two-handled heavy-based pan

Pogne, Pognon, Pougnon Various regional tarts of *brioche* pastry filled with fruit/pumpkin

Poids / .. lourds Weight /

Heavy weight, Heavy goods vehicle

Poids brut/net Gross/net weight

Poids et mesures Weights and measures

Poignée *[handful]* Small measure/amount (that fits into palm of hand); Handle (*Poigne* = grasp; *Poignet* = wrist)

Poil / A .. Hair, Fur / (fam.) Stark naked *[nu]*

Point (à ..) *[just right]* Point when pasta/vegetables/fish is perfectly cooked & must be immediately removed from heat; Medium-cooked meat (not *bleue,* not *saignante*); Perfectly ripe (fruit, cheese, etc.)

Pointe Point, Tip; Cut of beef (top rump)

Pointu, -e Pointed (knife, etc.)

Poirat Pear pie of Berry & Bourbonnais

Poire / Poiré Pear; Lean cut from topside of beef / Perry

Poire à four Basting pump

Poire cotonnée Sleepy pear: fruit beginning to deteriorate

Poire Williams Variety of pear; Pear brandy of Alsace

Poireau Leek

Poireau bleu de Solaize Purpleleafed leek from this region south of Lyon

Pois (petits ..) Peas

Pois anglais/de mai Garden peas

Pois cassés / .. chiches Split peas / Chickpeas

Pois gourmands/goulus *[greedy]* Mangetout/sugar peas

Pois mange-tout Mangetout peas

Poisseux, poisseuse Sticky, Greasy

Poisson / .. d'eau douce / .. de mer Fish / Freshwater fish / Saltwater fish

Poisson chat Catfish

Poisson d'Avril *[April fool]* Fish-shaped chocolate/sweetmeat/pastry made for 1st April (which, until 1564, was start of the year & under the sign of Pisces/*Poissons*)

Poissonnerie Fishmonger's (shop)

Poissoneux, poissoneuse Well-stocked (lake, etc.) with fish

Poissonnier, poissonnière Fishmonger

Poissonnière Fish kettle

Poitevine (à la ..) Poitou-style: often with chestnuts

Poitrine Breast; Belly (of pork); Brisket

Poivrade Sauce made principally with pepper; Baby artichoke eaten raw with salt (*à la croque au sel*)

Poivre (au ..) Dish/grill/sauce with crushed peppercorns

Poivre / Poivré, -e Pepper / Peppery, Spicy

Poivre d'âne Provençal name for *sarriette*/wild savory; Small cheese of Provence rolled in *sarriette*

Poivre giroflée Allspice

Poivrer to Add pepper

Poivrette Nigella seed: pepper substitute

Poivrière / Proivier Pepper mill/pot / Pepper tree

Poivron Capsicum: sweet pepper

Polenta Cornmeal porridge of northern Italy

Polonaise (à la ..) Polish-style: with chopped hard boiled egg, parsley & fried breadcrumbs

Polonaise (brioche ..) *Brioche* made with crystallized fruit & meringue & soaked in rum

Pomarine Jack-Be-Little pumpkin

Pomelo Citrus fruit (similar to grapefruit)

Pomerol Wine growing region of Bordeaux

Pommade *[ointment]* (term) Creamed butter & sugar

Pommard *AOC* Burgundy wine from the Côte-de-Beaune

Pomme Apple; (abbr. for *pomme de terre)* Potato; Knob; Head (of lettuce, cabbage, etc.)

Pomme [en l'air] Apple

Pomme à couteau/cuire Eating/cooking apple

Pomme d'amour Toffee apple

Pomme d'or Apple squash, Yellow Bird squash; Tomato

Pomme de laitue Heart of lettuce

Pomme de terre / Fécule de .. Potato / Potato flour

Pomme de terre-céleri Arracacia root, Celery potato: starchy root vegetable of Colombia

Pomme sauvage Crab apple

Pommé, -e Well rounded, Hearty (lettuce, cabbage, etc.)

Pommeraie Apple orchard

Pommes (aux ..) (term) First rate

Pommes (aux/de ..) With/of apples

Pommes (tomber dans les ..) (fam.) to Pass out, to Faint

Pommes ... Potato/apple dish

Pommes à l'huile Potato salad

Pommes allumettes Matchstick-shaped fried potatoes

Pommes Anna Sliced potatoes, pressed, fried & turned in a covered pan

Pommes Annette As *pommes Anna* but cut in strips

Pommes au beurre Whole, cored & peeled baked apples served on slices of fried bread

Pommes au blanc Plain boiled potatoes

Pommes au lard Potatoes sautéed with fatty bacon, onions & herbs

Pommes Berny *Pommes duchesse* with chopped truffles, coated with flaked almonds & fried

Pommes bonne femme Whole baked cooking apples, filled with butter & sugar

Pommes boulangères Sliced potatoes cooked in stock in the oven with finely sliced onion & bacon

Pommes château Blanched olive-shaped potatoes sautéed in butter, used as garnish (for steak)

Pommes Chatouillard Twice-fried potato 'ribbons'

Pommes chips Potato crisps *[chips]*

Pommes collerettes Cylinder-shaped fried potatoes cut with grooving knife

Pommes copeaux Fried potato 'ribbons'

Pommes dauphines Balls of potato purée mixed with choux pastry & deep-fried

Pommes dauphinoises Sliced potatoes cooked in the oven with milk/cream

Pommes de terre à chair ferme Waxy (firm) potatoes

Pommes de terre à l'eau/anglaise Boiled potatoes

Pommes de terre à la sarladaise Thinly-sliced potatoes sautéed in goose fat, sp. of Périgord

Pommes de terre à la vapeur Steamed potatoes

Pommes de terre au four Baked potatoes

Pommes de terre Darphin Potato cake or *paillasson* (made with grated fried potatoes)

Pommes de terre en chemise Jacket/baked potatoes

Pommes de terre en robe des champs Potatoes boiled in their skins

Pommes de terre fondantes Potatoes shaped into little balls & fried in butter

Pommes de terre mousseline Flesh of baked potatoes mashed with egg yolks, butter & cream

Pommes de terre normande Sliced potatoes baked in milk with onions, leeks & cheese topping

Pommes de terre primeurs New potatoes

Pommes de terre sautées Sautéed potatoes: chopped cooked potatoes tossed in butter with shallots & parsley

Pommes de terre soufflées Deep-fried potato wedges

Pommes Duchesse Purée potato mixed with butter & egg yolk, piped into shapes & baked

Pommes farcies Stuffed baked apples

Pommes gratinées Apples poached in syrup then browned in the oven with breadcrumbs & ground almonds

Pommes nouvelles New potatoes

Pommes paille Straw potatoes

Pommes Parisienne Nut-sized blanched potatoes tossed in meat glaze

Pommes paysanne Potatoes with bacon, mushrooms & onions

Pommes Pont-Neuf Thick chip potatoes

Pommes purée Creamed potatoes [*purée*]

Pommes sautées Sautéed potatoes

Pommes savoyarde *Pommes dauphinoises* cooked with stock

Pommes séchées Dried apple slices

Pommes soufflées Whole baked apples filled with soufflé mixture & scooped-out flesh

Pommes St-Florentin *Pommes duchesse* with chopped ham, coated with vermicelli & fried

...ned in the empty box and left

...l all the ice has evaporated.

...es, please call the

...ce Team on 01467 629666

Beez

member to
ive me piano
lessons Love

Sean

Pommes tapées Dried & pressed apples; (also, but unofficially) Mashed potato

Pompadour Various dishes named after the favourite mistress of Louis XV

Pompe *[pump]* Tartlet/pie with regional variations, esp. of the Centre & Midi

Pompette Tipsy

Pomponnette Small filled fried rissole hors d'œuvre

Pondre / Pondu / Ponte to Lay an egg / Laid / Laying

Pont l'Evèque Soft pale yellow cow's-milk cheese of Normandy

Pont-Neuf *[new bridge]* Parisian tartlet filled with frangipane, glazed & topped with pastry cross; (See also *Pommes P-N*)

Populage Marsh marigold (buds used like capers)

Porc / Pur .. Pork / Pure pork meat; (fam) The real thing

Porcelaine Porcelain: fine china

Porcelet Piglet

Porché Stew with pigs' trotters, etc. sp. of Brittany

Poreux, poreuse Porous

Port Port, Haven, Harbour; Mountain pass in the Pyrenees

Porte-cuillère Spoon rest

Portefeuille (en ..) *[in a wallet]* (term) Food folded (omelettes, etc.), split & stuffed (veal chops, etc.) or layered; Whole fish with spine bone removed

Porter to Carry, to Bear, to Bring, to Raise (the heat, etc.)

Porter un toast to Raise a toast (orig. a piece of toast offered to the guest of honour after guests had drunk the spiced wine it was soaked in)

Porte-serviette Towel rail

Portion Portion, Helping, Share, Part

Portion congrue (Lit: barely enough to live on), Tiny portion

Portionneur à glace Ice cream scoop

Porto Port: red-wine liqueur of Portugal

Porto flip Egg-flip: cocktail with port

Port-salut Pasteurized cow's-milk cheese of Mayenne

Portugaise (à la ..) Portuguese-style: usually with tomatoes

Portugaises Variety of oyster

Pot Pot, Jar, Jug, Tub, Container; In Beaujolais, a trad. 50 cl. bottle of wine

Pot (à la fortune du ..) Potluck: to eat a simple meal

Pot (avoir du ..) to Have good luck

Pot de vin / Pot-de-vin Jug of wine / (fam.) Bribe

Pot gradué Measuring jug

Potable Drinkable

Potage Thick/clear soup (trad. liquid from the cooking pot) (*soupe* contains vegetables, meat, etc.)

Potager Edible (esp. vegetables); Vegetable/kitchen garden (*Maraîcher* = market garden)

Pot-au-feu Trad. a 3-in-l stew (meat, vegetables & soup); Stockpot; Beef for boiling

Potée Various regional stews/soups cooked in an earthenware pot; Potful, Jugful

Poterie à feu Earthenware

Potimarron Large deep orange/yellow variety of edible squash

Potiron Pumpkin

Potjevfleisch [pot of meat] Dish of various meats (esp. veal, pork & rabbit) in jelly, sp. of Flanders

Poubelle Waste bin

Pouce / Manger sur le .. Thumb / (fam.) to Have a quick bite/snack, to Eat on the run

Pouce-pied Goose-necked barnacle: fleshy mollusc resembling a 'bunch' of toes

Pouding English-style (usually steamed/bread) pudding (See also *Pudding*)

Poudre / .. à récurer Powder / Scouring powder

Poudre (en ..) Powdered, Ground

Poudreuse à sucre Sugar shaker

Pouillard Young partridge/pheasant

Pouilles (vins des ..) Puglia wines (of southern Italy)

Pouilly-Fuissé White wine of Burgundy

Pouilly-Fumé White wine of the Loire

Poulailler Hen-house

Poulard Variety of wheat

Poularde Large fattened (hen) chicken

Poule / .. couveuse Hen; Boiling fowl / Broody hen

Poule de mer John Dory fish [Saint-Pierre]

Poule naine Bantam

Poule-au-pot As *pot-au-feu* but with chicken

Poule-des-bois Chicken of the Woods mushroom

Poulet Chicken; (fam.) Walnut kernel

Poulet d'élevage Battery chicken

Poulet de Bresse AOC chicken with blue legs of Burgundy

Poulet de grain Free-range chicken

Poulet fermier Farm chicken

Poulet jaune [yellow] Maize-fed chicken

Poulette / Sauce .. Pullet, Young chicken / Light white sauce

Poulpe Octopus [pieuvre]

Pountari Auvergne dish of pork stuffing & prunes; Dessert with prunes

Pounti Baked hash with egg, sp. of Cantal

Poupart Edible crab

Pourboire Tip

Pourlécher (se ..) to Lick one's lips

Pourpier Purslane (used as spinach or a garnish)

Pourpre Crimson

Pourri, -e Rotten, Gone bad, Spoiled

Poursuivre to Continue, to Proceed

Pourvoyeur, pourvoyeuse Purveyor

Pousse-café (fam.) Spirit taken after coffee

Pousse-pied (See *Pouce-pied*)

Pousser to Push; (term) to Prove (dough)

Pousse-rapière [*sword*] Aperitif made with *Armagnac*

Pousses / .. de soja Shoots, Sprouts / Bean sprouts

Poussin Chick; Spring chicken

Poussoir / .. à chinois Push-button / Pusher, Rammer (for sieve/*chinois*)

Poutargue Creamed fish roe paste (used as base for tara-masalata/*tarama*)

Poutine, Poutina Dish of tiny fried fish (esp. sardines & anchovies), sp of Nice

Praire Variety of clam

Pralin Praline: caramelized chopped/crushed nuts

Praline Praline paste (ground hazelnuts, sugar & cocoa or cocoa butter) used in confectionary

Praliné Genoese sponge cake layered with *praline*

Praliné, -e Covered/coated with *pralin*

Praliner to Cover/coat with *pralin*

Pralines Nuts rolled in caramel-ized sugar; Belgian chocolates

Praslines de Montargis *Pralines* named after the Comte du Plessis-Praslin (hence the spelling)

Pratiquer to Carry out, to Do [something]

Pré Meadow

Préalable / Au .. Prior / To begin with, First (before)

Préchauffer to Heat [up], to Warm up

Préciser to Make clear, to State, to Specify

Précoce [*precocious*] Early (fruit, etc.), Premature

Préconiser to Recommend

Précuit, -e Precooked

Préférence [de] Preferably, For choice

Prélever to Sample, to Set apart, to Deduct

Prémices [*beginnings*] First fruits, etc.

Prendre to Take, to Get

Préparer to Prepare, to Cook

Pré-salé [*salt meadow*] Lamb grazed on sea-shore, giving tender meat with salty flavour

Presqu'île [*almost an island*] Peninsula

Presse / .. agrumes Squeezer / Citrus fruit press

Presse-fruits Juice extractor

Presse-purée Potato masher

Presser to Press, to Squeeze; to Hurry

Pressing Dry-cleaner's

Pression Pressure; (abbr.) Draft beer

Pressoir Press (for grapes, etc.)

Présure Rennet: curdled milk from calf used to coagulate milk in cheese making

Prêt à l'emploi/cuire Ready to use/cook

Prétranché, -e Sliced

Prévoir to Anticipate, to Expect

Prime First, Prime, Premium, Dominant

Primerose Hollyhock [*rose trémière*]

Primeur Brand new, the First; (term) On promotion

Primeurs First/early/forced fruit & vegetables

Primevère Primrose, Primula, Cowslip

Princesse Rich garnish with asparagus tips & truffle

Printanière Garnish of sliced spring vegetables

Printemps / Printanier Spring / of Spring

Prix / .. choc! Price / Amazing price!

Prix coûtant Cost price

Prix fixe Set price (menu/meal)

Produits laitiers Milk products

Profiteroles Choux pastry buns filled with cream/ice cream, served with hot chocolate sauce

Profond, -e / Peu .. Deep / Shallow

Progrès Meringue cake with butter cream

Prolonger to Prolong, to Extend, to Lengthen

Prôner to Recommend, to Extol

Propriétaire Owner (esp. of vineyard, etc.), Landlord

Proscrire to Ban

Protéine Protein

Provençale (à la ..) Provençal, of Provence: with ingredients of the South of France

PROVENCE Large region in the SE, reaching from the Med. to the Alps, with a colourful cuisine of sun-ripened fruit & vegetables, herbs & fish

Provision Provision, Store, Stock, Supply

Pruine Bloom: natural white substance found on plums, grapes, etc.

Prune / Prunier Plum / Plum tree

Prune d'Ente Variety of plum used for Agen prunes

Pruneau Prune

Prunelle Sloe (berry); Sloe gin

Psalliote Agarics (genus of wild mushroom)

Puant de Lille Strong-smelling cheese of the North

Puant, -e / Puanteur Stinking, Foul smelling / Stench, Stink

Pub, Publicité Advertising, Publicity

Puces Fleas

Pudding Various English-style desserts; Small iced cake made of stale bread/brioche

Puer to Stink (of), to Reek (of)

Puissance Power, Strength, Force

Puits Well (for water, oil, etc.)

Puits (faire un ..) (term) to Make a 'well' in flour during pastry making

Puits d'amour [*love well*] Hollowed-out puff pastry tarts filled with jam or confectioner's custard (named after comic opera)

Puits de sel Saltpan

Puligny-Montrachet White wine of Burgundy

Pulpe / Pulpeux, pulpeuse Pulp, Flesh / Pulpy, Fleshy

Pumpernickel German-style rye bread

Punaise *[drawing pin]* Bug, Insect

Punch Punch (drink); Drive, Energy

Puncher to Imbibe cake with sugar syrup & alcohol

Pure Pure, Clear, Sheer

Purée Creamy-textured sieved food; Creamed potatoes

Purée Argenteuil Creamed white asparagus

Purée Clamart Creamed green peas

Purée Condé Cream red beans

Purée Conti Creamed lentils

Purée Crécy Creamed carrots & rice

Purée Dubarry Creamed cauliflower

Purée Esaü Creamed lentils

Purée favorite Creamed French beans

Purée Freneuse Creamed turnips

Purée Musarde Creamed flageolet beans

Purée Palestine Creamed Jerusalem artichokes & potatoes

Purée Parmentier Creamed potatoes

Purée Rachel Creamed artichoke hearts

Purée Saint-Germain Creamed peas

Purée Saxone Creamed turnips, potatoes & onions

Purée Soubise Creamed onions

Purée Vichy Creamed carrots

Pyrolyse (four à ..) Pyrolysis oven (designed to self-clean by intense heat)

BASIL

Quadrillage Chequer-work, Check pattern

Quadrillé, -e Squared (Square = *carré*)

Quadriller to Score, to Scorch, to Decorate food in criss-cross design

Qualité Quality

Quantité Quantity, Amount

Quart Quarter, Fourth; (term) a Quarter-litre of wine

Quartier District; Quarter (of beef); Segment (of orange)

Quasi / Quasiment Almost / Practically

Quasi de veau Cut of veal (rump)

Quatre-épices Four spices (ground pepper, nutmeg, cloves & ginger); Nigella (black cumin)

Quatre-quarts [*four quarters*] Pound cake (made with equal amounts of flour, sugar, butter & eggs)

Quenelle Light forcemeat dumpling of fish (often *brochet*/pike) or white meat

Quenotte Child's word for tooth

QUERCY Region comprising the *départements* of Lot & Tarn-et-Garonne with a rich cuisine similar to its neighbour Périgord

Quetsche Variety of sweet mauve plum of Alsace

Queue Tail; Stalk, Hull (of strawberry); Saucepan handle; Queue

Queue de bœuf Oxtail

Quiche Savoury tart filled with egg & cream mixture

Quiché Toasted bread spread with anchovies, sp. of Marseille

Quiche lorraine Classic egg tart with ham & onion, sp. of Lorraine

Quiche tourangelle *Quiche* filled with *rillette*, sp. of Touraine

Quignon Chunk, Hunk of bread; Crust end of loaf

Quillet Small round butter-cream sponge cake

Quincaillerie Hardware; Hardware shop

Quinconce Zig-zag, Criss-cross pattern

Quincy *AOC* dry white wine from Berry, similar to Sancerre

Quinquina Various bitter-flavoured wine-based aperitifs

Quint Fifth

Quintal Measure of 100 kilos

Quote-part Share, Quota, Portion

Quotidien, quotidienne Daily, (fam.) Daily paper, Every day

Rabais Rebate, Discount

Rabattable Adjustable; Folding

Rabattre to Lower; to Fold

Rable Saddle of rabbit/hare

Rablot Small mackerel

Rabote, Rabotte Apple/pear in pastry of Picardy/Champagne

Raccourci Cut down (in size), Shortened, Shrunk; Short cut

Racé [*distinguished*] (wine term) Breeding

Racines Roots; Root vegetables

Racler / Raclures to Scrape / Scrapings

Raclette [*hoe*] Scraper; Semi-hard cow's-milk cheese; Dish of melted *raclette* cheese served with potatoes & gherkins

Raclette électrique Table machine for melting *raclette* cheese & keeping potatoes hot

Racornir to Become hard or shrivelled

Radis / .. noir Radish / Black radish

Raffermir to Firm up, to Harden

Raffiné, -e Sophisticated, Elegant, Refined

Raffinerie Refinery

Rafraîchir to Refresh; to Cool quickly under cold water

Rafraichisseur Cool box or compartment

Ragondin Coypu

Ragoût Stew; Creamy garnish/filling

Ragoûtant, -e (peu ..) Unsavoury, Unappetizing

Raiderie Street market, Grand sale [*braderie*]

Raidir to Stiffen, to Tense, to Tighten; (term) to Seal meat in hot fat

Raie / Raiteau Skate (fish) / Small skate

Raifort Horseradish

Raisiné Sugarless grape jam of Burgundy

Raisins Grapes (A grape = *grain de raisin*)

Raisins de Corinthe Currants

Raisins de cuve Grapes grown for wine making

Raisins de Malaga Muscat raisins

Raisins de Smyrne Sultanas

Raisins de table Dessert grapes

Raisins secs Dried vine fruit (raisins, etc.)

Raite, Raito, Rayte Thick spicy Provençal sauce for fried fish

Raiton Small skate

Rajouter to Add

Rale Rail: family of large wading birds (corncrake, etc.)

Rallonger to Thin out (sauce, etc.)

Ramasse-miettes Small brush (often with pan) for clearing crumbs off table

Ramasser to Collect (eggs, etc.), to Pick up

Rambourg Variety of apple

Ramboutan Rambutan: exotic fruit similar to lychee

Rame [*oar*] Stake, Stick, Prop (for beans, etc.)

Rameau Branch, Twig

Rameaux (les ..) Palm Sunday (Sunday before Easter)

Ramener to Bring back

Ramequin Ramekin dish; Food cooked in a ramekin dish; Tartlet of cream cheese

Ramier Woodpigeon

Ramollir / Ramolli, -e to Soften / Soft, Softened, Creamed

Ramoneur Chimney-sweep

Rance Rancid

Rancio Slightly rancid smell of sweet wine

Rang Row (of onions, etc.); (term) Restaurant staff *[commis]*

Range-couverts Cutlery holder

Ranger / Bien rangé, -e to Put away, to Arrange / Tidy

Râpe Grater

Rapée Potato pancake

Raper / Rapé, -e to Grate / Grated (cheese, etc.)

Rapure Large overgrown oyster

Raquette Grey partridge

Rare / Rarement / Rarissime Scarce / Rarely, Seldom / Extremely rare

Râs al-hânout Spice mixture (cinnamon, cloves & black pepper) used in N. African cuisine

Ras, -e Level (spoonful); Short (cut)

Rasade Glassful

Rascasse Scorpion fish

Rase Scraper, Peeler

Rasoir *[razor]* Razor shell clam; Gadget for shaving truffles, etc.

Rassasiant Satisfying meal, Filling food

Rassasier to Satisfy (one's hunger), to Feed up

Rassir To allow foods (dough, meat, etc.) to rest & develop flavour

Rassis Settled; Stale (bread, etc.)

Rassise Stage when butchered meat becomes tender & flavoursome

Rat / Rate Rat; Star-gazer: Med. fish / Female rat; Spleen

Rata / .. aux choux Poor food / Bubble-&-squeak

Ratafia Rumetoft: homemade liqueur; Small macaroon

Ratatiner (se ..) / Ratatiné, -e to Shrivel up / Shrivelled

Ratatouille Provençal stew of southern vegetables

Raton *[young rat]* Little cream cheese pastry

Ratte Small yellow-fleshed potato, orig. of Le Touquet region

Rave Collective name for root vegetables; Rape, Coleseed

Ravier Small dish (for pickles & hors-d'œuvres, etc.)

Ravigote Classic hot/cold spicy sauce (for brawn, etc.)

Ravigoter to Perk (something) up, to Refresh

Raviole, Raviolle Stuffed pasta squares (ravioli) of Nice & Corsica; Spinach & cheese dumplings of Savoie

Ravitaillement Provision of fresh supplies

Rayé, -e Striped, Grooved

Rayon Shelf *[étagère]*; Department (of shop/store); Row (of onions, etc.)

Rayon de miel Honeycomb

Rayonnage Shelving

Réaliser to Achieve, to Produce, to Effect

Reblochon Yellow-skinned cow's-milk cheese of Savoie

Rebord Edge, Border, Lip (of cup), Rim

Reboucher to Replace bottle top/cork; to Fill in

Rebours (à ..) Against the grain; Working backwards

Récépissé, Reçu Receipt

Recette Recipe; Receipts, Takings

Recevoir to Receive; to Entertain

Réchaud Hot plate; Small stove; Chafing dish; Chef to Prince Condé in C18th

Réchauffer to Reheat

Rêche Rough (skin, etc.), Harsh

Récolte Harvest (of grapes, etc.), Crop

Recoudre [sew up] Close up

Recourir à to Use, to Resort to

Rectifier to Adjust seasoning, etc.

Récurer to Scour, to Scrub

Réduire (faire .. à/de) to Reduce to/by

Réforme Reform sauce: *poivrade* with gherkins & hard-boiled eggs

Refroidir to Cool; to Refresh: cool quickly under cold water

Régalade (boire à la ..) to Drink without lips touching the bottle

Régaler to Entertain, to Treat (someone), to Feast

Régime Diet; Bunch (of dates, bananas, etc.), Cluster, Stem

Régime jockey Strict diet

Réglisse Liquorice

Reguigneu Sliced ham dipped in beaten egg & fried, sp. of Avignon & Arles

Régulièrement Regularly, Evenly, Steadily

Réhoboam Champagne bottle size (6 btls/4.5 ltrs)

Reims (biscuit de ..) Small light [pink] biscuit to accompany champagne (Reims is in Champagne)

Reims (pâté de ..) Hot/cold pork pie from this region renowned for its *pâtés*

Reine (à la ..) Queen's-style: various chicken dishes

Reine de Saba Queen of Sheba: light chocolate gâteau served cold with custard

Reine-Claude Greengage (favourite fruit of François l's queen, Claude)

Reinette Variety of dessert apple

Réjouir to Delight, to Rejoice

Réjouissance Festivity, Merry-making, Rejoicing

Relâcher [to loosen] (term) to Thin down with liquid

Relais [relay] Inn, Roadside restaurant

Relais routier Transport café

Relent Smell, Whiff, Odour

Relever [to lift up] to Season, to Spice, to Sharpen

Religieuse [nun] Chocolate-covered double round éclair

Rémoise (à la ..) Reims-style: often with champagne

Remonter to Re-emulsify: restore sauce that has curdled

Rémoulade Spicy mayonnaise sauce

Remplacer to Replace

Remplir to Replenish, to Fill up

Remuer to Stir

Renard Fox

Rendement Yield, Production, Output

Rennaise of Rennes in Brittany

Renne Reindeer

Renouveler to Renew, to Repeat, to Revive

Renverser to Spill, to Tip, to Overturn

Répandre to Spill, to Scatter, to Empty

Répandu, -e Widespread, Prevalent, Common

Répartir to Divide, to Share out, to Spread over

Repas / .. froid Meal / Cold meal, Snack

Repas à la fourchette Fork meal, Buffet

Repas éclair Quick meal

Repasser to Sharpen (knife, etc.); to Iron/press

Repère Reference [mark]; Lute: flour & water paste to seal lid [lut]; Flour & egg white 'glue' for cake decorations

Replier to Fold up, to Tuck in, to Close up

Reposer to Rest, to Relax (dough, meat, etc.)

Requin Shark

Réservation Reservation, Booking

Réserve/ En .. Storage compartment, Storeroom; Stock; (term) Quality wine / Stored, In store

Réserve (de ..) Can be kept/stored

Réserve du patron Fancy name for 'house wine'

Réserver to Keep, to Put/set aside; to Reserve (a table, etc.)

Réserver au chaud to Keep (food/dish) warm

Réserver au frais to Keep (food/preparation) cool

Resquilleur, resquilleuse Gate-crasher; Queue-jumper

Resservir / Se .. to Serve up again / to Help oneself to more

Restaurant Place with refreshments (to 'restore' oneself), Eating-house

Restaurateur, restauratrice Keeper of a restaurant

Reste / Restes Rest of, Remainder / Left-overs

Resto, Restif (fam.) Restaurant

Rétablir to Restore, to Re-establish

Retailler to Cut (something) again, to Re-cut

Retirer to Remove, to Take off, to Take out

Retourner *[to return]* to Turn over

Réveiller to Wake up, to Enliven, to Whet (the appetite)

Réveillon Christmas Eve; New Year's Eve; Traditional meal after Midnight Mass

Revenir (faire ..) to Brown (in hot fat) before further cooking; to Cook (liver, etc.) quickly over high heat

Revesset 'Green' *bouillabaisse* of Toulon (with sardines, spinach, anchovies & sorrel)

Revigorer to Invigorate, to Refresh

Rhizome Rhizome: root-like stem (ginger, etc.)

Rhum ambré/blanc Dark/white rum

Ribol Variety of black dessert grape

Ribote Bout of drinking, Drinking spree

Richelieu Garnish & various grand dishes; Layered sponge cake topped with crystallized fruit & dedicated to the Cardinal's great-nephew

Riesling Grape variety & white wine of Alsace & Germany

Rigodon Sweet brioche pudding or savoury crustless quiche, sp. of Burgundy

Rigole Channel (in carving board, etc.)

Rigoler to Have fun, to Enjoy oneself, to Have a laugh

Rigotte Goat/cow's-milk cheese of various regions

Rigueur / De .. Rigour / Indispensable, Obligatory

Rillauds, Rillons, Rillots Belly/shoulder of pork cubed & cooked in lard, sp. of various regions

Rillettes Potted meat of various regions: fatty spread of shredded pork/rabbit/duck/goose/poultry

Rimotte Cold porridge of Périgord cut into cubes

Rince-cochon (fam.) *Kir communard*: red wine & cassis in the Beaujolais region

Rince-doigts Finger bowl

Rincer la dalle (se ..) (fam.) to Whet one's whistle (*dalle* = flagstone)

Rioler to Arrange strips of pastry on tarts, etc.

Ripaille Hearty fare/feast; White wine of Savoie

Ris de veau Sweetbread: thymus gland & pancreas of calf (N.B: rice = *riz*)

Rissole Small sweet/savoury item cooked in hot fat [*rissoler*]

Rissole de Bugey Small Christmas pie of turkey & herbs

Rissoler to Brown by quickly frying in hot fat

Rive River bank

Riversaltes AOC *vin doux naturel* from Roussillon

Riviera Coastal region (esp. the Côte d'Azur & the Italian Gulf of Genoa)

Riz Rice

Riz au lait Rice pudding

Riz blanc Polished white rice

Riz complet Brown rice

Riz étuvé Par-boiled rice

Riz long-ferme American long-grain rice

Riz long-tendre Italian rice: for risotto

Riz parfumé Long-grain fragrant rice

Riz précuit/cuisson rapide Pre-cooked rice

Riz rond Pudding rice: short round grains for desserts & paella

Riz sauvage Wild rice: long thin black 'aquatic grass'

Rizière Rice field, Paddy field

Robe *[appearance]* (wine term)
Colour

**Robe des champs/de chambre
(en ..)** Jacket potato (Lit: as in
the fields/in a dressing gown)

Robert (sauce ..) Classic white
wine & vinegar sauce

Robinet Tap

Robinette Scad (fish) *[saurel]*

Robot [ménager] Food processor
(Blender = *mixeur*)

Robusta Species of coffee
(stronger & containing more
caffeine than Arabica)

Robuste (wine term) Robust, full
bodied & assertive

Rocamadour Small soft
sheep's-/goat's-milk cheese of
Périgord

Rocambole Sand leek

Rocher *[rock]* Rock cake; Praline
chocolate

Rocou Annetto:
yellow/orange/red food
colouring

Rogatons Leftovers; Scraps

Rogner to Trim, to Pare

Rognon Edible animal kidney
(Human kidney = *rein*)

Rognonnade Loin of veal with
kidney attached

Rognons blancs (term) Testicles
[testicules]

Rognures Trimmings (cut away
morsels/pastry, etc.)

Rollot Strong cow's-milk cheese
of Picardy

Romaine Cos lettuce

Romaine (à la ..) Roman-style:
often with spinach, cheese &
small birds

Romanée-Conti *AOC*
Burgundy wine from the
Côte-de-Nuits

Romarin Rosemary

Rompre / Rompu to Break up,
to Snap / Broken, Worn out

Romsteck, Rumsteak Rump
steak

Ronce Bramble; Burr

Ronce-framboise *[blackberry-
raspberry]* Loganberry

Roncin Bread pudding of
Franche-Comté; Type of
cheese fondue made with
beaten eggs & served with
potatoes, sp. of Lorraine

Rond de bœuf Round of beef:
meat cut comprising topside,
silverside & rump

Rond de gigot (term) Slice of
leg of lamb

Rond de serviette Napkin ring

Rondeau Sauté pan used in
restaurants

Rondelle *[washer]* Round slice
(sausage, lemon, etc.)

Rongeur Rodent

Roquebert Popular name for
Roquefort cheese

Roquefort World-famous blue
ewe's-milk cheese of
Rouergue

Roquette Rocket (salad plant)

Roquille Candied orange peel

Rosace *[rose window]* Dish
presented in circular pattern

Rosbif Roast beef (usually rare,
sliced & cold)

Rose / Rosé, -e, Rosâtre Pink;
Rose / Rosy, Pinkish (colour)

Rosé (vin ..) Rosé/pink wine:
made from black & white

grapes (NOT from red & white wine!)

Rose à l'arête [*pink to the bone*] Fish cooked very lightly

Rosé des prés Field mushroom

Rosé des Riceys Rosé wine (often vintage) of the southern Champagne region

Roseau Reed

Rosée / Goutte de .. Dew / Dewdrop

Rosette Semi-sweet *AOC* white wine of Bergerac

Rosette de Lyon Fine-quality *saucisson*, orig. of Lyon

Rosquille, Rousquille Iced aniseed cake in figure of eight

Rossini Various dishes named after the composer (esp. tournedos steaks garnished with *foie gras*)

Rot / Roter Belch, Burp / to Belch, to Burp

Rotengle Rudd: freshwater fish similar to roach

Roteuse (fam.) Bottle of champagne

Rôti, -e / Rôtissage Roast; Roasted / Roasting, Spit-roasting

Rôtie Slice/round of toast [*un toast*]

Rotin Rattan, Cane (furniture)

Rôtir to Roast, to Toast, to Scorch

Rôtissoire Rotisserie; Dutch oven

Rouelle Round slice of meat esp. veal/lamb

Rouennaise (à la ..) Rouen-style: with duck/duckling

ROUERGUE Old province south of the Auvergne with a cuisine rich in tripes & cheeses

Rougail Highly spiced seasoning/sauce used in West Indian cooking

Rouge / Rougeâtre Red; Red wine / Reddish (colour)

Rouget [barbet] Red mullet

Rouget grondin Red gurnard [*grondin rouge*]

Rouille [*rust*] Garlic & paprika mayonnaise of Provence, esp. used with *bouillabaisse*

Roulade Roll (shape); Various stuffed & rolled preparations

Rouleau [à pâtisserie] Rolling pin

Rouleau de printemps Spring roll (of Chinese cuisine)

Rouler / Roulé, -e to Roll up/out / Roll, Rolled

Roussâtre Russet (colour)

Rousse Egg yolk (due to its reddish colour) in Provence

Roussette Grape variety & white wine of Savoie; Dogfish: small fish of shark family [*saumonette*]; Carnival fritter, sp. of Beauce

ROUSSILLON (See *Languedoc-Roussillon*)

Roussin Cob, Plough-horse

Roussir [*to scorch*] to Brown in hot fat (meat, onion, etc.)

Routier [*lorry driver*] Roadside/transport restaurant [*relais*]

Rouvrir to Re-open, to Open again

Roux Basic liaison (equal amounts of flour & fat) for sauces, etc.

Roux blanc White *roux* for cream/white sauces

Roux blond White *roux* cooked until lightly golden

Roux brun White *roux* cooked until lightly browned

Roux, rousse Reddish brown (colour)

Rove Goat of the Alpilles (small chain of mountains in Provence)

Royale (à la ..) Various dishes with unusual or sophisticated ingredients

Royale *[royal]* Shapes cut from egg-based purée as garnish for clear soup; Royal icing

Royans Sardines in Charentes (Royan is on the Gironde esturary)

Ruban Ribbon; Ribbon stage: when egg yolks beaten with sugar blend smoothly & form a ribbon

Ruche / Rucher Beehive, Hive / Apiary

Rude Rough, Coarse, Severe

Ruifard Fruit pie flavoured with Chartreuse, sp. of Dauphiné

Rully *AOC* Burgundy wine of the Côte Chalonnaise

Ruminer to Chew the cud

RUNGIS (marché de ..) Vast wholesale food market just south of Paris that replaced *Les Halles*

Russe (à la ..) Russian-style: with caviar or Russian salad

Russule verdoyante Green Russula mushroom

Rutabaga Swede (root vegetable)

Ruthénoise (à la ..) Rodez-style (in Rouergue): tripe, game pâtés, cheese

Sabardin Chitterling sausage, sp. of the Lyonnais

Sabayon Zabaglione: Italian dessert of warm egg yolks & wine; Sauce for fish & shellfish

Sablé, -e Sandy texture (See also *Pâte sablée*)

Sabler to Rub in the dry ingredients when making short crust pastry

Sablés Crumbly sweet biscuits with regional variations (orig. from Sablé-sur-Sarthe)

Sableux Sandy (texture)

Sablier Egg timer

Sabodet Coarse sausage, sp. of Lyon & Dauphiné

Sabot [*clog*] Deep oval oven dish

Sabot fendu Cloven hoof

Sabre Scabbard: Med. fish used for soup

Sachertorte Renowned rich chocolate cake of Vienna

Sachet de thé Teabag

Sacristain Classic twisted puff pastry biscuit

Safran / Safrané, -e Saffron / With saffron

Sagou Sago

Sagourne Dish of sliced fried pancreas, sp. of Tours

Saignant, -e [*bleeding*] Underdone, Rare (meat)

Sain, -e Healthy, Wholesome, Sound

Saindoux Lard

Sainfoin Clover-like plant grown for fodder

Saint-Amour Ruby-coloured light *AOC* Beaujolais wine

Saint-Aubin Red & white Burgundy wines from Côte-de-Beaune

Saint-Cochon (la ..) Day (in various regions) when the pig was killed & pork was eaten fresh

Sainte-Maure Cylindrical goat's-milk cheese of Touraine with straw running through its length

Sainte-Menehould Various dishes (esp. pig's trotters) with mustard

Saint-Emilion Robust red Bordeaux wine (considered more like a Burgundy than a Bordeaux)

Saint-Estèphe Red *AOC* Bordeaux wine from Médoc

Saint-Florentin Cow's-milk cheese from the Yonne; Rich Kirsch sponge cake

Saint-Genix Brioche cake with pink pralines, sp. of Savoie

Saint-Germain Various dishes with green peas; Preparation for fillets of sole & brill

Saint-Glin-glin (fam.) Never-ever (because there is no such saint!)

Saint-Honoré Patron saint of pastry cooks; Gâteau of short-crust pastry surrounded by choux buns & filled with whipped cream

Saint-Hubert Patron saint of hunters; Various dishes with game

Saint-Jacques (abbr.) Coquille Saint-Jacques

Saint-Jean (la ..) Midsummer's Day

Saint-Joseph Red & white Côtes-du-Rhône wine of the Ardèche

Saint-Marcellin Soft cow's-milk cheese of the Dauphiné

Saint-Martin (été de la ..) Indian summer

Saint-Martin (la ..) Saint's feast day (11 Nov.) when, by trad., pig is killed & prepared as ham for Easter

Saint-Nectaire Semi-hard nutty-flavoured cow's-milk cheese of the Auvergne

Saint-Nicolas (la ..) Feast day (6 Dec.) of patron saint of butchers (& children) when breads & spiced biscuits are made in the shape of a man/boy

Saint-Nicolas-de-Bourgueil Fruity red & rosé wine of Touraine (similar to *Bourgueil*)

Saintongeaise of Saintes in Charente-Maritime

Saint-Paulin Semi-soft pasteurized cow's-milk cheese with orange rind

Saint-Pierre John Dory: fish with huge mouth & 60% bones

Saint-Sylvestre (la ..) New Year's Eve; Saint's feast day (31 Dec.)

Saint-Véran White *AOC* Burgundy wine of Mâcon made from Chardonnay grapes

Saint-Vincent (la ..) Feast day (22 Jan.) of the patron saint of wine growers

Saisir *[to seize]* to Seal (meat, etc.)

Saison / En pleine .. Season / At the height of the season

Saison bat son plein (growing) Season is in full swing

Saké Sake: Japanese rice wine

Salade (faire une ..) to Make a salad; (fam.) to Spin a yarn

Salade / .. verte Lettuce, Salad with lettuce / Green salad

Salade composée Salad with meat, eggs, etc.

Salade de ... Salad (of other than leaf ingredients)

Salade du groin d'âne *[donkey snout]* Dandelion salad of Lyon

Salade niçoise Salad with tomatoes, green beans, olives, anchovies & hard-boiled eggs, sp. of Nice

Salade russe Russian salad: diced mixed vegetables in mayonnaise

Saladerie Salad bar

Saladier Salad bowl

Saladier lyonnais Salad of trotters, chicken livers, pickled herring & hard-boiled egg, sp. of Lyon bars

Salaison Salting, Immersing in brine; Salt meat/fish

Salamandre Salamander: grill-oven of restaurants; Metal instrument for caramelising

Sale Dirty; Nasty, Horrid

Saler / Salé, -e to Salt, to Add salt / Salted, Salty (Salt = *sel*)

Salers *AOC* cheese of the Auvergne (orig. made with milk of Salers cows), similar to *Cantal*

Salers (race ..) Breed of red-brown cow with impressive horns

Salicorne Glasswort, Marsh samphire

Salière Salt mill/cellar

Salin Saline; Salt marsh

Salir to Dirty, to Pollute

Saliver to Salivate, to Drool (over)

Salle / .. à manger Room; Hall; Dining room of restaurant / Dining room

Salmanazar Champagne bottle size (12 btls/9 ltrs)

Salmigondis Mix of almost anything (left-overs, etc.)

Salmis Game stew

Saloir Salting tub (for salting pork, etc.)

Salon Living room, Lounge, Drawing room; Trade show

Salon de l'agriculture Agricultural Show

Salon de thé Tea room

Salon-salle à manger Living-cum-dining room

Salpêtre Saltpetre: potassium nitrate (used in brine)

Salpicon Finely chopped ingredients bound by sauce/syrup

Salpiconner to Cut/chop ingredients very finely (esp. for *salpicon*)

Salsifis Salsify, Oyster plant [*scorsonère*]

Sancerre Red, rosé & (mostly) dry white *AOC* wine of the Loire Valley

Sanciaux bourbonnais Type of pancake with diced ham

Sandre Pike-perch: large fish of perch family

Sandwich Probably the best-known snack in the world, with multiple regional, national & international variations

Sang Blood

Sangler [*to strap*] (term) to Pack ice & coarse salt round bowl in ice cream making

Sanglier Wild boar

Sanguette Blood from chicken, cooked in pan with onions, etc. (delicacy of various regions)

Sanguine Blood orange

Santé Health; 'Cheers!'; 'Healthy' meat & vegetable soup

Santons Nativity figures (esp. of Provence)

Sapin Fir/Christmas tree

Sapotille Sapodilla: apricot-flavoured tropical fruit

Sar, Sard Sea fish of Provence, related to sea bream [*lou sar*]

Sarcelle Teal: small wild duck

Sarde (à la ..) Sardinian-style; Meat coated with tomato *demi-glace* served with rice croquettes

Sardine Small fish of herring family

Sardoche (fam.) Sardine

Sargue Sargus: fish similar to sea bream

Sarladaise of Salat in Périgord

Sarments Vine twigs/cuttings

Sarrasin Buckwheat

Sarriette Savory (herb)

Sartagnado, Sartagnono Dish of small fried pressed fish, sp. of Nice

Sasser to Sift; to Peel thin-skinned vegetables by rolling them in a cloth with salt

Sauce Hot/cold seasoned liquid used to enhance food

S

152

Sauce allemande Basic white sauce made with veal/poultry stock

Sauce béarnaise Rich sauce with egg yolks, vinegar & butter

Sauce béchamel Basic white sauce roux

Sauce chasseur Mushrooms, shallots & white wine added to *sauce demi-glace*

Sauce courte *[short]* (term) Thick sauce

Sauce de soja Soy sauce

Sauce demi-glace Basic sauce of reduced *sauce espagnole*

Sauce espagnole Classic sauce of meat stock & brown roux used as base for many other sauces

Sauce hollandaise Hot butter & egg sauce with added vinegar or lemon juice

Sauce longue *[long]* (term) Thin sauce

Sauce Madère Madeira sauce

Sauce Mornay *Sauce béchamel* with egg yolk & grated cheese

Sauce piquante Spicy sauce made with vinegar & gherkins

Sauce rémoulade Mustard-flavoured mayonnaise/sauce

Sauce suprême Classic sauce made with chicken stock & cream

Sauce tournée Curdled sauce

Sauce velouté Basic white sauce: white roux with white stock

Sauce vinaigrette Oil & vinegar dressing

Saucer to Pour sauce over

Saucière Sauceboat

Saucisse Sausage (most often fresh & uncooked) (See also *Saucisson*)

Saucisse (chair à ..) Sausagemeat

Saucisse de Francfort Frankfurter: sausage of pork & veal

Saucisse de Strasbourg Sausage with smoked beef & pork

Saucisse de Toulouse Pork sausage esp. used in *cassoulet*

Saucisson Cooked/dried/salted sausage

Saucisson d'Arles Dry pork & beef sausage with garlic

Saucisson de Lyon Peppery dry pork sausage *[rosette]*

Sauge Sage

Sauge-ananas Pineapple sage

Saugrenée Seasoned herb butter added to vegetables

Saumâtre Brackish (water); Bitter & salty (taste)

Saumon / .. blanc Salmon / Hake *[merlu]*

Saumon fumé Smoked salmon

Saumonette Dog fish (usually skinned & headless) *[roussette]*

Saumur Still & sparkling wine of the Loire Valley

Saumur-Champigny Red wine of Saumur in the Loire Valley

Saumure Brine, Pickle

Saunier Salter: salt worker/maker

Saupiquet Meat/game with a wine & vinegar sauce

Saupoudrer to Sprinkle, to Dust, to Dredge

Saur, Sauret Salted, smoked herring, sp. of Boulogne

Sausselis Small savoury puff pastry hors d'œuvre

Sausson Almond, anchovy & mint paste used in hors d'œuvres

Sauté *[jumping]* Dish of sautéed meat/fish/vegetables

Sauter (faire ..) to Toss (pancakes, potatoes, etc.)

Sauternes Renowned fragrant sweet white wine of Bordeaux

Sauteuse Sauté pan: deep frying pan

Sautoir Large high-sided sauté pan

Sauvage Wild, Natural

Sauvagin, -e Fishy (smell/taste)

Sauvagine Collective word for waterfowl

Sauvignon Grape variety & white wine made from it (on its own or blended)

Savamment Knowingly, Wittingly, Skilfully

Savant Clever, Erudite

Savarin Ring mould; Baba (yeast cake) cooked in a ring mould

Saveur Savour, Taste, Flavour, Tang

SAVOIE Savoy: mountainous region in the SE, bordering Switzerland & Italy, with a cuisine rich in dairy produce, charcuterie, game & lake fish

Savoie (biscuit de ..) Light sponge cake made with beaten egg whites

Savoie (gâteau de ..) Brioche cake baked with pink pralines

Savoie (vins de ..) Wine, often sparkling, from the mountain vineyards of this region in the SE

Savoir se tenir à table / Ne pas .. To have good table manners / To have bad table manners

Savoir-faire Know-how

Savoir-vivre Manners

Savon / .. noir Soap; Bar of soap / Soft soap

Savon à barbe *[shaving cream]* (fam.) Inferior/insipid cream

Savon de Marseille Household soap

Savoyarde (à la ..) Savoie-style: potato gratin & egg dishes

Scarabée Beetle

Scarole Escarole: salad green similar to curly endive

Scel-o-frais Clingfilm

Schenkele Christmas finger biscuit of Alsace

Schweppes (brand name) Tonic water

Sciacce Corsican pasty, trad. for All Saint's Day

Sciure Sawdust

Scorsonère Black salsify, Oyster plant

Seau à champagne/glace Champagne/ice bucket

Seau, seaux / .. à charbon Bucket, Pail / Coal scuttle

Sébaste Mediterranean fish (family of scorpion fish)

Sébile Begging bowl

Sec, sèche / Séchage Dry / Drying

Sèche-linge Tumble-drier

Sécher / Séché, -e to Dry / Dried

Sécheresse Drought; Dryness

Secouer to Shake

Seiche, Sèche Cuttlefish

Seigle Rye

Seille Bucket, Pail *[seau]*

Séjour Stay, Sojourn, Period of time; Living room

Sel / Fleur de .. Salt (See also *Salé*) / Fine table salt

Sel chinois *[Chinese salt]* Mono-sodium glutamate

Sel de céleri Celery salt

Sel de cuisine Cooking/coarse salt *[gros sel]*

Sel de mer, Sel gris Sea salt

Sel de poisson Nuoc-mam: salty fish condiment used in Vietnamese cuisine

Sel fin/de table Table salt

Sel gemme Rock salt

Self Self-service restaurant

Selle Saddle (of venison, lamb, etc.)

Selon ... According to (size, weight, availability, etc.) (See also *SG*)

Sels Smelling salts

Semelle (dur comme de la ..) Hard as leather

Semoule Semolina: processed granules of ground wheat/*blé*, rice/*riz* or maize/*maïs*

Semoule de maïs Ground maize (Italian cornmeal = *polenta*)

Senteur Scent

Sentir to Smell, to Sniff (something)

Sépia Ink of cuttlefish; (fam.) Cuttlefish

Septentrional, -e Northern, of the North

Sept-œils *[seven eyes]* Lamprey: eel-like fish with 7 holes on its head *[lamproie]*

Serein Evening dew

Serfouir to Hoe

Seringue Syringe: for basting, piping or injecting brine, etc.

Serpent Snake

Serpillière Cloth, Sacking

Serpolet Wild thyme in Provence

Serre (fruit de ..) Hothouse variety (of fruit, etc.)

Serre / .. chaude Greenhouse / Hot house

Serré, -e Tight, Compact, Thick; (term) Sauce, etc. made thick by reducing liquid; Extra strong (coffee, etc.) (opp. of *allongé*)

Serrer to Squeeze, to Press; to Tighten; (term) Final whisking to obtain very stiff egg whites

Servante Maid-servant; Dumb waiter

Serveur / Serveuse Waiter, Barman, Carver / Waitress

Serviable Obliging, Helpful

Service Duty; Service charge; Tip *[pourboire]*

Service à table Waitress-service

Service compris Service included (in price)

Service de table Table-ware

Serviette Table napkin; Towel; Briefcase

Servir to Serve, to Wait table, to Help oneself

Set de table Place mat, Table mat (Table settings = *couverts*)

Séteau Small elongated type of sole

Sétoise of Sète (famous old fishing port of Languedoc)

Sève *[sap]* Liqueur of various regions

Sevré, -e Weaned

Seyssel Dry, light white wine of Savoie

SG: selon grosseur Depending on size (of lobsters, etc.)

Shiitake Shitake, Chinese mushroom

Sicilienne (à la ..) Sicilian-style: often fried meat, tomato & rice

Siffleur Baldpate (wild) duck

Sili mor Conger eel in Brittany

Sillon Groove

Silure Large freshwater fish of catfish family

Simple Plain, Simple; Single

Singe *[monkey]* (fam.) Corned beef

Singer (term) to Flour meat, etc. before browning in fat

Sirop / .. d'érable Syrup / Maple syrup

Sirop de citron/orange Lemon/orange squash

Sirop de menthe/fraise Mint/strawberry cordial

Siroper to Soak sponge, etc. in syrup, alcohol, etc.

Siroter to Sip; to Trickle (syrup, etc.)

Sirupeux, sirupeuse Syrupy, Sticky

Sitôt (que) As soon as, So soon *[aussitôt]*

Smitane Smetana: fresh soured cream

Sobre Sober, Temperate, Moderate

Sobronade Hearty vegetable soup of Périgord

Socca Type of hot chickpea flour pancake, trad. sold in the streets & markets of Nice

Socle Stand, Pedestal, Plinth, Base

Soda Soda water; Soda drink

Sohleb Porridge made from sorghum & ginger

Soigneusement Carefully, With care

Soissonnaise (à la ..) Soissons-style: with the large white haricot beans of Picardy

Soit That is, i.e.; Either ... or ...

Soja Soya, Soy

Sole Sole (fish); Base-plate, Bottom (of oven)

Sole de ligne Dover sole caught on the line – the real thing!

Soleil / Lever/coucher du .. Sun; Sunflower / Sunrise/Sunset

Solette Small/slip sole

Solidifier to Solidify

Solilemme Rich brioche of Alsace, similar to a teacake

Solognote (à la ..) Sologne-style: often a rich duck dish or marinated leg of lamb

Sommelier, sommelière Wine waiter/waitress, Wine consultant

Sommité *[leading light]* Plant tips/tops

Son Bran: husk of cereal grain

Sonde *[sounding rod]* Specially shaped cheese-tasting spoon

Sorbe / Sorbier Sorb apple *[alise]* / Rowan, Mountain ash

Sorbet Water-ice (orig. made with *sorbes*)

Sorgho Sorghum, Indian millet

Sot-l'y-laisse *[a fool leaves it there]* Chicken oyster: tasty morsel of meat on each side of poultry tail (too good to leave!)

Soubise / A la .. Onion sauce/purée / Dish with a *soubise*

Souche Stump, Stub; Pedigree, Lineage

Souchet Shoveller (wild) duck; Galingale: Med. plant

Souci d'eau Marsh marigold (buds used like capers)

Soucoupe Saucer

Soude Caustic soda

Souder *[to weld]* to Join (pastry, etc.) by pressing

Sou-fassum Stuffed cabbage in mutton stock, sp. of Nice

Soufflé Hot/cold savoury/sweet preparation made light with whisked egg whites

Souffler to Blow out (candles, etc.); to Whisper

Soufre Sulphur

Soupape Valve, Safety valve (of pressure cooker)

Soupe Soup (containing meat/vegetables/bread). *Soupe* was orig. a thick slice of bread covered with broth/*bouillon* (See also *Potage*)

Soupe au lait Bread & milk

Soupe d'épeautre Spelt broth: rustic mutton & brown wheat soup, sp. of Provence

Souper *[to take soup]* Supper

(trad. consisting of *soupe*), Light evening meal (trad. *dîner* at midday being the main meal), Supper party; to Sup, to Have supper

Soupeser to Weigh something in the hand

Soupière Soup tureen, Soup bowl

Soupirail, soupiraux Vent, Small cellar-style window

Souple Versatile, Adaptable, Supple

Source Source, Spring

Souricière Mousetrap

Souris Mouse, Mice; Prized 'sweet' knuckle on leg of lamb

Sous Under, Below

Sous vide Vacuum-packed

Sous-alimentation Malnutrition

Sous-alimenté, -e Undernourished

Sous-chef Second-in-command

Sous-marin Submarine: large long sandwich, sp. of Quebec

Soutirage (term) Draining off (in cheese/wine production)

Soutirer to Draw off (liquid)

Spaghetti vegetal Spaghetti marrow

Spaghettini Flat spaghetti

Spalla Italian salted & dried pork sausage

Spatule Spatula

Spätzle, Spatzele, Spetzli Small rich dumpling of Alsace (often tossed in butter)

Spécial, -e, spéciaux Special, Exceptional

Spéciales Seed oysters raised in salt marsh beds *[claires]*

Spécialité, e Speciality, Special dish

Spéculos, Speculoos Thin gingerbread biscuits, sp. of Belgium

Spiritueux Spirits, Spirituous liquor

Sprat Sprat *[anchois de Norvège]*

Spunchade Sorbet made with meringue mix [& liqueur]

Squille Squilla: large shrimp-like crustacean

Stabilisant Stabilizing agent (egg yolk, pectin, etc.)

Stagnante Stagnant (water)

STC: service et taxes comprises Service & tax included

Steack, Steak Steak *[bifteck]*

Steak-frites Steak & chips

Stephanois of Saint-Etienne (large town SW of Lyon)

Sterlet Small sturgeon

STG: spécialité traditionnelle garantie Denotes product is guaranteed to be of traditional origin

Stocker to Store, to Stock

Stockfisch Stockfish: dried salt cod used in *stoficado*

Stoficado Dish of mashed salt cod & potato, sp. of Aveyron

Strasbourgeoise (à la ..) Strasbourg-style: dishes with sauerkraut, foie gras, bacon, etc.

Streusel Streudel: sweet/savoury filling in pastry roll, sp. of Viennese cuisine

Strier to Streak, to Make streaky

Stufato, Stufatu Corsican ragout of beef, pork & ham served with pasta

Suave *[genteel]* Sweet, Pleasant, Soft

Subric Small savoury/sweet croquette (orig. cooked on hot bricks = *sur briques*)

Suc Sap (of plant)

Suçarelle Snail dish of the SE

Succédané Substitute (artificial sweetener, coffee, etc.), Ersatz

Succès *[success]* Classic cake of almond meringue with butter cream

Succulent, -e Delicious, Succulent

Succursale Branch (of shop), Outlet

Sucer to Suck

Sucette Lollipop; Dummy

Suçon Stick of barley sugar

Sucre Sugar

Sucre adant/de luxe Sugar crystals

Sucre brun Brown sugar

Sucre candi/casson Candy/coffee sugar

Sucre cristal/cristallisé Granulated sugar

Sucre d'orge Barley sugar

Sucre de canne Cane sugar

Sucre de pomme Apple-flavoured candy-stick, sp. of Rouen

Sucre en morceaux Lump sugar

Sucre en pain Sugar loaf: moulded into cone shape

Sucre en poudre Caster sugar *[sucre semoule]*

Sucre en tablette Lump sugar

Sucre filé Spun sugar

Sucre gélifiant Jam sugar: fine powder with added pectin

Sucre glace Icing sugar

Sucre granulé/en grains Sugar nibs: for pastry decoration

Sucre roux Brown (demarara) sugar

Sucre semoule Caster sugar [*sucre en poudre*]

Sucre vanillé Vanilla sugar

Sucre vergeoise blonde/brune Soft light/dark brown sugar

Sucre vermicelles 'Hundreds & thousands': sugar decoration [*non-pareilles*]

Sucrer / Sucré, -e to Sweeten, to Sugar / Sweet, Sweetened

Sucrerie Sugar factory/refinery; Confectionary

Sucrette Sweetener

Sucrier Sugar bowl

Sucrin Variety of sweet melon

Sucs (de cuisson) Essence; Juice (of fruit, meat, etc.)

Sucs gastriques Gastric juices

Sud South

Suédoise (à la ..) Swedish-style: often a mix of meat/fish with fruit & cheese

Suédoise [*Swedish*] Dessert of fruit in jelly mould with cream

Suer (faire ..) to Sweat: cook vegetables on very low heat

Suif Suet

Suinter to Ooze, to Seep

SUISSE Switzerland; Swiss

Suite Continuation, Following on, Next

Suivant, -e Next, Following, the One after

Supérette Mini-market

Supérette automatique Vending machine

Supermarché Supermarket [*grande surface*]

Supion Cuttlefish; Squid (in the South)

Supplémentaire Supplementary, Additional, Extra

Supprimer to Leave out, to Cut out, to Remove

Suprême Dish/soup with breast & wing of chicken, or fillets of fish; Various dishes containing 'luxury' ingredients

Sur / Suri ,-e On; Sour / Turned (sour)

Sur lie (wine term) Bottled directly off the lees (esp. *Muscadet*)

Sûr, -e Sure, Certain

Sureau Elder (plant)

Suret, surette Sourish, Tart, Sharp

Surfin, -e Extra fine, Superior

Surimi Sticks of processed fish meat (crabsticks)

Surnager to Float

Surtout Centre-piece (of table); Especially, Above all

Surveillance Supervision, Control

Suze Gentian-based aperitif, orig. of the South

Svelte Slender, Slim

Syllabub Frothy dessert of whipped cream, sugar, white wine & brandy served in a tall glass

Sylvaner Grape variety &
white wine of Alsace

Syrah Grape variety of the
Rhône Valley producing full-
bodied red wine (*Hermitage,
Cornas,* etc.)

Tabac Tobacco, Tobacconist's

Tabac de cuisine *[cooking tobacco]* Powdered mushroom

Tabagie (fam.) Place reeking of stale tobacco

Table / Tablée Table / Sit-down lunch/dinner party

Table à flamber Trolley on which a *flambé* dish is prepared

Table à repasser Ironing board

Table basse Trad., a communal dining table; Informal meal offered in guesthouse, etc.

Table de cuisson Hob (of cooker)

Table roulante Trolley

Tablette Bar (of chocolate, etc.); Small table

Tablier Apron, Overall

Tablier de sapeur *[sapper's apron]* Dish of breaded fried tripe, flattened & cut square, sp. of Lyon

Taboulé Tabbouleh: salad made with *couscous*/bulgur grains

Tabouret [kitchen] Stool

Tacaud Bib: small bony Med. fish similar to cod

Tache Bruise, Stain, Mark, Spot

Tâche / Tâcher Task / to Try, to Do one's best, to Toil

Tacheté -e Bruised, Spotted, Speckled

Taco Mexican pancake (tortilla) rolled & filled

Tacot Bib: Med. fish *[tacaud]*

Tadorne Shelduck

Tahitienne (à la ..) Tahiti-style: often marinated raw fish fillets

Taille / .. fine Size, Height, Waist(-line) / Slim-line

Tailler to Cut, to Trim

TAILLEVENT C14th chef who wrote *Le Viandier* (one of the oldest cook books in existence)

Taillon Small shape (slice, etc.)

Tajine Various dishes of N. African origin; Conical ovenproof dish used for cooking a *tajine*

Talibur Sugar-filled apple baked in pastry, sp. of Picardy *[rabotte]*

TALLEYRAND Statesman (1754-1838) whose chef was the famous Carême & after whom many dishes are named

Talmouse Small savoury/sweet pastry with creamy filling

Talon *[heel]* Knuckle end of leg (esp. pork)

Tamarin Tamarind: spice used in jams & chutneys, etc.

Tambouille (fam.) Grub, Food

Taminier Black bryony

Tamis / Tamiser Sieve, Sifter / to Sieve, to Sift

Tampon Plug, Stopper; Pan scrubber

Tamponner to Dab, to Pat; to Fleck (sauce, etc.) with butter

Tanaisie Tansy

Tanche Tench: freshwater fish mostly used in soups & stews

Tangelo Citrus fruit (crossed tangerine & grapefruit)

Tangelo ugli Ugli fruit: citrus fruit (crossed *tangelo* & orange)

Tanin Tannin: tannic acid found in bark, tea & wine, etc.

Tant-pour-tant Basic mix of caster sugar & powdered almonds used in commercial pastry cooking

Tapenade Paste of black olives, capers, & anchovies, sp. of Provence

Taper to Hit, to Knock (See also *Poire tapée*)

Tapette à mouches Fly swat

Tapinette Fresh soft-cheese tart of Orléans

Tapioca Starch of manioc root *[perles du Japon]*

Tapisser to Coat, to Line (mould, etc.)

Tapoter to Pat, to Tap (on the table)

Tarama Taramasalata: Greek sp. of creamed fish roe, seasoning & olive oil

Tardive Late (harvest, potatoes, etc.)

Tarine, Tarentaise (race ..) Mountain cattle (that trad. give the milk for Beaufort cheese)

Tarnaise of the Tarn *département* in the SW

Tarse *[instep]* Tarsus: 'foot' of chicken, etc.

Tartare (à la ..) Minced/chopped raw ingredients (esp. beef/salmon) with raw egg, herbs & seasonings

Tarte Tart, Flan, Pie

Tarte alsacienne Latticed jam tart of Alsace

Tarte flambée Alsatian bacon & onion tart *[flammenküche]*

Tarte renversée Upside-down tart

Tarte Tatin Upside-down caramelized (trad. apple) tart, sp. of Sologne (made famous by the Tatin sisters)

Tartelette Tartlet, Small individual tart

Tartiflette Classic dish of sliced potato & onion with cheese, sp. of Savoie

Tartine Slice of bread spread with butter, etc.

Tartine de confiture Slice of bread & jam

Tartiner / A .. to Spread with a knife, etc. / for Spreading

Tartineur Special spreading knife with rounded end

Tartouffe Old word for potato

Tartouillat Dessert of apples/cherries baked in batter, (sometimes in cabbage leaves), sp. of Burgundy

Tartre Tartar: wine deposit; Scale, Fur (in kettle)

Tas / .. de foin Heap, Pile / Haystack

Tasse / Grande .. Cup / Breakfast cup/mug

Tasse à thé / .. de thé Tea cup / Cup of tea

Tasse bouillon Soup cup/bowl

Tasser to Press/pack down/into

Taste-vin, Tâte-vin Shallow wine-tasting cup

Tâter to Feel, to Touch, to Test

Taupe / .. de mer Mole / Porbeagle shark

Taureau, taureaux Bull

Tavel Renowned *AOC* rosé

wine from near Avignon in the southern Rhône Valley

Tavelé, -e / Tavelure Spotted, Blemished / Blemish

Taverne / .. anglaise Tavern (orig. a wine shop) / English-style restaurant popular in Paris in C19th

Tchin[-tchin] Cheers!

Teinte Shade, Colour, Hue

Telfairia Oyster nut (water melon) of Île de Réunion

Tellement To such a degree, So

Telline Variety of clam from the Camargue

Tempura Method of frying food in Japanese cuisine

Tendons Sinews, Tendons

Tendre / Tendreté Tender, Soft, Delicate / Tenderness (of meat, etc.)

Tendre-de-tranche Silverside of beef

Tendron Beef/veal meat cut from the back of the ribs, used in stews, etc.; Gristle

Teneur Content, Amount (of)

Tenir to Hold, to Keep

Terminaison Termination, Ending

Termites Termites, Woodworm

Terne Dull, Drab (colour)

Terrain Ground, Plot of land, Playing-field

Terre / Terreux / Terroir Earth / Earthy / Rural, Rustic

Terre cuite Baked clay (terracotta)

Terre réfractaire Heat-resistant clay

Terreau Loam, Leaf-mould

Terreux, Terreuse Earthy; Grubby; Dull (colour)

Terrible Awful, Terrible, Remarkable

Terrible (pas ..) Not too bad (but not too good, either!)

Terrine Coarse pâté (usually of mixed chopped meats) *[pâté en terrine]*; Dish used to cook/prepare a *terrine*

Terrine (en ..) Any preparation in a *terrine* dish

Terrinée Cold rice dessert, sp. of Normandy fairs

Terroir Land; (wine term) Tang of the soil

Terroir (produits du ..) Local produce

Tester / .. à l'aveugle to Test, to Taste / to Blind test

Têtard Tadpole

Tête / .. de veau Head / Dish of calf's head (stuffed or with spicy sauce)

Tête-bêche Head-to-tail

Tête-de-Moine *[monk's head]* Tangy Swiss mountain cheese 'shaved' with special rotating blade

Tête-de-nègre Chocolate-covered meringue sand-wiched with butter cream; Variety of Cep mushroom

Téter to Suckle

Tétine Udder; Teat

Tétragone Summer/Australian spinach

Tétras Grouse

Tex-Mex Texan-Mexican-style: usually hot & spicy

Thé / Théière Tea / Teapot

Thé complet English-style cream tea

Thermidor (homard ..) Lobster (or sole) dish created in Paris on 1st night of play by the same name

Thermomètre Thermometer

Thon / .. blanc Tuna / White tuna [germon]

Thonine Bonito, Skipjack tuna

Thonne Veal cooked with tuna fish

Thouarsais (vins de ..) Red, white & rosé wine from around Thouars in the Loire Valley

Tian Dish for & of a *gratin* in Provence

Ticket-restaurant® Luncheon voucher

Tiède Tepid, Lukewarm

Tiédir to Warm (something) up; to Cool down

Tielle Sétoise Squid tart of Sète in the South

Tiers / Aux/des deux .. One third / To/by two thirds

Tige Stem, Stalk

Tilleul Lime blossom, Linden flower (used in teas, etc.)

Timbale Drum-shaped mould; Dish cooked in a *timbale*; Metal tumbler/container

Tipule Daddy-long-legs

Tique Tick (insect)

Tire-bouchon Corkscrew

Tire-bouchon (en ..) Curly, Wrinkled

Tisane Herbal tea

Tisanière Lidded cup with filter to make *tisane*

Tisser / Tissé, -e to Weave / Woven

Tissu Cloth, Material, Fabric

Titan Titanic, Giant

Titre [title] (wine term) Strength

Toast (un ..) Piece of toast

Toasts Small slices of bread (for *canapés*, etc.)

Tofu Preparation of soya used in oriental dishes

Toile d'araignée Cobweb

Tokay d'Alsace Grape variety [pinot gris] & white wine of Alsace

Tôle Baking sheet/tray

Tomate Tomato; Aperitif of *pastis* with grenadine

Tomate cerise Cherry tomato

Tomate cœur de bœuf Beef-steak tomato

Tomate concassée Tomato pulp

Tomate olivette/roma Roma tomato

Tomber [to fall] (term) to Cook watery vegetables (spinach, etc.) over low heat with no added liquid

Tomber à glace (term) to Reduce/concentrate liquid

Tomber dans les pommes (expression) to Faint, to Pass out

Tombés (fruits ..) Windfalls

Tome, Tomme Various drum-shaped cheeses of goat's-, ewe's- or cow's-milk

Tomme de Savoie Strong nutty-flavoured semi-hard cow's-milk cheese of Savoie

Tomme fraîche Springy fresh Tomme cheese used in cooking, esp. for *aligot*; Another name for *Aligot* cheese

Tom-pouce *[Tom Thumb]* Small iced shortcrust pastry squares with butter cream

Tondre / Tonte to Shear (sheep), to Clip / Shearing-time

Tonneau Cask, Barrel

Tonus Tone, Energy

Topinambour Jerusalem/winter artichoke

Toque Chef's traditional tall hat

Torchon Cloth, Tea towel

Torchon (au ..) Wrapped in cloth/muslin to retain shape (esp. ham)

Tordre to Bend, to Wring, to Twist

Tordu, -e Twisted, Crooked, Dented (by bruising, etc.); Weird

Torréfacteur Coffee merchant; Roasting machine

Torréfaction / Torréfier Coffee roasting / to Roast (coffee)

Tors, -e Twisted, Crooked

Tortell, Torteil Brioche cake of Catalan

Tortiller to Twist, to Twiddle

Tortillon Dry petit four of twisted puff pastry

Tortue Turtle

Tortue (en ..) Dish of calf's head served with *sauce tortue* or *fausse soupe à la tortue*

Tortue (fausse soupe à la ..) Mock turtle soup: made with calf's head

Tortue (sauce ..) White wine sauce flavoured with tomato (orig. served with turtle)

Toscane (à la ..) Tuscany-style: with Parmesan cheese & ham

Totelots Pasta salad, traditional Good Friday dish in Lorraine

Tôt-fait Any dish quickly prepared; Pound cake

Touaille Roller-towel

Touffe Tuft, Wisp, Clump, Cluster; Bunch of stalks

Touffu, -e Thick, Bushy, Dense

Touiller (fam.) to Stir without due care; to Toss (salad, etc.) *[remuer]*

Toulousaine (à la ..) Toulouse-style: using ingredients of the SW, often sweetbreads & truffles

Toupin, Toupine Small earthenware/cast iron cooking pot of Savoie

Tour de main Knack

Tour de pâtisserie Marble/metal slab for rolling out pastry

TOURAINE Wine growing region in the Loire Valley centred on Tours (Vouvray, Montlouis, Chinon & Bourgueil, etc.)

Tourangelle (à la ..) Touraine-style: often with white wine

Tourbe Peat

Tour-de-main (en un ..) In a trice

Tourer la pâte (term) to Fold, turn & roll out puff-pastry dough

Tourgoule Normandy-style rice pudding *[terrinée]*

Tourifas Raw ham &

mushrooms fried on toast, sp. of Auvergne

Tourin, Thourin Rich onion/garlic soup of the SW with regional variations

Tournebroche Turnspit (for oven/barbecue)

Tournedos Thick steak taken from fillet of beef

Tourner / Tournage to Turn; to Mix; to Shape; to Fold; to Stir; to Go sour/off; to Over-ripen / Turning, Shaping

Tournesol Sunflower

Touron, Tourron Soft nougat sweetmeat of Spanish origin

Tourte Pie, Large covered tart

Tourte Lorraine Type of rich raised meat pie of Lorraine

Tourteau Common crab

Tourteau fromagé Blackened ball-shaped cake made with goat's-milk cheese & varying ingredients, sp. of Poitou-Charentes

Tourterelle Dove [*colombe*]

Tourtière Ovenproof (plain/fluted) flan/pie dish

Tourtillon Brioche cake of Bordeaux

Tourton, Tourtou Small buck-wheat *galette* of Limousin

Tout compris Everything included (in price)

Tout, -e, tous All, Every, Everything, Everybody

Toxique Toxic, Poisonous

Traçabilité Ability to trace/track back (esp. within food chain)

Traditionel, traditionelle Traditional, Traditional style

Train de côtes Rib of beef

Traire to Milk (a cow); to Draw (milk)

Trait [*trace*] Small (cocktail) measure of spirit/liqueur; Dash; Trait, Characteristic

Trait (cheval de ..) Draught horse

Traite Milking

Traiteur Caterer; Tall, lidded saucepan

Traiteur (rayon ..) Delicatessen

Tranchant Sharp (knife, etc.)

Tranche / Trancher Slice, Portion / to Cut, to Slice

Tranche grasse Top rump of beef

Tranche napolitaine Ice cream of three layers & flavours

Tranchelard Long pointed carving knife

Trancheuse Slicer, Slicing machine

Tranchoir Carving knife; Large wooden/carving board; Trencher: thick slice of bread to soak up meat juices

Transvaser to Decant, to Pour out

Travail Work, Job; Workmanship

Travail de fourmis [*ants*] (fam.) Laborious task

Travaillé, -e Elaborate (esp. of wine)

Travailler [*to work*] (term) to Beat/blend dough/batter mixture

Travaux Works, Road works

Travaux ménagers Housework

Travers Pork spare ribs

Trèfle Clover, Shamrock

Trèfle de chevalline Bird's-foot trefoil (used dried in marinades)

Treillage / Treille Trellis, Lattice / Climbing vine

Tremper to Soak, to Steep, to Dip, to Dilute

Tremper la soupe (term) to Pour soup over a hunk of bread

Trempette (faire ..) to Dip bread, etc. into soup, etc.

Trénels Stuffed mutton tripe dish of Aveyron

Trescat SW dish of mutton tripe with egg yolks

Tresser to Plait, to Braid *[natter]*

Tréteau Trestle

Trêve des confiseurs Confectioners' Truce: trad. break from war, work, sport, etc. (31 Dec. to 2nd Tues. of Jan.) for exchange of confectionary, etc.

Trévise Radicchio: Italian chicory

Tricandilles Strips of tripe

Tricholome Tricholoma: genus of mushroom

Trier / .. à la main to Sort, to Select / to Hand pick

Trinquer to Clink glasses, to Take wine with (someone)

Trinqueur, trinqueuse Drinker, Tippler

Tripaille Offal (tripe)

Tripe (à la ..) Egg dish with onions in béchamel sauce

Triperie / Tripière Tripe butcher's shop / Tripe butcher

Tripes / Tripette Tripe: stomach of ox/calf/sheep / Small tripe

Tripes à la mode de Caen Slow-cooked tripe dish, sp. of Normandy

Triple-sec Very dry liqueur (often orange-flavoured)

Tripotch, Tripotcha Spicy black pudding of the Pays Basque

Tripous, Tripoux Dish of braised tripe, sp. of central France

Troc Exchange, Barter, Swap

Trognon Core, Stalk (of cabbage, etc.)

Trois-frères Rich ring-mould cake made with rice flour or ground almonds (created by the three Julien brothers)

Trombone Paperclip (used to de-pip grapes!)

Tromper (se ..) to Be mistaken, to Be wrong

Trompette-de-la-mort Trumpet of Death, Horn of Plenty mushroom

Tronc Trunk (of tree, etc)

Tronçon Chunk, Stub, Stump, End; Middle section of flat fish

Tronçonner to Cut into pieces/chunks

Trop / De .. / En .. Too much/many / Over the limit / Excess

Trop (pas ..) Not too much

Trop perçu Overcharged

Trop plein Overflowing

Troquet (abbr. for *mastroquet*) Bistro, Wine bar

Trou / A .. Hole, Cavity / With holes

Trou (boire comme un ..) (fam.) to Drink like a fish

Trou normand [*Norman hole*]
Calvados sorbet served
between courses (to fill the
gap!)

Troubler / Troublé, -e to Become
cloudy (liquid, etc.); Cloudy

Trouer / Troué, -e to Make a
hole/holes / With holes

Troupeau Herd, Flock (of
sheep), Gaggle (of geese)

Trousser to Arrange poultry,
crayfish, etc. in trussing posi-
tion [*troussé*]

Truc Gadget; Knack, Trick

Trucha Omelette with spinach &
Swiss chard, served with
tomato *coulis*, sp. of Nice

Truelle [*trowel*] Fish or cake slice

Truffade, Truffado Potato &
Tomme cheese pancake, sp. of
Auvergne

Truffe / Truffé, -e Truffle: prized
black fungus / With truffles

Truffer to Stuff or implant
(turkey, etc.) with truffles

Truffes Chocolate truffles

Truie Sow: female pig

Truite / Truitelle, Truiton Trout
/ Small trout

Truite à chair rose Pink trout

Truite arc-en-ciel Rainbow trout

Truite au bleu Trout cooked in
vinegar (skin turns blue)

Truite de lac Brown trout

Truite de mer Sea trout

Truite des gaves Mountain river
trout (of the Pyrenees)

Truite fario Common trout

Truite saumonée Salmon trout

Trumeau Leg of beef

Tsarine (à la ..) Czarina-style:
garnish of cucumber in cream
sauce for poultry/fish

Tsigane, Tzigane Gipsy [*gitan*]

TTC: toutes taxes compris Tax
included

Ttoro, Tioro Spicy fish soup or
fricassée of the Pays Basque

Tubercule Tuber

Tuer to Kill, to Slaughter, to
Butcher

Tuile [*roof tile*] Thin curled
almond biscuit

Tulipe [*tulip*] Tulip-shaped
(wine glass, mould, pastry,
etc.)

Turban Dish arranged in a
circle or cooked in ring mould

Turbigo Lambs' kidneys in
white wine & tomato

Turbiner [*to turbine*] to Mix ice
cream/sorbet ingredients
during freezing process

Turbot Turbot: large flatfish of
Med. & Atlantic

Turbotière Fish kettle for large
flat fish (esp. turbot)

Turbotin Small turbot

Turc, Turque (à la ..) Turkish-
style: often with aubergines

Turin, Turinois Uncooked cake
of chestnut purée, chocolate &
Kirsch

Turion Spear of asparagus

Tussilage Coltsfoot

Typé Typical

U

Un par un, une à une One by one

Unilatérale (à l'..) Cooked on one side only (esp. fish steaks)

Uniquement Exclusively, Only

Unitaire Unit (price, etc.)

Unité Unity; Unit

Universel, universelle Universal, All-purpose

Urne Urn

Usage Use, Practice

Usager User

User / Usé, -e to Use / Worn out

Usine Factory (Factory-made = *industriel*)

Ustensile Utensil

Utile (se rendre ..) to Make oneself useful

Utile / Etre .. Useful / to Be helpful

Utilisable Usable

Vacances Holidays (*Vacance* = vacancy)

Vacancier, vacancière Holidaymaker

Vachard Cow's-milk cheese of the Auvergne (*vacherin* in other regions)

Vache / Vachette *[calfskin]* Cow / Young cow

Vache à eau Water bottle (orig. of hide)

Vache à lait, Vache laitière Dairy cow

Vacherie Dairy farm

Vacherin Cow's-milk cheese of Franche-Comté & Savoie; Rich gâteau of meringue & cream, often with chestnut purée or strawberries

Vacherin Mont d'Or Creamy cow's-milk cheese of the Jura

Vairon Minnow

Vaisselle Crockery; the Dishes, the Washing up

Vaisselle (lave-..) Dishwasher

Vaissellier Dresser: trad. kitchen furniture for everyday tableware

Valençay Soft pyramid-shaped goat's-milk cheese; Red, white & rosé wine of the Loire

Valenciennes (à la ..) Various dishes of the North (rabbit, etc.)

Valet *[knave]* Manservant, Valet

Valet de ferme Farm-hand

Valisette Pack, Small case

Vallée / Vallon Valley / Vale, Small valley

VALLEE de la LOIRE Loire Valley: region that reaches from the Auvergne to the Atlantic, best known for its *châteaux*, wine & soft fruit

VALLEE du RHONE Rhône Valley: region running south from Lyon to the Med.

Vallonné, -e Undulating, Hilly

Valois Garnish of potatoes & artichoke hearts; Béarnaise sauce made with meat glaze

Vanette, Vanneau Queen scallop *[pétoncle]*

Vanille / Vanillé, -e Vanilla / Vanilla flavoured

Vanilline Vanillin: vanilla flavour (natural/synthetic)

Vanneau / Œufs de .. Lapwing, Peewit / Plover's eggs

Vanner *[to winnow]* (term) to Stir/whisk hot sauce or cream until cool & smooth, & to prevent skin forming

Vannerie Basket-making/work

Vanter / Se .. to Praise / to Boast, to Brag

Vapeur / A la .. Steam / Steamed

Varech Kelp, Seaweed

Varié, -e Varied, Assorted; Adjustable

Vase Vase, Vessel

Vaseux, vaseuse *[murky]* Woolly; With a sore head! (*vase* = sludge)

Vasque Wash hand basin, Shallow bowl

VDQS: vin délimité de qualité supérieure 2nd category of *appellation/AOC* wines

Veau Veal; Calf

Végétal, -e, végétaux Vegetable, Plant

Végétalisme Veganism: strict vegetarian diet excluding all animal products

Végétarien, végétarienne Vegetarian

Veille (avant ..) Two days before

Veille (la ..) / .. au soir / .. de Noël The day before / The night/ evening before / Christmas Eve

Veillée Evening (of entertainment); Wake

Veiller to Watch over, to See to

Veilleuse (en ..) Oven, gas, light, etc. on lowest setting

Veilleuse *[side light]* Pilot-light (for gas); Night-light

Veine / Veiné, -e French cut of beef from the neck, used for stewing / Veined, Streaked

Velours *[velvet]* Thick smooth carrot soup

Velouté (sauce ..) Basic smooth white sauce made with veal/chicken/fish stock

Velouté, -e Velvety texture; Thick, smooth soups, etc.

Venaco Strong goat's-/ewe's- milk cheese of Corsica

Venaison Venison; Large game animals generally

Vendanges Vine harvest

Vendanges tardives *[late harvest]* Wine of Alsace made from grapes left longer on the vine, giving higher sugar levels

Vendangeur, vendangeuse Grape harvester

VENDEE Coastal area of Poitou in the West

Vendéenne (à la ..) Vendée-style: often game, fish, cabbage or speciality breads & cakes

Vendôme Cow's-milk cheese of Orléans

Vendre / A .. to Sell / For sale

Vendredi Saint Good Friday

Vénéneux, vénéneuse Poisonous

Vénitienne (à la ..) Venetian style: dishes served with *sauce vénitienne*

Vénitienne (sauce ..) *Sauce allemande* with tarragon, vinegar, green butter & herbs

Ventadour Dish of tournedos steak or *noisette* of lamb garnished with bone marrow & truffle

Vente (en ..) Available (for sale)

Vente au détail / .. en gros Retail / Wholesale

Vente directe Sale (of wine, etc.) to the public by the grower

Ventre Stomach, Belly

Ventrèche Rolled spiced belly of pork

Venus Cockle

Ver / .. solitaire Worm, Grub, Maggot / Tapeworm

Ver à bois Woodworm *[termite]*

Véranda Veranda, Covered terrace, Conservatory

Verdâtre Greenish

Verdeur Acidity, Tartness, Rawness

Verdier Dish of hard-boiled eggs stuffed with *foie gras* & covered with a rich *béchamel* sauce

Verdure *[greenery]* Green vegetables/salad; Mix of green herbs

Verdurette *Vinaigrette* sauce with herbs & hard-boiled egg

Vergeoise (sucre ..) Soft brown sugar

Verger Orchard

Verifier to Check

Verjus *[green juice]* Verjuice: acid juice of large unripe grapes

Vermeil Silvergilt

Vermicelle Vermicelli: long fine strands of pasta

Vermouth Aromatic wine made in France & Italy

Vernir *[to varnish]* to Glaze pastry with milk or egg yolk

Vernis Variety of clam

Vernissé, -e Glazed (pottery, etc.)

Véronique Veronica, Common speedwell; Brooklime

Verre / .. de … / .. à pied Glass / Glass of … / Stemmed glass

Verre à feu Heat-resistant glass

Verre gradué Measuring glass/jug

Verrerie Glassware

Verres à dégustation Specifically shaped glasses, esp. for fine wines (Bordeaux, Bourgogne, Cognac, etc.)

Verrière, Verrine Bell-glass: small glass mould

Verser to Pour (out), to Turn out/over

Vert, -e / Au vert Green / Eels with parsley, spinach, sorrel & herbs, sp. of the North

Vert-cuit Very lightly cooked food

Verte (sauce ..) Green mayonnaise (with purée of herbs)

Vert-pré Garnish of small green vegetables or with *sauce verte*

Verveine Verbena

Vesse de loup géante Puffball, Giant puffball

Vessie Bladder

Viande / A la .. Meat / Method of cooking Cep mushrooms

Vichy (à la ..) Young sliced carrots cooked in [Vichy] water

Vichy (sel de ..) Bicarbonate of soda

Vichyssoise (crème ..) Cold vegetable (trad. potato & leek) cream soup

Victuailles Provisions, Victuals

Vidange Waste; Emptying; Air space in bottle between the cork & the wine

Vide / Vider Empty / to Empty; to Clean (fish, etc.)

Videler to Form a neat pastry edge with the fingers

Vide-pomme Apple-corer

Vidrecome Loving cup: two-handled drinking vessel

Vieil, vieille (See *Vieux*)

Vieille / .. de mer Grouper / Wrasse (sea fish)

Vieilles vignes *[old vines]* (term) Wines made from mature vines

Vieillir / Vieillissement to Age / Ageing

Viennois Viennese; Various sweet soft breads & pastries

Viennoise (à la ..) Vienna-style: coated with breadcrumbs & fried

Viennoise (escalope ..) Wiener

schnitzel: veal escalope coated in egg & breadcrumbs

Viennoiseries Bakery products other than bread (*croissants, brioches*, rolls & buns, etc.)

Vierge [*virgin*] Unadulterated, Pure (olive oil, etc.)

Vieux croûton (fam.) Old duffer

Vieux jeu Old-fashioned

Vieux rose [*old rose*] Dusty pink (colour)

Vieux, vieil, vieille Old, Aged, Ancient, Worn

Vif, vive Lively, Keen, Vivid, Sharp

Vif (à ..) Raw; Cooked very quickly

Vif (à feu ..) On a high heat (gas, etc.)

Vigne / Vignobles Vine; Vineyard / Vineyards; Wine region

Vigne noire Black bryony [*tamier*]

Vigneron Wine-grower, Wine-maker

Vigneronne (à la ..) Wine-grower's-style: usually with grapes

Villageoise (à la ..) Villager's-style: poached white meat/poultry with *sauce villageoise*

Villageoise (sauce ..) Rich white sauce with purée of onion

Villages [*villages*] Denotes specific 'parcels' of agricultural land or vineyards within a region

Villleroi Sauce to coat foods before bread-crumbing & deep-frying

Vin Wine

Vin blanc White wine; (fam.) A glass of white wine

Vin blanc cassis White wine with *cassis* [*kir*]

Vin blanc limé White wine with lemonade

Vin champagnisé Sparkling wine

Vin chaud Mulled wine

Vin cuit Fortified wine such as sherry, etc.

Vin d'honneur Wine/champagne offered at receptions & civic occasions, etc.

Vin de bleuet Liqueur made with blueberries

Vin de coucher Newly-weds' toast to their guests

Vin de curé Toast offered to priest at a christening

Vin de fruits Country (fruit) wine

Vin de garde Wine that should be laid down to improve with age

Vin de liqueur Fortified wine (port, etc.); Sweet wine

Vin de messe Consecrated wine

Vin de paille Dessert wine of the Jura made from grapes dried on straw [*paille*]

Vin de palme Wine made from grapes grown in palm groves

Vin de palus Wine made from grapes grown on salt marshes (esp. of Bordeaux)

Vin de pays Regional wine made from specified vines

Vin de plaine Wine made from grapes grown on flat ground

Vin de primeur Very young fresh wine

Vin de queue Wine made from pressed grape stalks

Vin de table Everyday wine, usually blended

Vin doux Sweet wine

Vin doux naturel Sweet wine fortified with brandy [VDN]

Vin du cru Locally made wine (*cru* denotes specific locality of vines)

Vin en primeur Wine bought as 'futures' (often not even bottled at time of purchase)

Vin fin Quality/'fine' wine

Vin gris Very pale-coloured rosé wine

Vin Jaune Yellow-coloured *AOC* wine of the Jura

Vin liquoreux Sweet wine

Vin mousseux Sparkling wine

Vin nouveau New wine to be drunk young

Vin ordinaire Everyday wine

Vin perlant/perlé Lightly sparkling wine

Vin pétillant Sparkling wine

Vin primeur Young, new wine (esp. Beaujolais)

Vin rosé Pink wine made from black & white grapes (the black skins are quickly removed)

Vin rouge Red wine

Vin vert Young white wine of the South

Vin vieux Mature wine

Vinaigre Vinegar (*vin aigre* = sour wine)

Vinaigrette Seasoned oil & vinegar sauce for salads & cold dishes; French dressing

Vinaigrier Bottle with glass/cork stopper for serving vinegar; Vinegar manufacture

Vinasse (fam.) Cheap wine, Plonk

Vincent (sauce ..) Mayonnaise with herbs & chopped hard-boiled egg

Vinicole Wine-growing area/region

Vinification Process of wine making

Violacé, -e Purplish (colour)

Violet Purple; Sea squirt [*figue de mer*]

Violette Violet (candied violets are a sp. of Toulouse)

Violine Crimson-purple (used to describe colour of wine)

Violon Violin-shaped fish of skate family

Visitandine Small rich cake of ground almonds & egg whites

Vitamine Vitamin

Vitelotte Kidney potato

Viticole To do with wine; Wine industry

Viticulteur Vine-grower

Viticulture Art of vine growing

Vive Weever fish [*vipère de mer*]

Viveur [*reveller*] Spicy red dishes with cayenne/beetroot

Vivier Stew: fish-tank (in a restaurant, etc.)

VO / VSOP Very old / Very special/superior old pale: denotes age of Cognac, Armagnac & Calvados (5 yrs.+)

Voiler *[to veil]* (term) to Encase in spun sugar

Voiture *[car]* Cheese/dessert trolley

Voiturier Car-parking porter (at hotel, casino, etc.)

Volaille / Volailler Poultry, Fowl / Poultry merchant/shop

Vol-au-vent Puff pastry case light enough to 'fly in the wind' filled with sauce-bound ingredients

Volnay Red Burgundy wine from the Côte-de- Beaune

Volonté (à ..) *[at will]* Unlimited, As required

Volontiers Readily, Gladly, Easily

Volupté (sensual) Pleasure, Delight

Vosgienne (à la ..) Vosges-style: usually with plums

Vosne-Romanée Renowned red Burgundy wine (along with Romanée-Conti, etc.) from the Côte-de-Nuits

Vougeot Red Burgundy wine from the Côte-de-Nuits

Voute Vaulted roof (of cellar, etc.)

Vouvray White wine, still & sparkling, of Touraine in the Loire Valley

Vrac (en ..) Loose (not packed); in Bulk (goods)

Vrai, -e True; Real, Genuine

Vras Wrasse

Vulgaire Vulgar, Common, Ordinary

Waldorf Mixed salad with fruit & walnuts; Dish of conger eel

Walewska (à la ..) Rich dish of poached fish with lobster & Mornay sauce

Washington Garnish of creamed sweetcorn for poached chicken

Waterfisch (sauce ..) Hot or cold [aspic] sauce for freshwater fish

Waterzooï Stew of freshwater fish & eel, sp. of Flanders

Welshe Welsh rarebit; Soft cheese of Alsace, ripened in *marc de gewürztraminer*

Williams (poire ..) Variety of pear; Liqueur made from pears

Witloof [*white leaf*] Flemish name for chicory [*endive*]

Xavier Cream/consommé soup with sliced chicken/egg

Xérès Sherry

XO Extra old: denotes age of Cognac, etc.

Yack Yak: longhaired pack animal of central Asia

Yaourt Yoghurt [yoghourt]

Yaourt à boire Drinking yoghurt

Yaourt à la grecque Greek yoghurt

Yaourt aromatisé Flavoured yoghurt

Yaourt aux fruits Yoghurt with fruit

Yaourt brassé [stirred] Smooth yoghurt

Yaourt de chèvre Goat's-milk yoghurt

Yaourt ferme [firm] Set yoghurt

Yaourt maigre Low-fat/slim-line yoghurt

Yaourt nature Natural/plain yoghurt

Yaourt sucré Sweetened yoghurt

Yaourtière Yoghurt-making machine

Yassa Spicy Senegalese dish of grilled meat/chicken/ fish marinated in limejuice

Yoghourt Yoghurt [yaourt]

York (jambon d'..) English-style ham (cooked on the bone)

Yorkaise (à la ..) Dish with York ham

ZAC: zone d'activité commerciale Commercial centre (ZAC can also be abbr. for various other urban zones)

Zarzuela Catalan fish/seafood ragout

Zébre / Zébrer Zebra / to Mark with stripes, to Streak

Zébrine Variety of striped aubergine

Zéphyr [light wind] Various light & frothy dishes (soufflés, cakes, etc.)

Zéro Naught, 'Off' (on stove, etc.)

Zeste Zest: outermost skin of citrus fruit; Membrane of walnut

Zester to Peel/remove the zest of citrus fruit

Zewelewai Onion tart of Alsace

Zikiro Pays Basque dish of skewered mutton basted with garlic/vinegar/chilli-flavoured water

Ziminu Type of bouillabaisse of Corsica

Zinc Zinc; [zinc] Counter, Bar

Zingara Italian gypsy-style: sauce/garnish of ham & tomato

Zuppa inglese [English soup] Italian name for trifle

Other books in THE COOKTIONARY® series:

THE COOKTIONARY COMPANION

PRODUCE & PREPARATIONS, INGREDIENTS &
INSTRUCTIONS FOR A KITCHEN IN FRANCE

THE COOKTIONARY FOR KIDS

AN A-Z OF FOODY WORDS, FAVOURITE FOOD IN
FRENCH, GAMES TO PLAY BETWEEN MEALS, FUNNY
THINGS THEY EAT IN FRANCE

THE COOKTIONARY IN FRANCE

A HANDBOOK FOR COOKS AT HOME OR ON HOLIDAY
IN FRANCE

COOKTIONARY CONTACTS

Internet: www.thecooktionary.com

E-mail: the.cooktionary@wanadoo.fr

Post: Franglivres, 90 rue de Flandres
60490 Conchy-les-Pots, FRANCE

COOKTIONARY is a Registered Trade Mark

WIN A COOKTIONARY FRIDGE MAGNET!

FIND A FUNDAMENTAL FRENCH FOOD
WORD THAT IS NOT IN THE COOKTIONARY

YOU COULD WIN
A *FRIDGE MAGNET!*

Send the Word, your Name and Address, by Post
to: Cooktionary Magnet,
90 rue de Flandres, 60490 Conchy-les-Pots, France

Or by e-mail to: the.cooktionary@wanadoo.fr

The word you submit may be included in a
subsequent edition of

THE COOKTIONARY